THE SLOW VIOLENCE OF IMMIGRATION COURT

The Slow Violence of Immigration Court

Procedural Justice on Trial

Maya Pagni Barak

NEW YORK UNIVERSITY PRESS
New York

NEW YORK UNIVERSITY PRESS
New York
www.nyupress.org

© 2023 by New York University
All rights reserved

References to Internet websites (URLs) were accurate at the time of writing. Neither the author nor New York University Press is responsible for URLs that may have expired or changed since the manuscript was prepared.

Please contact the Library of Congress for Cataloging-in-Publication data.
ISBN: 9781479821037 (hardback)
ISBN: 9781479821044 (paperback)
ISBN: 9781479821082 (library ebook)
ISBN: 9781479821051 (consumer ebook)

New York University Press books are printed on acid-free paper, and their binding materials are chosen for strength and durability. We strive to use environmentally responsible suppliers and materials to the greatest extent possible in publishing our books.

Manufactured in the United States of America

10 9 8 7 6 5 4 3 2 1

Also available as an ebook

To migrants around the world fleeing violence,
to those who hold out hope for justice,
and to Dolores

CONTENTS

Introduction

Although undocumented migration has garnered significant attention since the 1980s, the Executive Office for Immigration Review (EOIR)— the U.S. immigration system's central adjudicating body—had managed to remain outside the spotlight, which is no longer the case. This book rests upon immigration stories as told by Central Americans, their family members, and the attorneys who represent them. Experiences with immigration court help us understand how immigrants view the fairness and legitimacy of the law. Thus, their perceptions, experiences, and reactions serve as a starting point from which to explore the inner workings of U.S. immigration courts and to reimagine justice and legitimacy from a cross-cultural perspective.

Notably, working in immigration court has been likened to "trying capital cases in traffic court."[1] Consisting of 67 courts and 460 judges,[2] the EOIR adjudicates hundreds of thousands of cases each year, the vast majority of them deportation cases, which technically are referred to as "removal" cases.[3] Of these, approximately 70% will end in a deportation order[4]—an unsurprising fact given that most people don't qualify for any form of relief from deportation. More than two-thirds of all immigration matters involve Latin Americans. Behind Mexico, among nations represented in immigration court matters, El Salvador, Guatemala, and Honduras have consistently held the second, third, and fourth spots for years.[5] Between 2004 and 2018, the United States deported 1.1 million Central Americans.[6] For many, deportation means leaving one's family, possessions, and career behind, possibly forever. For those brought to the United States as children, it means leaving the only country they have known. For others, deportation can be a matter of life or death.

Journeys through immigration court are often rather bleak, and the realities portrayed in this book are no exception. Even immigrants with viable legal claims to relief from deportation find themselves fighting an uphill battle, often lacking financial resources and access to legal counsel. Many face additional barriers to courtroom success, such as limited English proficiency and other cultural, class, gender, and racial divides. The strain of being placed in deportation proceedings weighs heavily upon immigrants and their families.

The pressures of the system are also felt by immigration attorneys, most of whom are overworked, underpaid, underresourced, and charged with protecting their clients from deportation, a fate that for some clients is akin to a sentence of death. Of course, there are the occasional bright spots, like the attorney who successfully prevented her client's unlawful deportation not once, not twice, but three separate times; on the third occasion he was pulled from a plane headed for El Salvador literally moments before takeoff. Not surprisingly, however, most of the deportation stories found within this book end with a deportation order and, along with it, a sentence of life in the shadows should one choose not to comply.

These narratives alone would be compelling. Yet this book represents more than a compilation of deportation stories. It is an examination of the ways immigrants make sense of immigration court and the immigration system. It is also an exploration of how immigrants experience legal processes, deportation proceedings, immigration court, and the immigration system writ large. With such high stakes and such poor odds, how do immigrants make sense of and assess the complicated legal bureaucracy they find themselves thrust into when facing deportation? More important, how does this pivotal experience—like the experiences of Jessica and her son, Eddy—shape immigrants' views of immigration court and its actors, the immigration system, and the legitimacy of and compliance with United States law?

I offer surprising answers to these questions by bringing immigrant and attorney voices to the forefront, illuminating people's understanding of the law and the world around them on their own terms. To many, the immigration system—and immigration court more specifically— appears to be plagued with issues of due process, fairness, and legitimacy. Most onlookers would likely suspect immigrants to take issue with the deportation process. Yet like Jessica, most immigrants interviewed for this project found immigration court to be quite fair, at least *procedurally*. Contrary to their expectations and the stories they had heard, judges, attorneys, interpreters, and other court employees were polite, respectful, and unbiased. Many felt listened to or at least not ignored or antagonized by those in the courtroom.

Perhaps more shocking, immigrants frequently asserted that the United States has the right—and the duty—to establish laws that protect the safety of those residing within its borders. This right, they held, extends to the realm of immigration law and specifically deportation. Indeed, immigrants discussed the high value they placed upon the "rule of law" in the United States. After all, government corruption, political instability, and high crime rates in their home countries were what prompted many—including Jessica, her mother, and her son—to come to the United States in the first place.

Despite believing in the fairness of their lived immigration court experiences, as well as the fairness of deportation in an abstract sense, the overwhelming majority of immigrants interviewed for this project said that, under no circumstances, would they comply with a deportation order; in fact many (including Jessica) had already violated a deportation order. In the end, critiques of immigration court and the immigration system, as well as compliance with deportation orders, rested upon questions of equity, ethics, and morality—not process or being treated "fairly."

It is generally believed that perceptions of fair process foster satisfaction with undesired legal outcomes, beliefs in state legitimacy, and compliance with the law.[7] Indeed, fair process is typically found to outweigh several factors pertaining to obedience to the law, including equity and outcome desirability. For example, someone who believes that they are treated with respect during a traffic stop should be more likely to pay—as opposed to dispute—a traffic ticket than someone who feels that they are treated unjustly by a police officer (e.g., believing one was stopped for "driving while Black"). Along these lines, immigrants who find immigration court to be fair should accept and comply with deportation orders. Similarly, if immigrants believe that the state has a legitimate authority to deport unwanted individuals from its territory, they should accept and comply with orders of deportation. Yet I did not find this to be the case.

Why does the immigration context appear to defy expectations? How can seemingly incongruent perceptions of fair process, outcome satisfaction, state legitimacy, and legal compliance be reconciled? Engaging with both criminological and sociolegal literature, in this book I reveal how and why the normative rules of fairness, legitimacy, and compliance do not apply in the immigration context. Joining an emergent body of "second wave" scholarship addressing the absence of culture, diversity, and identity in traditional procedural justice and legitimacy literature, I make the case for a holistic reimagining of procedural justice, specifically that culture, experience, and positionality toward the law all play a role in shaping assessments of legal encounters. This framing provides a plausible explanation for group and individual-level variations in fairness assessments of the law and serves as a basis for radically reimagining deportation altogether.

In this book I also identify important policy implications. In recent years, activists, attorneys, and even judges have made the case for addressing immigration court's procedural shortcomings. Specifically, arguments have been made in support of a number of enhanced due process strategies drawn from the criminal justice system, such as appointed counsel for indigent immigrant respondents and/or the elimination of mandatory detention.[8] Yet as immigrant experiences and perceptions can attest, emphasis on due process enhancements may be altogether misguided. The vast majority of immigrants who find themselves facing deportation do not qualify for relief under the law as it currently stands. Enhanced procedural fairness and due process protections fail to address the absence of a path to legalization for the vast majority of immigrants "illegally" residing in the United States.

Although it is difficult to argue against due process, I demonstrate that neither immigrant satisfaction nor legal compliance will be achieved through procedural reforms alone. Instead, only a radical reimagining of deportation, coupled with comprehensive immigration reform offering viable pathways to legalization and citizenship for all immigrants, can put a stop to the slow violence of immigration court.

Research Methods

Between 2014 and 2016, I enmeshed myself in various immigration networks across metropolitan Washington, DC. During this time, I attended local festivals and community events, observed hearings in immigration court, volunteered with immigrant rights organizations, and connected with key members in local Central American and legal communities to gain insight into the inner workings of immigration court. Through chance meetings, "cold recruiting,"[9] and "convenience" and "snowball" sampling,[10] I eventually conducted formal, in-depth interviews with 36 attorneys and immigrants who wanted to share their immigration court stories, stories that form the basis of this book.

Interviewing attorneys and immigrants is no easy task. Attorneys were often incredibly busy, managing dozens of clients and cases—some matters of life or death—with very limited resources. Many immigrants were initially quite hesitant to speak to me about the very personal details surrounding their legal circumstances. I was both a stranger and, as a White American and nonnative Spanish-speaker, a community outsider. I was stood up by attorneys and immigrants on more than one occasion. Yet once interviews were secured, immigrants and attorneys openly shared the details of their lives and experiences with the immigration system, ranging from the intimate to the mundane.

Interviews were conducted in English and Spanish in accordance with participant preferences. All attorney interviews were conducted in English. All but one immigrant interview was conducted in Spanish. Interviews typically lasted over an hour, with many stretching to cover entire afternoons or evenings. In most cases, I met with individuals in their homes or offices. A handful of participants requested that we meet in a coffee shop or restaurant. A few preferred to speak by phone. Although I met with most interviewees just once, I spoke with others on multiple occasions. I also kept in touch with several participants for some time, inquiring periodically about case updates and life events.

Interviews were conversational in nature[11] and tailored to participants, with related, yet distinct, questions asked of attorneys and immigrants. Interviews covered such topics as migration stories, legal education, immigration law and policy, deportation hearings, legal defense strategies, and future plans. The interview questionnaire can be found in the appendix ("Interview Protocols"). I was most interested in learning how those having intimate experiences with immigration court—either through representing clients facing deportation or by virtue of facing deportation themselves—perceived the overall fairness of the court and the larger immigration system. I was also curious to uncover how the legal knowledge attorneys and immigrants hold, the legal encounters they have, and the stories they tell shape and reflect their assessments of the law.[12]

Including both immigration attorneys and immigrants in this study was central from the project's inception. Attorneys provide a window into the inner workings of immigration court through the lens of professionals who have been socialized into American legal culture. Immigrants confronting their own or their family members' possible deportations, by contrast, exist in the "space between" legal cultures, bringing an understanding of fairness and the law rooted in their home countries to bear upon their experiences in the United States.

Insights gained from interviews were bolstered by regular visits to two East Coast immigration courts, where I observed dozens of deportation hearings.[13] At the time, the two courts were quite similar. For example, both courts had between five and ten judges. Both courts handled similar caseloads and had comparable backlogs, and by the end of my fieldwork both were scheduling cases as far out as five years. The two courts were also relatively average when compared with immigration courts across the country, with staffing numbers and caseloads near the national means.

Despite the similarities, the two courts differed in two key ways: asylum grants and deportation rates. One of the courts had a lower than average deportation rate and a higher than average asylum grant rate. For example, the year I began fieldwork, this court had a deportation rate of 42% as compared with the national average of 51% and an asylum grant rate of 71%, more than one and a half times the average grant rate that year.[14] The other court under study had an above average deportation rate that same year but an average asylum grant rate.[15] Still—then and now—Guatemalans, Hondurans, and Salvadorans claim the top-three spots for deportation by nationality in both courts.[16]

For a time, I became a regular fixture in these two courts. With few exceptions, immigration court hearings are open to the public. This afforded me access to the court itself plus a variety of immigration hearings. I frequently chatted with security guards, interpreters, lawyers, and other staff. Many court employees could not understand my fascination with what to them was just another drab, monotonous federal courtroom. Judges were initially intrigued by my presence and occasionally engaged me in conversation between proceedings. On more than one occasion I was called upon by lobby security guards to perform informal translation. A few court staff made clandestine attempts to secure interviews for me with court interpreters and attorneys from the Department of Homeland Security (DHS), who are contractually forbidden from participating in such interviews.[17] After the novelty wore off, however, most court regulars simply ignored me. Although such ethnographic encounters inform this book,[18] it is the voices of attorneys and immigrants, as captured during formal interviews, that drive the arguments presented in the chapters that follow.

All interviews and observations were conducted under a strict human subjects protection plan. This permitted those I interviewed to share freely without fear of identification or reprisals, especially with regard to information about ongoing immigration proceedings, violations of civil and criminal law, and the precariousness of one's legal status. Similarly, it created a safe space for immigration attorneys to discuss the local immigration bar and courts openly and honestly. I asked attorneys to refrain from discussing privileged information and cautioned them if the conversation seemed to veer in that direction. I use pseudonyms throughout the book to protect immigrants and attorneys. I have also removed any identifying references to judges and other court staff and disguised various identities and locales presented in interview narratives.

I stand by my reputation as a researcher in confirming that interviews took place as described and that interview participants were open and honest. This is further evidenced by the rich detail and raw emotion filling the pages of this book. As other researchers have described,[19] the confidential nature of our interviews—and the fact that I was a virtual stranger—was freeing for many of the immigrants and attorneys I interviewed, affording them a rare opportunity to unload some of their most personal concerns, experiences, and opinions without fear of judgment or reprisal.

Although I cannot reveal the identities of those I interviewed, I can provide a brief summary of my sample. Interviews were limited to Guatemalan, Honduran, and Salvadoran immigrants currently or previously in deportation proceedings and their family members, as well as licensed attorneys who practice immigration law. Approximately half of those I interviewed were women and half were men. Interview participants ranged in age from their early twenties to their late sixties. Most of the immigrants I interviewed were in their thirties and forties, and most immigration attorneys interviewed were also in their thirties and forties.

Of all 37 interview participants, 17 were attorneys and 20 were immigrants. Most attorneys had little if any legal experience outside immigration law. One attorney had been a criminal prosecutor for a short period prior to practicing immigration law, and another was a criminal defense attorney for many years before transitioning into immigration work. All but one attorney, who worked for DHS as the immigration equivalent of a criminal prosecutor, represented immigrant clients. About half the attorneys interviewed were in private practice, although they acknowledged taking the occasional pro bono case (i.e. working without a fee), while the other half worked in nonprofit organizations. All of the attorneys I interviewed regularly represented clients in deportation proceedings and as such were particularly well positioned to assess matters of fairness in immigration court.

Immigrant participants had various immigration statuses and were all part of mixed-status families, meaning that they had some family members residing in the United States without authorization, others who were American citizens by birth, and still others who fell somewhere in between. Although interviews centered upon the deportation experiences of participants and their direct family members, many of those interviewed could name at least several close family members or friends who had been deported or who were facing deportation.

Most interview participants initially entered the United States without inspection (i.e., "illegally") and were living in the United States without a valid immigration status when their deportation proceedings were initiated. Most had been to immigration court at least once by the time we met, and all had spent time in immigration detention. Approximately one-third had been convicted of minor criminal offenses or traffic violations, including drunk driving; in all such instances, involvement with the criminal justice system triggered the deportation process.

About half of these individuals had ongoing cases and were awaiting final deportation decisions. Of these, three were in simultaneous proceedings with their children. The other half had already received some form of relief from deportation or had been ordered deported. Of those ordered deported, some actually never left, while others left and returned without authorization. Indeed, two immigrants I interviewed were facing deportation for a second time after illegally returning to the United States.

Eight immigrant participants discussed the ongoing deportation experiences of close family members, often their own children or partners. Three of these individuals had been ordered deported in the past but had never attended a hearing in immigration court, either having been deported via fast-tracked hearings on the border or having failed to appear for their scheduled deportation hearings. These three individuals had standing orders of deportation when we met.

I do not claim that this is a representative sample of attorneys or immigrants. Sampling was purposive in nature, ensuring that those with whom I spoke would be able to draw upon intimate experiences with the immigration system. However, the characteristics and experiences of those I interviewed are consistent with what is generally known about immigration attorneys and Central American immigrants living in the United States. For example, recent data from the American Immigration Lawyers Association (AILA)[20] and the National Immigration Lawyer Survey (NILS) project suggest that the immigration bar is relatively diverse with respect to gender, race, and ethnicity.[21] The NILS project also reported a high percentage of immigration attorneys in nonprofit practice (38%), which is consistent with findings that female attorneys are more likely to work in government, nonprofit, and social justice–related and social work–related specialties than their male counterparts[22] and that women and minorities are more likely to serve disadvantaged populations,[23] such as immigrant populations.

Similarly, the immigration system's omnipresent grasp on immigrant families and communities has been well documented. Nearly 17 million immigrants in the United States live in mixed-status families comprising individuals with and without varying types of authorization to reside in the United States.[24] Such families find themselves in a precarious position, with the threat of deportation looming large not only for undocumented members but also for those with temporary or nonimmigrant visas, who may be forcibly removed from the country for something as simple as a clerical error, missed deadline, or unexpected change in immigration policy. Cecilia Menjívar equates this experience to that of "legal limbo," noting that such "liminal legality" (along with the accompanying vulnerability to deportation) is a defining characteristic of Central American immigrants' lives in the United States.[25]

The United States deported approximately 4 million immigrants from 2006 to 2016.[26] Many of these individuals were placed in detention during the deportation process. Of those who faced deportation in 2020, for example, 82% spent at least some time in immigration detention.[27] Although just under half of all those deported have prior criminal convictions, most convictions are for nonviolent or immigration-related offenses.[28] Of those ordered deported, many either remain in the country or return without authorization. Thus, it is not surprising that, on several occasions, I sat down to interview an immigrant about a child's or spouse's ongoing deportation only to learn that they, too, had firsthand experiences with deportation.

In the end, I did not set out to discover a one-size-fits-all understanding of procedural justice. I set out to do just the opposite: to uncover the complex and nuanced relationships between fairness and the American immigration system, relationships that I suspected would be quite subjective. Unlike most procedural justice research,[29] in this book I provide a glimpse at the ways people think about and evaluate fairness and the law as told through individual accounts and observations of lived experiences with immigration court.

Outline of the Book

The book contains six chapters, the conclusion, and an epilogue. Chapter 1, "Modern-Day Deportation," includes one family's immigration story to set up the social and historical contexts of modern-day deportation policy in the United States, including the deportation of immigrants from the Northern Triangle, consisting of Guatemalans, Hondurans, and Salvadorans. Together, Central Americans represent the largest group of immigrants placed in deportation proceedings each year after Mexicans. Thus, this chapter provides a brief overview of the sociopolitical history of Central American migration, as well as the structure of the United States immigration system, setting the stage for a discussion of fairness in immigration court. Chapter 1 also introduces the concept of procedural justice, or process fairness, offering an integrated review of relevant literature and setting the stage for a discussion of immigrants' and attorneys' assessments of fairness in immigration court.

Drawing upon the experiences and perspectives of immigration attorneys, chapter 2, "Justice and Immigration Court," introduces readers to America's immigration court. This chapter includes a basic explanation of the rules and procedures associated with immigration court and the deportation hearing in addition to evaluations of said rules and procedures from the perspectives of the attorneys I interviewed. Unlike the immigrants I spoke to, the attorneys found great procedural faults within the deportation hearing, immigration court, and the immigration system.

In chapter 3, "Tracing Immigrant Legal Consciousness," I use migration stories to illuminate the importance of culture, context, and community in assessments of legal actors, encounters, processes, and systems. The concept of *immigrant legal consciousness* is introduced and situated among existing scholarship on legal consciousness and sociolegal status (e.g., "disabled," "undocumented immigrant," "welfare recipient," etc.) broadly understood. Unlike those born and raised in the United States who are socialized into the dominant American legal culture, immigrants experience dual socialization—first in their countries of origin and later in the United States. With limited exposure to formal sources of legal knowledge in the United States (e.g., K–12 education), immigrants come to learn about American law and legal systems through stories told by family and friends as well as reports in the media. As immigrant communities are somewhat insular, and because most immigrants go to great lengths to avoid encounters with the law, especially if undocumented, deportation stories—and myths—take hold. Although gossip and storytelling have long been considered central components of legal consciousness, the role of storytelling in the construction of immigrant legal consciousness is greatly amplified. Ultimately, legal narratives from the immigrant community prime immigrants to assess their deportation hearings, immigration court, and the immigration system.

In chapter 4, "Who Says the Court Can't Be Fair?," immigrants' procedural justice assessments unfold through immigration court narratives. Evaluations of court actors and procedures are generally positive as immigrants recount being treated professionally and respectfully in most cases. Divergence between immigrant and attorney perceptions of procedural justice is also discussed. Connections are drawn to satisfaction and compliance—or lack thereof—with deportation orders. Unlike what is found in most procedural justice studies, immigrants' evaluations of fair process are not necessarily linked to outcome satisfaction. Instead, immigrants' assessments of the *distribution* of justice (i.e., which individuals and classes of people get deported and which do not) are as important as, if not more important than, assessments of process fairness when it comes to feeling satisfied with the outcome of their deportation hearings.

In chapter 5, "Deportation Hearings, Legitimacy, and the Rule of Law," I present immigrants' perceptions of state legitimacy, including the power to deport, exacerbating contradictions between this project and most procedural justice studies. Analysis is situated in legal narratives from immigrants' home countries, serving as a backdrop against which immigrants evaluate fairness and legitimacy. These countries are often paralyzed by government corruption, gang violence, and what many perceive as an absence of law and order. Immigrants express limited concern over process fairness when discussing state legitimacy in the abstract or the legitimacy of specific immigration policies such as deportation. A strong belief in the rule of law is widespread among those interviewed. Legitimacy is instead linked to notions of ethics and morality. Connections are drawn between legitimacy and compliance as apparent incongruities—immigrants believing in the state's power to deport (some) immigrants yet refusing to comply with their own deportation orders—are explored. Compliance with immigration law is thus not a question of fair process but instead is a question of the *substantive* fairness of immigration law. Immigrants reveal that compliance with the law in this context is predicated upon the existence of viable pathways to legalization for "deserving" (i.e., noncriminal) immigrants.

In chapter 6, "The Case for Substantive Justice," I synthesize the relationship between procedural justice and legal consciousness, offering a robust critique of dominant procedural justice framings and calling for a postmodern revitalization of procedural justice theory. In this chapter I review the limitations of procedural justice theory and reassert the relevance of culture and identity in evaluations of the law and legal actors. Exploring America's obsession with procedural protections in the criminal justice system, as well as culturally, I then offer a challenge to the value of procedural fairness and due process protections in the immigration system. Demands for enhanced due process and procedural fairness within immigration court are framed as little more than "criminal justice creep," a gentler form of *crimmigration*. Although procedural justice may afford an air of fairness and legitimacy, by no means does it guarantee justice. I make clear that, without a sincere and intentional reimagining of procedural justice, we risk its weaponization.

After reviewing the preceding chapters, in the conclusion and epilogue, I extend the book's central arguments beyond the immigration court context and reflect upon a question that is central to the discussion at hand: What is the value of procedural justice in the face of a substantively unjust immigration system? The answer is a challenge to both the normative assumptions of mainstream procedural justice and the commonly held assertion that issues with the immigration system, immigration court, and deportation can be addressed through the advancement of due process protections (e.g., the right to indigent defense) and bureaucratic changes (e.g., hiring additional immigration judges). As evidenced by this book, fair process will likely do little to enhance immigrant compliance with deportation orders. What's more, fair process masks the spectacle of violence taking place in the U.S. immigration system on a daily basis. To truly address the harms of immigration court and the immigration system we must stop relying upon strategies that foster *perceptions* of justice in the service of social control and begin to foster *real* justice in the service of collective well-being and human dignity.

1

Modern-Day Deportation

Each year, hundreds of thousands of immigrants are moved through immigration court, experiencing the entire system through the lens of deportation. Most will be ordered deported—an outcome welcomed by very few, if any. For many, deportation is a definitive experience with the American legal system, a pivotal moment with the state itself. As evidenced by Jessica's story, deportation—both real and imagined—is not simply a singular event; it is a thread woven through the narrative of one's life.

Jessica's Story

In spite of everything, Jessica is an optimist. She peered through the blinds cautiously before welcoming me, a complete stranger, into her nondescript basement apartment. Like many of the immigrants I interviewed for this book, I connected with Jessica through an immigration attorney. I knew that Jessica was awaiting her teenage son's upcoming deportation hearing. I also knew that his hearing had already been postponed three times—that year. Still, we had communicated only briefly prior to my visit. Although it is not a particularly unsafe area, Jessica later explained that she rarely leaves her apartment, concerned about Immigration and Customs Enforcement (ICE) agents and neighborhood gangs. Indeed, her apartment complex would serve as the backdrop for a gang homicide not long after our meeting.

Although a careful individual, Jessica's positivity and warmth quickly became apparent. She ushered me into her dimly lit living room, her younger child (a U.S. citizen) watching cartoons in the background, and motioned for me to take a seat on her large green couch. As I listened to Jessica recount her family's migration journey, she spoke with purpose. Despite her older son's upcoming hearing, Jessica was unfazed. This was not her first encounter with the system, and she was determined to handle her son's deportation hearing differently than she—and her mother—had handled her own.

Jessica was born in El Salvador during the civil war, which began in 1980. The war came on the heels of five decades of military rule, seven military coups d'état, and nearly 20 years of social unrest.[1] Fought between the Farabundo Martí National Liberation Front (FMLN) and the Salvadoran government, the conflict lasted 12 years and resulted in mass internal displacement and external migration, as well as the deaths of more than 75,000 Salvadorans.

It is estimated that upward of 300,000 Salvadorans fled to the United States during the war.[2] The United States supported the Salvadoran government in the war, making it politically difficult to extend Salvadoran migrants fleeing the war refugee status.[3] Most Salvadorans who came to the United States during the period did so illegally. Some came on their own while others were aided by coyotes, paid smugglers familiar with border-crossing routes. Still others came to the United States as part of the Sanctuary Movement, a multidenominational network of religious organizations that assisted undocumented immigrants with their resettlement in the United States, often providing legal advice, material goods like clothing and food, and temporary shelter.

In Guatemala, as in El Salvador, the increasing concentration of resources and the growing desperation of disadvantaged sectors of the population throughout the twentieth century exacerbated long-standing tendencies toward political instability, military rule, and violent repression.[4] In Guatemala, the 1954 military overthrow of President Jacobo Árbenz and subsequent 1960 revolt by a group of junior military officers sparked 36 years of state-sponsored repression and violence during which upward of 200,000 people were killed or disappeared and between 500,000 and a million people were displaced.[5] It is estimated that over 90% of the human rights violations that were committed under military rule in Guatemala took place between 1979 and 1984, coinciding with increased emigration to Canada, Mexico, and the United States.[6]

Among this wave of unrecognized Central American refugees was Jessica's mother, Maribel. Facing an impossible choice, Maribel left Jessica in El Salvador with her grandparents. She hoped to start a better life for the two in America and eventually bring Jessica to live with her. Like many of the Salvadorans fleeing the war, Maribel entered the United

States without permission by crossing the United States–Mexico border; she was not apprehended. Once in the United States, Maribel eventually found work and a new husband, with whom she would have three more children, all U.S. citizens.

The passage of the Immigration Reform and Control Act of 1986 (IRCA) provided Maribel and her husband, also an undocumented immigrant, with a path to legalization. IRCA served three primary functions: to increase United States Border Patrol funding, to create employer sanctions for the hiring of undocumented immigrants, and to grant amnesty to several million undocumented immigrants residing in the United States, many of whom were Central American. Through IRCA, Maribel and her husband acquired green cards and were eligible for citizenship. With her immigration status "fixed," Maribel now had the opportunity to bring Jessica to the United States legally. However, achieving this goal would be neither cheap nor easy.

Navigating the Immigration System

Today, approximately one in every five Salvadorans lives in the United States.[7] Salvadorans represent the largest group of Central American immigrants in the United States, with population estimates between 1.3 and 1.4 million.[8] This is followed by Guatemalans, who number upward of 850,000, and Hondurans, totaling around 600,000.[9] These three populations also represent a significant portion of undocumented immigrants residing in the United States. The DHS estimates that around 730,000 Salvadorans, 620,000 Guatemalans, and 450,000 Hondurans are currently in the United States without authorization, giving them the second, third, and fifth largest undocumented populations in the United States behind Mexicans.[10]

Most of these people, whether documented or not, have come to the United States over the past several decades. Although civil wars and state violence drove much of the Central American migration of the 1970s and 1980s—as in Maribel's case—by the 1990s many looked to the United States to escape failing economies and a series of natural disasters.[11] Hurricane Mitch, which occurred in 1998, was one of the most severe of such natural disasters. Honduras, an impoverished country with high unemployment and underemployment rates,[12] was hit particularly hard by the hurricane, prompting mass migration to the United States.[13] Three years later, in 2001, El Salvador experienced not one but two earthquakes and numerous aftershocks. More than 150,000 homes were leveled and nearly 200,000 more were damaged, along with important infrastructure, including 23 hospitals, 121 health-care units, and 1,566 schools.[14] This prompted additional Salvadoran migration to the United States, where many had existing family ties.[15]

Like the hundreds of thousands of Central Americans living in the United States, Jessica migrated for multiple reasons. Principal among these reasons, however, was family reunification.[16] In the summer of 2003, Jessica, along with a small group of other undocumented immigrants, attempted to cross the United States–Mexico border. "It was like a scene out of a movie," she explained. All of a sudden, two large helicopters appeared in the sky, shining bright spotlights down upon them. Before the group fully realized what was happening, they were surrounded by Border Patrol agents.

Unlike most of her travel companions, however, Jessica had another option. She was already in line for a family-sponsored visa that would have allowed her to enter the United States legally and would have put her on a path toward citizenship. The problem was that her visa was not materializing quickly enough. Because the number of visa applications far surpasses the number of available visas each year, Jessica could expect to wait nearly a decade for her family-based visa.[17]

Making matters more complicated, Jessica was in an abusive relationship. Her home life was quickly deteriorating. She was concerned for the safety of herself and her toddler. After discussing her options with her mother, the pair decided to pay a coyote to sneak Jessica into the United States illegally. Like her mother before her, Jessica would leave her son with his paternal grandparents and make the difficult journey through Guatemala and Mexico to the United States. And like her mother before her, Jessica intended to create a better life for her and her child, whom she hoped would join her once she was established in the United States. However, the trip ended with Jessica detained and in the custody of U.S. Border Patrol.

Today, Border Patrol is one of about a dozen federal agencies that are primarily responsible for administering and enforcing immigration law in the United States. Initially housed under the Department of Labor and later the Department of Justice, the now defunct Immigration and Naturalization Services (INS) once handled all immigration matters, from visa processing to policing to the adjudication of conflicts in court. In 2003, the INS was dismantled and restructured as three separate entities under the newly created Department of Homeland Security: United States Citizenship and Immigration Services (USCIS), which oversees lawful immigration to the United States; Customs and Border Protection (CBP), which monitors and processes the movement of people and goods across borders; and Immigration and Customs Enforcement (ICE), which enforces federal immigration law, investigates the illegal movement of goods and people, and prevents terrorism within the nation's interior. Additional immigration needs were dispersed to other agencies, including the Department of Health and Human Services, which provides assistance to and helps settle refugees, in addition to being responsible for the care and custody of unaccompanied immigrant youth; the Department of Labor, which determines labor needs and issues labor certifications; and the Department of State, which issues visas at consulates worldwide.

All three DHS agencies—the USCIS, CBP, and ICE—are further subdivided into various programs. For example, ICE is split between two operating components: Homeland Security Investigations (HSI) and Enforcement and Removal Operations (ERO). HSI investigates a wide range of illegal activities, including immigration crimes; human rights violations and human smuggling; smuggling of narcotics, weapons, and other types of contraband; financial crimes; cybercrime; and export enforcement issues.[18] ERO primarily deals with unauthorized immigration and is composed of several easily distinguishable operations. Fugitive Operations and Criminal Alien Program are two of the most prominent ERO operations and are used to apprehend, process, detain, and deport unauthorized immigrants.[19] ERO is also responsible for housing detained immigrants awaiting trial or deportation, including those lawfully seeking asylum.

After her apprehension at the border, Jessica was detained for several months. She explained that, although she did not mind being detained, it was difficult to adjust. The detention facility was freezing. The food was bad. The employees were not the friendliest. Still, Jessica managed to build several strong friendships with other detained women. She even celebrated a birthday with these women. However, as time went by, Jessica watched many of these same women being pressured into accepting "voluntary departure," a deportation alternative available to eligible noncitizens allowing them to leave the country of their own accord. Voluntary departure typically involves fewer and less severe negative consequences than does deportation.[20]

Immigration officers repeatedly told Jessica—as they did other detainees—that she had no chance at remaining in the United States legally. They said she would have to spend months, even years, in detention if she decided to fight her case in court, where she would inevitably lose. "No matter where you go or where you try to hide," immigration officers would yell, "we have your fingerprints and we will find you." The strain of detention coupled with the constant intimidation of *la migra* (a Spanish-language slang term for immigration enforcement officers, short for "immigration") was too much for many to handle. Still, Jessica was determined to remain in the United States. After several months in detention, she was finally given a hearing date in immigration court and released to her mother.

Many of the hundreds of thousands of immigrants who face deportation in immigration court each year have had experiences with at least one other immigration agency at one point or another.[21] Some, like Jessica, are apprehended by the CBP during a border-crossing attempt. Others are picked up by ICE after a warrant is issued for their arrest or perhaps during a random traffic stop. In some cases, immigrants violate the terms of their USCIS-issued visas, triggering a deportation hearing. Of these, some are also held in detention. For example, in 2018 34% of all completed immigration court cases involved detained individuals, down from 53% in 2010.[22]

When released pending a deportation hearing, immigrants are now subject to varying levels of supervision, not unlike that experienced by probationers and parolees in the criminal justice system. For instance, the Intensive Supervision Appearance Program (ISAP)[23] involves weekly or biweekly check-ins with an immigration case manager and home visits. Some ISAP participants are required to wear an electronic monitoring bracelet with GPS technology or perform telephonic check-ins using voice recognition software as part of the Electronic Monitoring Device program. In 2012 alone, a total of 40,452 immigrants were placed under

ISAP supervision.[24] ISAP has since expanded, more than doubling to 87,439 immigrants under supervision by January 31, 2021, and nearly tripling to approximately 240,000 immigrants under supervision by May of the following year.[25]

Supervision programs such as ISAP were not yet in full swing when Jessica was apprehended in 2003. Jessica left immigration detention with a court date and nothing more, instructed to appear but accountable only to herself. At the time, Jessica did not speak English and did not have a driver's license. She had been in the United States for a matter of months and knew next to nothing about the American legal system. When she asked her parents about getting to the hearing, her stepfather told her it was a waste of time and refused to drive her. "Forget about going to court and try to find a job," she recalled him saying. Jessica was already nervous about going to court—she had never been in court before and was afraid that, if she went, she would be deported. Between her fear and, as she explained, "not knowing any better," she did not argue with the advice. Jessica did not attend her hearing, which took place in her absence two hours from her mother's home.

Jessica eventually learned of the consequences of her missed hearing, but by then it was too late. It is standard practice for immigration judges to order individuals deported in absentia when they fail to appear for a hearing. Without being sure, Jessica assumed this was what had happened in her case—as she recalls, she had already ignored multiple letters from the court.

It is difficult to predict what the outcome of Jessica's deportation hearing might have been had she been supported by her parents or represented by an attorney, let alone just shown up. Options for relief from deportation are limited. Legal pathways to come to the United States are also limited.

Today, obtaining relief from deportation has become increasingly difficult, as has coming to the United States legally. Through a series of executive orders, case decisions, and rule changes, the Donald Trump administration denied visas on the basis of country of origin with the highly controversial "Muslim ban";[26] eliminated discretionary relief from deportation through administrative closure;[27] established the "Migrant Protection Protocols" requiring those seeking asylum at the southern border to remain in Mexico until their asylum hearings;[28] and implemented a broad interpretation of existing public charge rules that restricts both admission to the United States and the ability to obtain Lawful Permanent Resident status (i.e. "green cards").[29]

The Trump administration also closed more than a dozen international USCIS offices, adding to already lengthy visa application backlogs.[30] A case-closure quota was implemented for immigration judges.[31] Asylum qualifications also narrowed as the administration used the "self-referral authority" to reopen and refer immigration cases to the United States Attorney General for new decisions altering existing precedent. Indeed, in 2018, then–Attorney General Jeff Sessions ruled that gang violence alone would no longer serve as grounds for asylum.[32]

Even before such policy changes, Jessica was quite fortunate to have qualified for a visa, a visa she inadvertently gave up that day on the border when she was taken into custody by Border Patrol agents. Unlike Jessica, many Central Americans cannot obtain visas to come to the United States. Long-term visas require specific family or employment ties. Temporary visas require substantial financial resources—substantial enough to prove that one is not secretly planning an extended stay. For those who do qualify, annual quotas and long waits can be discouraging; many simply find an alternative way to enter the United States.[33] Consequently, like Jessica, some immigrants choose to enter the United States "without inspection." This is a civil offense and a criminal misdemeanor.[34] It is also grounds for deportation.

Deportation is not reserved for individuals without legal authorization to be in the United States. Immigrants with valid visas or residency, commonly referred to as "green card holders," can be deported for visa violations, criminal convictions, or admissibility issues that were overlooked when they were initially granted permission to enter the United States. Being deportable, however, does not mean that deportation is inevitable—even if it is likely.

Common forms of relief from deportation include adjustment of status, asylum and withholding, cancellation, and stays of deportation. Because the United States is party to the United Nations Convention Against Torture, relief from deportation may also be afforded to individuals who would likely be subject to torture, either at the hands of or due to the inaction of government actors, if returned to their country.[35] Immigration judges are required to interpret deportation grounds in favor of immigrants; however, they have the discretion to grant—or not grant—relief.[36]

Central Americans in particular have been eligible for a handful of country-specific relief options over the years. Temporary Protected Status (TPS) is one such form of relief. TPS is a temporary and renewable legal status designated by the secretary of homeland security and granted to noncitizens from a country to which it is deemed unsafe to return due to circumstances like ongoing armed conflict, environmental disasters or epidemics, or "other extraordinary and temporary conditions."[37] TPS was extended to Hondurans and Salvadorans throughout the 1990s and 2000s.[38] It is estimated that there are currently more than 327,000 Hondurans and Salvadorans with TPS in the United States.[39]

Despite similar country conditions throughout the 1980s and into the present, Guatemala has never been granted a TPS designation.[40] Some Guatemalans, however, are eligible for immigration relief under the provisions of the Nicaraguan Adjustment and Central American Relief Act (NACARA). NACARA was passed by Congress in 1997 and offers a special form of cancellation of removal (deportation) to eligible Guatemalans, Salvadorans, and members of the former Soviet Union and its successor republics who entered the country prior to 1990.[41]

As a Salvadoran, Jessica may have qualified for relief from deportation through TPS, but she will never know for sure—immigration outcomes vary significantly due to individual circumstances and the discretionary powers of immigration judges; it is unlikely that she would have qualified for any other form of relief. At the time, all Jessica knew was that, although she may have avoided deportation, she had also lost a chance at fast-tracking her legal status in the United States. Only years later would Jessica learn that her illegal entry and deportation order permanently ruined her chances at the family-based visa her mother applied for on her behalf years earlier. When her visa application did finally reach the top of the pile, the USCIS would request copies of Jessica's fingerprints. A fingerprint search would reveal her past encounter at the border and her missed immigration hearing, along with the fake name she gave the Border Patrol agents who arrested her.

Still, none the wiser, Jessica remained hopeful that her pending visa application would eventually be approved and she could legalize her status. In the meantime, she decided to get a job, keep a low profile, and dedicate herself to bringing her son to the United States as quickly as possible—she did not want to repeat her mother's mistakes.

Going to Court

Jessica eventually moved to the East Coast, found a new partner—an undocumented Guatemalan man—and had a second child. "One day, when he is an adult," she stressed excitedly, "he will be able to sponsor visas for his father and me to live in the United States legally." Jessica has managed to find restaurant work on and off over the years. She linked her precarious employment situation to her immigration status—or lack thereof—lamenting the way things turned out. As Jessica saw it, if she had papers, she could have found stable employment. More important, she would have been to bring her older son, Eddie, to the United States legally.

Reuniting with Eddie in the United States was always part of Jessica's plan, just as it had always been her mother's plan to reunite with her. Unfortunately, the realities of daily life, coupled with the workings of immigration policy, made this more difficult than Jessica expected. She began asking around and wound up in several consultations with immigration attorneys, each of whom told her that it was impossible to fix her immigration status. Without legalizing her own status, they explained, there would be no way to bring Eddie to the United States. Jessica was disheartened by the news. She felt increasing pressure to get Eddie out of El Salvador—and fast.

When Jessica left Eddie, her two-year-old, in El Salvador in 2003, the nation was still in the midst of recovering from the devastating effects of civil war. A series of tough-on-crime policies enacted to address growing gang violence (e.g., Plan Mano Dura and Super Mano Dura) further entrenched organized crime and repressive state violence.[42] Sílvia Roque, a researcher with the Center for Social Studies at Portugal's University of Coimbra, explains that gang violence and violent governmental and nongovernmental responses to it "fed each other, embedding war and terror in everyday [Salvadoran] life."[43]

By the spring of 2014, the fragile 2012 truce between the notorious Barrio 18 and Mara Salvatrucha-13 (MS-13) gangs began to fall apart; gang violence exploded.[44] In 2015, the murder rate in El Salvador—

which is smaller than the state of Rhode Island and has just over 6 million inhabitants—rose to 104 homicides per 100,000 people.[45] The summer of 2015 was, in fact, the bloodiest in Salvadoran history, far exceeding the violence experienced during the whole of El Salvador's civil war. It was at this point that El Salvador surpassed Honduras to become the most violent country not at war in the world.[46] During this time, El Salvador averaged 700 murders per month,[47] the equivalent of more than 23 murders per day or nearly one every hour.[48]

Gang violence is not a new phenomenon in Central America. Indeed, it was widespread throughout the region by the late 2000s. Although El Salvador, Guatemala, and Honduras all face serious gang problems, the conflict produced by El Salvador's rival gangs—Barrio 18 and MS-13—is arguably the most severe. Both gangs trace their origins to 1980s Los Angeles, where groups of young Salvadoran civil war refugees began forming cliques to protect themselves from the city's existing Black and Hispanic gangs. Over time, these Salvadoran cliques adopted the practices of American gangs. Many members were deported back to El Salvador after being arrested on gang-related charges. Once in El Salvador, the two street gangs quickly proliferated, uniting with former FMLN and government combatants—some of whom had been child soldiers—with military training and weapons left over from the war.[49] Today, entire neighborhoods, jails, and prisons across El Salvador are gang-controlled.[50] Citizens are often forced to pay "rent,"[51] which is a euphemism for extortion, or join the gangs. Failing to cooperate can lead to death. Police and military often tolerate, and even collaborate with, the gangs.

Barrio 18 and MS-13 are also well established in Guatemala and Honduras, where, along with other street gangs, they have grown in numbers and power.[52] Gang extortion, harassment, and forced conscription are now commonplace.[53] As in El Salvador, serious problems of corruption and impunity in Guatemala and Honduras have exacerbated crime and insecurity in recent years.[54]

Thus, when Eddie and his half-brother found themselves being harassed by MS-13 members, it was simply seen as a fact of life. Eddie continued going to school, but he stopped spending unnecessary time outside his grandmother's home. Things changed, however, when Eddie's half-brother was killed after refusing to join the gang. Jessica panicked. She realized that her son's life was in imminent danger. She felt she had no choice but to send money for him to be smuggled to the United States, joining tens of thousands of unaccompanied minors seeking refuge from soaring gang-related violence, government corruption, and political instability in Central America over the prior decade.[55]

In 2014, Eddie was one of 68,000 unaccompanied minors who were apprehended at the United States–Mexico border; of these, 75% were from El Salvador, Guatemala, and Honduras.[56] After a brief period in dentition, Eddie was released to Jessica. Like his mother more than a decade earlier, he was given a date in immigration court and ordered to appear.

Jessica stressed that she does not want to be guilty of the same mistakes her mother made with her immigration case. After Eddie's release, Jessica carefully collected and stored the documents he had received during his apprehension and detainment. As new documents pertaining to his case arrived in the mail, she safely filed them away. She remarked on the time and care she took to prepare for Eddie's first hearing, marking it in her calendar, coordinating rides to and from the court—she has never obtained a driver's license—and making sure that he arrived promptly on time.

Following Eddie's first hearing, Jessica heeded the immigration judge's advice and began searching for an attorney to take his case. A woman of little means, she knew that most immigration attorneys would be prohibitively costly. Recalling the hundreds of dollars she spent on mere consultations in the past, Jessica asked around and was finally referred to a local nonprofit legal aid organization specializing in youth cases. She obtained a lawyer for Eddie, free of charge. "The lawyer believes that Eddie has a viable case," Jessica remarked continuing, "and a real shot at relief." Her eyes lit up as she spoke.

Still, the case would not be easy. Eddie's attorney planned to argue that he qualified for asylum. Although many who have come to the United States as part of this recent wave of migrants hope to be granted asylum, uncontrollable gang violence—the driving force behind their migration—often fails to meet its basic requirements.[57] Applying for and receiving asylum is a complicated and difficult process. Individuals must establish that they have experienced persecution in the past or that they have a well-founded fear of future persecution should they return home.

Importantly, this persecution must occur on account of one's race, religion, nationality, political opinion, or membership in a particular social group. This "nexus" requirement is often the greatest hurdle for gang-based asylum claims, leaving many Central American immigrants with little recourse for relief from deportation.

When I left Jessica's apartment that afternoon after we spoke, Eddie's hearing—and the family's future—were pending. It was unclear when he would finally have his merit hearing, let alone if he might be able to legalize his status in the United States. At the time, the court that was assigned Eddie's case was scheduling cases as far out as five years—to 2020, at the time this was being written.[58] I stayed in touch with Jessica for nearly a year, hoping to be able to attend her son's next deportation hearing, but it was postponed again and again. Indeed, I stayed in touch with a number of Central Americans with pending deportation cases while researching this book, hoping to interview them once they had gone to court. Their hearings would inevitably be rescheduled, and we would eventually lose touch. I never did find out how Eddie's case concluded or, for that matter, if it ever did.

Procedural Justice and Immigration Court

Jessica's experiences with the immigration system are not unique. Such stories have come to dominate news media in recent years as debates over immigration reform reignited under the administrations of Barack Obama and Donald Trump, including Deferred Action for Childhood Arrivals (DACA)/Deferred Action for Parents (DAPA), the unaccompanied minor crisis, the border wall, family separation, and so on. What's interesting about Jessica's story is not the cycle of migration it highlights, the way it exemplifies the destabilizing role of the United States in Latin American countries through civil war and deportation-as-crime-control policies, or the traumatic violence it embodies. Instead, what is most interesting about Jessica's experience is the fact that, in spite of everything, she still believes in the fairness of immigration court and the US legal system, at least from a *procedural* perspective.

"Procedural justice" refers to the fairness of a given process. In particular, it centers upon the way regular people perceive their treatment by those in positions of power and control. Assessments of procedural justice can be distinguished from outcome satisfaction, as well as the *distribution* of outcomes or resolutions (or "distributive justice").[59] Procedural justice can also be differentiated from substantive justice, or fairness tied to general ethics or morality.

Introduced by the noted social psychologist John Thibaut and the University of Virginia professor of law emeritus W. Laurens Walker, procedural justice has captivated criminologists, legal scholars, and psychologists for decades. In a series of psychological experiments and simulations comparing adversarial and inquisitorial forms of conflict resolution in the United States and Europe, Thibaut and Walker found that perceptions of fairness greatly influence satisfaction with hypothetical legal encounters.[60] Indeed, in some circumstances, perceptions of fairness appeared to be *the* determinant of overall satisfaction with simulated dispute resolutions.

Like Thibaut and Walker before them, subsequent scholars have arrived at similar conclusions when studying procedural justice in a variety of contexts including the classroom,[61] criminal sentencing,[62] incarceration,[63] restorative justice programs,[64] traffic stops,[65] and the workplace.[66] Time and again, it appears that perceptions of fairness feature prominently in individuals' evaluations of their interactions with authorities, dispute resolution, and the law. In many cases, the fairness of a given legal process matters more than its outcome, whether or not it is considered desirable or as "good as the next guy's."

"When people interact with the legal system in some way, or when they bring a dispute to the legal system for resolution," as the psychologists and legal scholars Rebecca Hollander-Blumoff and Tom Tyler explain, "they care deeply about the fairness of the process that is used to resolve their encounter or dispute, separate and apart from their interest in achieving a favorable outcome. Individuals are more satisfied with, and are more likely to adhere to, dispositions that are reached through procedures that [they] feel are fair."[67] Fair treatment signals that the law is legitimate and moral, strengthening normative attachments to it.[68] Fair treatment can also signal messages about those involved in a legal encounter and counteract marginalization and stigmatization.[69] Faced with uncertainty—say, regarding the trustworthiness of a police officer or a hearing outcome— perceptions of fair treatment make the situation more tolerable.[70]

Ultimately, people expect fair processes to lead to fair outcomes. Moreover, fair processes create obligations to obey. When a legal process is deemed fair, people are more likely to believe in the legitimacy of the authorities and the system involved, as well as to comply with authorities and their decisions.[71]

A number of factors influence evaluations of process fairness, including authorities' behavior and motivations, decision quality, and opportunities for error correction, in addition to opportunities for participation and representation.[72] For example, people are more likely to view legal authorities as legitimate[73] and cooperate with them when treated respectfully.[74] They are more likely to be satisfied with unfavorable outcomes when decision makers appear unbiased or caring.[75] And they are more likely to abide by the rules or comply with a legal decision when they have the chance to tell their side of the story.[76] What's more, authorities' ability to explain their actions in accordance with appropriate laws or rules can mitigate perceptions of bias that might lead one to find a legal encounter unfair.[77] For instance, a judge citing the law when justifying a sentencing decision, or a police officer referencing the speed limit when justifying a traffic ticket, may lead to enhanced perceptions of fairness.[78]

Still, people tend to evaluate fairness differently in formal and informal settings,[79] in cooperative and uncooperative situations,[80] and in dispute resolution and nondispute contexts.[81] For example, fairness of police encounters is judged differently than that of court hearings.[82] Moreover, different groups of people may evaluate procedural justice differently. Although early studies of procedural justice found little evidence of variation in assessments by race,[83] subsequent studies have found that Black Americans are more likely to evaluate encounters with the police as procedurally unjust than White Americans.[84] Yet overall, when individuals feel that authorities are trustworthy, have treated them politely and respectfully,[85] and have listened to and believed them,[86] they are more likely to feel that a legal encounter has been fair. As Tom Tyler, one of the foremost procedural justice scholars, summarizes: "The key factor shaping public behavior . . . is the fairness of the processes legal authorities use when dealing with members of the public."[87]

"Second Wave" Procedural Justice

The concept of procedural justice originates from within this American sociolegal context. Most procedural justice research has been conducted in the United States and similarly situated countries.[88] The Anglocentric nature of procedural justice is its "tell" and its downfall. Fairness is a socially constructed reality.[89] What is considered fair to one person or in one culture, procedurally or otherwise, may be thought unfair by another. The weight given to fair process may also vary by person, place, and time, as well as positionality in relation to the law and the state. Viewing procedural justice from a critical, feminist, postmodern lens brings its flaws into stark relief.

Until recently, most procedural justice research, like most mainstream criminological research,[90] has been limited to generalized comparisons of allegedly homogeneous groups of conventional *citizens*. These citizens are typically presumed to exist in an allegedly homogeneous American, Western, or colonizing culture.[91] Their perceptions of justice, outcome satisfaction, legitimacy, and compliance are then examined through an apolitical, positivist, Western orientation.[92] This research pays little attention to sociolegal status[93] or to the complexities of identity, culture, and society.[94]

For example, racial and ethnic comparisons in procedural justice scholarship are typically limited to analyses of "Blacks" versus "Whites" or broad categorizations of "majority" versus "minority" populations.[95] Such framings ignore the multifaceted nature of race and ethnicity in the United States—let alone around the world. Gender is often treated as little more than a control variable.[96] Sexual orientation, until quite recently, was entirely absent from procedural justice research.[97]

Without meaningful inclusion of identity in procedural justice studies, discussion of intersectional identity has been out of the question.[98] This is not only exclusionary but signifies the outdated nature of mainstream procedural justice literature as intersectional identity has garnered substantial attention in other fields of study for years.[99] Overall, procedural justice literature frequently offers a myopic, ahistorical, apolitical, and asocial view of fairness and the law. To assume that procedural justice operates the same way across culture, experience, and identity is naive at best and arrogant at worst.

Increasingly, however, scholars are examining the impacts of culture, identity, and legal socialization on perceptions of procedural justice, state legitimacy, and compliance with the law. A "second wave" of procedural justice research has emerged,[100] disrupting traditional models of the concept. This literature reveals the relationship between fairness and the law to be much more nuanced than initially presumed. Not only do identity, culture, religion, and sociopolitical history influence assessments of process fairness; they shape the importance of procedural justice itself.

For instance, perceptions of fairness, legitimacy, and compliance have been found to vary by gender identity and sexual orientation. People identifying as members of the lesbian, gay, bisexual, and transgender (LGBT+) community tend to have more negative opinions of the police with regard to procedural justice, trust, and legitimacy than those identifying as heterosexual.[101] Similarly, transgender individuals expect to be treated poorly by police, whether or not they've had encounters with them in the past, which in turn shapes their evaluations of the police.[102]

Procedural justice assessments and impacts are also highly contextual. For example, although procedural justice evaluations weigh heavily on young people's beliefs in state legitimacy and compliance with the law,[103] these beliefs and evaluations vary by community context, such as in high-crime urban areas and among at-risk and delinquent youth.[104] These views are also dynamic, changing as children age.[105]

At times, distributive or substantive justice may outweigh procedural justice with respect to compliance and legitimacy.[106] For example, incarcerated individuals have been found to prioritize the equitable distribution of outcomes across inmates over process fairness when evaluating the legitimacy of legal authorities,[107] as well as to privilege dispute outcomes over fair process.[108] This is likely related to the high stakes of the prison context and the fact that inmates are held in close quarters for stretches of time, allowing them to compare and contrast their sentencing outcomes or the disciplinary actions they face in prison.

As part of this second wave, procedural justice research has also spread around the world with interesting results. Traditional procedural justice models have found some support in places such as Australia,[109] Belgium,[110] Brazil,[111] China,[112] Israel,[113] Jamaica,[114] Kenya,[115] Slovenia,[116] Sweden,[117] Trinidad and Tobago,[118] Turkey,[119] and the United

Kingdom.[120] Yet there is mounting global evidence challenging the procedural justice status quo.

For example, opportunities to provide input appear to have less bearing on procedural justice assessments in societies that normalize power inequality between authority figures and nonauthority figures (e.g., China, Hong Kong, and Mexico) than in those that do not (e.g., the United States and Germany).[121] Similarly, cultural and religious beliefs in India and China may lead distributive justice to outweigh procedural justice in the context of organizational commitment and satisfaction.[122]

In post-Soviet countries, such as Slovenia, procedural justice remains a predictor of police legitimacy, but the effects of legitimacy on compliance are limited.[123] Similarly, the criminologists Kristina Murphy and Adrian Cherney find that, although fair process is generally associated with enhanced perceptions of police legitimacy among ethnic minorities in Australia, it has little effect on willingness to cooperate with the police and may matter less to members of these communities than to those of Anglo-Saxon heritage.[124] In Scotland, where the public generally holds favorable opinions of the police, procedural justice interventions have been found to *decrease* overall satisfaction with police encounters and have no impact on perceptions of legitimacy.[125]

Such variation highlights the historical tendency to overlook context in procedural justice research.[126] Indeed, Justice Tankebe, a Cambridge criminologist, contends that the power of procedural justice is not universal but culturally specific.[127] Examining police-citizen encounters in postcolonial Ghana, he finds that public cooperation with the police depends more heavily upon instrumental factors, such as perceptions of police effectiveness in fighting crime,[128] than it does upon fair process.[129] Tankebe stresses that assumptions about procedural justice are grounded in American cultural experiences and norms. As he explains, these assumptions cannot be made in Ghana, where, for instance, police suffer from a crisis of legitimacy and police-citizen encounters take place within a "sociopolitical context in which abuse and torture might be the consequences of a failure to obey police directives."[130]

Following this logic, researchers have begun to question whether or not procedural justice models operate as expected among immigrant communities, which exist at the intersection of multiple legal cultures and systems. Drawing upon Tankebe's work, the criminologist Daniel

K. Pryce finds that, like Ghanaians residing in Ghana, Ghanaian immigrants residing in the United States are influenced both by procedural justice and effectiveness when assessing the police.[131] Still, as Pryce and his colleagues, the criminologists Devon Johnson and Edward R. Maguire, stress, "little is known about [procedural justice's] effects in immigrant communities, and particularly immigrant communities whose residents may have struggled with police brutality and corruption in their country of origin."[132]

Although traditional procedural justice models have received some support in the immigration context,[133] nascent explorations—like the one found in the pages of this book—indicate that the relationship between the two is complex. For instance, the experience of migrating may predispose immigrants to hold *favorable* views of legal authorities and legal systems in receiving countries, as they are seen to offer improvements over countries of origin.[134] Vicarious procedural justice assessments vis-à-vis family, friends, and the media may have more influence on immigrant compliance with the law and legal authorities than personal experience.[135] Still, procedurally just treatment may be more meaningful to immigrants than nonimmigrants, particularly with regard to willingness to report crime.[136] Ultimately, contrary to mainstream understandings, second-wave studies suggest that there is no one-size-fits-all approach when it comes to procedural justice.

Conclusion

Although growing in number, studies exploring procedural justice across varying cultures, contexts, and identities are still the exception rather than the rule.[137] This emergent body of second-wave procedural justice scholarship cannot help but direct our attention to the underlying assumptions that are often made about the ways people experience and evaluate matters of fairness and the law. It also reveals the many gaps that remain in our understanding of the relationship between lived experience, fairness, and the law. In particular, little is known about the ways that those who exist on the margins of American culture, those who exist outside American culture, and those who find themselves caught between two or more cultures—such as immigrants like Jessica—think about the law.

Contrary to what might be expected by the average onlooker or procedural justice scholar, Jessica found immigration court to be procedurally just. She was not interested in court reforms or additional due process protections within the immigration system. She was pleased with the treatment that she and her son received from the immigration judge, attorneys, and interpreter handling her son's deportation hearing. As will be explored further in chapter 5, Jessica believed in the state's authority to deport *some* immigrants—those who violate criminal law—from the country.

Again, Jessica was knowingly in violation of the law when we spoke. At the time, she was residing in the country without authorization and despite her previous deportation. Yet all the fair process in the world would not get Jessica to accept an order of deportation—not for herself and not for her son. She simply wished there was a way to "give everybody papers" so that they had a chance at making a life in the United States. She longed for substantive immigration reform, meaningful reforms that included amnesty, family reunification, and a life outside the shadows for millions of undocumented immigrants and the millions more who dream of coming to America. Jessica was not alone—similar sentiments were expressed by nearly every immigrant I interviewed.

Jessica's experience begs a number of questions. How do immigrants make sense of the law? Specifically, how does the immigrant experience shape evaluations of procedural justice and legitimacy in the United States? What effects might this have on immigrants' compliance with the law? Does this vary by migration story, length of time in the United States, or visa status? What cultural and legal expectations and experiences do immigrants carry with them from their home countries to their encounters with American law, legal actors,[138] and legal institutions? As is often said in conversations about capital punishment in the context of the criminal defense, death is different.[139] Might deportation also be different? Might the traditional relationship between fair process, legitimacy, and compliance break down in the face of deportation, a fate that, for many, signifies social and even literal death?

Before addressing such questions, however, it is necessary to establish a baseline from which to gauge immigrants' perceptions of justice and legitimacy in the immigration court context. Chapter 2 provides a basic review of the rules and procedures within immigration courts and deportation hearings. It also explores the procedural justice assessments of immigration lawyers, a group of individuals who have been deeply socialized into American cultural and legal norms by virtue of their profession. Unlike Jessica and the other immigrants I spoke to, these attorneys found great procedural faults within deportation hearings, immigration courts, and the immigration system, making it all the more difficult to comprehend why it is that immigrants appear so fond of the immigration court system and its actors.

2

Justice and Immigration Court

"It's kind of a glacial pace," says Charles, who oversaw a law school's immigration clinic at the time. He continues: Clients "are really shocked at the time that passes between hearings in immigration court. . . . [They say], 'This is America! I thought this was the best country in the world and it takes all these months to get things done—or years. This is crazy!'"

Long hearing scheduling and waiting times in immigration court were just one among several commonly cited grievances flagged by those I interviewed. When I spoke with Charles, the immigration court had a national backlog surpassing 500,000 cases. Six years later, the court's backlog approached two million cases—1,809,953 pending cases at the time of this writing.[1] Now, as was also the case when I began this study, hearings are often scheduled months—even years—in advance, and they are commonly delayed or postponed. This is despite the fact that the number of judges employed by the court system jumped from 237 to 460 between 2016 and 2020,[2] as well as the recent implementation of case-completion quotas.[3]

The increased backlog can be traced, in part, to the recent rise in Central American migration discussed in chapter 1. It can also be traced to shifts in immigration policy and practice under the Trump administration. For example, although the deportation of immigrants with criminal records was prioritized under President Obama, the Trump administration was determined to pursue any and all deportation cases. Indeed, Trump officials moved to restrict, and then eliminate, "administrative closure," a discretionary practice affording judges a means of removing a hearing from the docket without granting a decision in light of pending decisions that could affect case outcome or because they are considered low-priority cases.[4] The push to pursue more deportation cases, predictably, increased court caseloads—and backlogs.

Still, the ever-increasing backlog should come as little surprise to those familiar with the history and workings of America's immigration court system, which is designed neither to handle large caseloads nor to be particularly fair. Infamously likened to "trying death penalty cases in traffic court,"[5] the immigration court system has long suffered from both administrative and procedural shortcomings.

U.S. Immigration Court and the Deportation Hearing

For most of U.S. history, immigration matters were not decided by an independent court but were instead handled by immigration inspection officials employed by the now defunct Immigration and Naturalization Service (INS). These officials were not technically judges or required to have a law degrees.[6] In 1962, the Department of Justice established a staff of trial attorneys to represent the government in immigration matters, and a decade later "special inquiry officers" were designated as "immigration judges" by regulation.[7] The Executive Office for Immigration Review (EOIR, i.e., the immigration court) was finally established as an independent body within the Department of Justice in 1983, severing the ties—for the most part—between immigration enforcement and adjudication.

The court is the judicial arm of the immigration system and is responsible for adjudicating hundreds of thousands of immigration cases annually through the interpretation and administration of federal law. The system comprises 67 courts[8] and two adjudication centers.[9] Immigration courts are trial-level tribunals tasked with interpreting and applying federal immigration law[10] and conduct a variety of proceedings, appellate reviews, and administrative hearings. The system receives hundreds of thousands of cases each year, most of which involve Central American immigrants.[11] The vast majority of cases on the court's docket are deportation hearings.[12]

The United States Supreme Court has consistently held that immigration matters, including deportation and detention, are civil, not criminal, in character.[13] As such, immigrants facing deportation and detention are not afforded many of the due process protections guaranteed to defendants in criminal proceedings.[14] For example, immigrants do not have a right to indigent defense in immigration proceedings (whereas criminal defendants are appointed a lawyer if they cannot afford one). Moreover, evidence obtained without a proper warrant or in violation of the landmark case *Miranda v. Arizona* can be admitted in immigration hearings, with the exception of egregious Fourth Amendment violations.[15] Immigrants do have the right to present evidence and cross-examine witnesses in immigration court or to appeal bond and deportation decisions.[16] They are granted some Fifth Amendment protections, including the right to a "fundamentally fair" deportation hearing.[17]

Under some circumstances, the rights of immigrants facing deportation are further restricted. For example, specific classes of immigrants, such as those convicted of certain felony crimes, may be subject to administrative deportation by an immigration officer, expedited prison hearings, and/or judicial deportation when connected to a federal criminal case at sentencing.[18] Suspected terrorists are also subject to different deportation procedures that are not handled by immigration court but instead by a special terrorist deportation court.[19] Typically, though, deportation proceedings are held in immigration court. From 2016 to 2021, the court averaged roughly 350,000 new deportation cases per year.[20]

A deportation hearing, or "removal" hearing,[21] is initiated when DHS files a "Notice to Appear" (NTA; Form I-862) or in some cases a "Notice of Referral to Immigration Judge" (Form I-863) with the immigration court after it has been served on a noncitizen or anyone in the United States who does not hold American citizenship but who may hold a visa or lawful permanent residency.[22] DHS has "virtually unfettered prosecutorial discretion" to file such charges with the court.[23] DHS can issue a Notice to Appear to a noncitizen upon her arrival to the United States, as well as to a noncitizen already present in the United States. Aside from logistical information, the NTA contains both the noncitizen's acts or conduct alleged to be in violation of the law and the charge(s) against the noncitizen, along with the statutory provision(s) alleged to have been violated.[24]

Deportation proceedings are divided into initial hearings and merits hearings. *Initial hearings* are the immigration equivalent of a pretrial hearing and cover matters such as pleadings, scheduling, bond determinations, and related tasks like advising an immigrant of her rights and explaining the charges leveled against her. This is also when a decision is made as to the immigrant's deportability; if an immigrant's deportability is contested, the judge may schedule a separate hearing on the question of deportability. Initial hearings are slotted on "Master Calendars,"[25] in which numerous hearings are scheduled in one day. For example, it is not unusual for a judge to complete two dozen initial hearings—before lunch—on a Master Calendar day.

During a deportation hearing the government is represented by an ICE trial attorney.[26] It is the ICE attorney's burden to establish an immigrant's alienage and deportability.[27] Generally, an immigrant may be subject to deportation if she entered the United States without authorization, overstayed a valid visa, or was convicted of certain types of criminal offenses. Again, there is no constitutional right to appointed counsel in immigration court. Although immigrants have the right to effective assistance of counsel in immigration court under the Fifth Amendment, lack of representation does not violate due process.[28] When immigrants cannot hire an attorney or acquire pro bono representation, they must represent themselves pro se (i.e., without assistance of counsel).

The difficulties of obtaining immigration representation have been highlighted by numerous scholars. For example, between 2007 and 2012, 37% of all immigrants in deportation proceedings, and just 14% of all detained immigrants, were represented by an attorney.[29] As of May 2021, only about 6% of all immigrants currently in deportation proceedings, and just 22% of all detained immigrants, were represented by an attorney.[30] Similarly, the difficulties of acquiring *quality* legal representation in the immigration context have also been demonstrated,[31] including the dangers of *notario* fraud.[32] This is especially noteworthy as immigrants with legal representation are far more likely to obtain relief from deportation than those without representation.[33]

It is an immigrant's responsibility to demonstrate eligibility for relief if she chooses to contest her deportation. Alternatively, if eligible, immigrants can choose to leave the United States voluntarily. Immigration judges are required to inform immigrants of any apparent relief eligibility.[34] If the immigrant is not petitioning for relief, a decision to deport the immigrant or to terminate the proceedings will be made during the initial hearing. Petitions for relief from deportation are heard at individual merits hearings; a decision to grant or deny relief (and remove the immigrant) is made at that stage.

Common forms of pursuing relief or forestalling deportation include: adjustment of status, asylum[35] and withholding, cancellation, motions to reopen or reconsider, and stay of deportation. Because the United

States is party to the United Nations Convention Against Torture, relief from deportation may also be afforded to individuals who would likely be subject to torture, either at the hands of or due to the inaction of government actors, if returned to their country.[36] Additional forms of relief from deportation are extended to individuals from certain former Soviet countries, from countries that have recently experienced a natural disaster, and victims of various crimes.[37] Judges are required to interpret deportation grounds in favor of immigrants; however, immigration judges have the discretion to grant—or not grant—relief from deportation.[38] Typically, less than a quarter of deportation cases end in some form of relief allowing immigrants to remain in the United States, but this varies from court to court and judge to judge.[39] If an immigrant fails to appear at any of her scheduled hearings during the deportation process, the judge can—and often does—issue a deportation order in absentia.

The Board of Immigration Appeals (BIA) has jurisdiction regarding decisions in most deportation cases.[40] Since the early 2010s, the BIA has received between approximately 30,000 and 40,000 cases each year—this number jumped to nearly 50,000 in 2018—with the vast majority being appeals of judges' decisions.[41] Immigration appeals were originally subject to review by a panel of five immigration judges, but reforms instituted by former U.S. Attorney Generals Janet Reno and John Ashcroft reduced review to a single judge; BIA judges are not required to write an opinion if upholding a lower court decision.[42]

Some immigration decisions are eligible for judicial review—such as those involving constitutional claims and legal questions. Review eligibility, however, was severely limited by federal legislation passed in the 1990s and early 2000s.[43] Decisions pertaining to relief from deportation, among others, are generally excluded from judicial review. Despite this, a handful of immigration appeals eventually make their way up to the United States Supreme Court.

Detention

Increasingly, immigrants facing deportation are held in detention for the duration of at least some—if not all—of the hearing process, which can last months or even years.[44] Immigration detention has been likened to "criminal detention but without the constitutional protections."[45] Immigration detention is a form of civil confinement, not punishment, making it exempt from many protections guaranteed in the criminal justice system. Indeed, there is no constitutional right to release on bond, and some classes of immigrants are subject to mandatory detention.[46]

The list of individuals subject to mandatory detention has expanded significantly over decades, in large part due to the passage of the Anti-Terrorism and Effective Death Penalty Act (AEDPA) and the Illegal Immigration Reform and Immigrant Responsibility Act (IIRIRA). Today, mandatory detention applies to anyone who has committed a "crime involving moral turpitude," defined as a crime involving fraud or vile, base, or depraved conduct that is generally intended to harm and violates accepted moral standards;[47] committed any drug-related, firearms-related, money laundering–related, or prostitution-related offense; committed an "aggravated felony," which, under federal immigration law, includes some criminal misdemeanors; or has two or more criminal convictions.[48] Individuals whom DHS believes are drug traffickers or have engaged in any terrorist-related activities are also subject to mandatory detention.[49]

In cases where detention is not mandatary, bond decisions are left to the discretion of immigration judges.[50] Although judges in criminal proceedings must consider a defendant's ability to pay when determining a bail amount, immigration judges are not required to consider financial means when setting bond.[51] As such, it is not unusual for immigrants who have been granted bond to remain in detention due to the inability to pay.[52]

Most attorneys I interviewed explained that representing detained clients is more difficult than representing nondetained clients. As Dimitri, an immigrant himself who had practiced law for over 40 years, summarizes, "detained clients pose a lot of obstacles." For one, detention facilities are often located hours away from court—and attorneys' offices—in rather remote areas. This makes it hard for attorneys to visit clients and speak with them in person. Harry, an attorney with more than 15 years' experience, elaborates that "if I'm going to be doing stuff efficiently . . . I'm not going to go [to the detention facility]. . . . So everything's done by phone and by mail. . . . Obviously there are advantages to going down there and seeing them in person. . . . I could do that, but it would be a different relationship, financially. It's just not possible to do that for what I'm charging."

Another attorney paid for an "open line" with area detention facilities so that her clients could always reach her by phone, which she believed helped to build better relationships with clients. Several attorneys stressed that, when working with detained clients, it is important to find someone on the outside—a family member or friend—who can help transport important documents (e.g., birth or marriage certificates, official immigration paperwork, and other types of evidence). Despite various strategies of accommodation, a couple attorneys revealed having been unable to locate detained clients on various occasions after ICE moved them from facility to facility—without warning—during their deportation proceedings.[53]

Interpretation

English is the language of record in immigration court. The majority of individuals in immigration proceedings, however, have limited English proficiency (LEP). The Federal Court Interpreters Act (1978) requires the use of interpreters in federal proceedings, whether civil (e.g., immigration court) or criminal. Executive Order 13166 and Title VI of the Civil Rights Act also require federal agencies to ensure that LEP individuals have "meaningful access" to courts.[54] Lower federal courts have upheld the right to interpretation for LEP individuals in criminal court, but the Supreme Court has not weighed in on the matter.[55]

Those in immigration court with English abilities deemed "inadequate to fully understand and participate in [deportation] proceedings" are provided interpreters.[56] "Especially in immigration proceedings," explains Eugenio Mollo Jr., an immigration attorney and University of Toledo lecturer in law, "interpreters are a focal point in the judicial process. They are arguably more representative of a client than [their] attorney. An interpreter is the direct spokesperson for the [immigrant]."[57]

EOIR employs about 80 staff interpreters and upward of 1,500 contract interpreters.[58] Many courts use "in-house" interpreters for Spanish language needs. For other languages, contract interpreters are brought in, sometimes traveling across the country. When this isn't an option, telephonic interpretation services are used. EOIR's reliance on privately contracted interpreters has been heavily criticized by interpreters, legal practitioners, and labor rights activists due to exploitative working conditions for interpreters and reductions in interpretation quality.[59]

Judges are responsible for determining when interpretation is required and what language is appropriate, often relying on immigrants' attorneys, if being represented, for assistance. There is no indigenous language screening mechanism in immigration court, and immigrants are generally assumed to speak the dominant language of their country of origin.[60] Immigrants' primary languages are routinely misidentified during initial encounters with CBP,[61] and such misidentification may follow them to detention[62] and immigration court.[63] When this occurs, the provision of incorrect interpretation dramatically hinders courtroom communication[64] and can go undetected for most or even all of the court hearing.

All interpreters take an oath "to interpret and translate accurately" and are overseen by the EOIR's Language Services Unit, which conducts "quality assurance programs."[65] Immigration court interpreters are not required to be certified by the Administrative Office of the United States Courts or to take the standard certification exam by the Consortium for Language Access in the Courts.[66] Instead, immigration courts conduct internal interpreter screenings and rely upon private contractors to screen and certify language interpreters.

Although interpretation facilitates hearings and makes legal processes more accessible, it also mediates and modifies communication between parties.[67] "Good" interpretation speeds up hearings and reduces the risk of serious misunderstandings and errors.[68] "Bad" interpretation can be detrimental. As Muneer I. Ahmad, clinical professor of law and director of the Jerome N. Frank Legal Services Organization at Yale Law School, explains, even with increasing professionalization, "the quality of courtroom interpretation varies greatly, and demand for qualified interpreters vastly outstrips supply."[69]

Linguists and legal scholars have noted many issues with interpretation ranging from minor communication errors and lack of language proficiency to paraphrasing and interjections of personal opinion to implicit and explicit bias.[70] For instance, interpreters' use of linguistic hedge words—such as "um," "uh," or "well"—has been found to negatively impact the way immigrants are perceived, undermining their credibility and testimony.[71] In another study, immigration court observers in New York noted multiple instances in which interpreters made anti-immigrant statements in open court, including that immigrants should "get the f--- out" and referring to them as "freeloaders."[72] In short, a lot of "bad" interpretation takes place in courts across America, and immigration court is no different.[73]

Despite the many critiques of court interpreters, attorneys I interviewed generally agreed that the quality of interpretation in the immigration courts under study was good. Still, as one attorney explained, interpretation is "more art than science," involving the transmission not only of words but also of cultural and emotional meaning. Interpretation is "inescapably subjective."[74] It is also an inherently political act.

As María Rosario Martín Ruano, associate professor of translation and interpretation at the University of Salamanca, contends, "neutral" interpretation simply does not exist.[75] As she explains: "[I]nasmuch as translation entails a refracted reception of alien idiosyncrasies, and to the extent that the ensuing relocation of meaning is inevitably influenced by the dominant ideologies, established identity constructions, and accepted social discourses and narratives prevailing in the target context, the renderings resulting from literal translation . . . might be perceived as blunt, weird or exotic, [reinforcing] negative perceptions of the foreign culture as radically Other."[76]

Instead, effective interpretation requires language proficiency *and* "culturally specific performance," including emotional simulations bordering on "theatrics."[77] The use of slang and colloquial expressions, style, and local or regional differences in language structure, vocabulary, meaning, pronunciation, and accent create cultural and linguistic barriers between speakers, interpreters, and listeners.[78]

Along these lines, attorneys I spoke with stressed that, even with the best interpreters, some words and phrases lose their meaning when translated. No matter how good court interpreters are, explains Marisa, a midcareer attorney with a high volume of deportation defense cases, "it's always better for your client if they can speak English—the impact of what they're saying is more direct and the best translator in the world can't convey all the nuances." In addition to being fluent, attorneys emphasized that interpreters must account for emotion, intonation, and pauses, which is more difficult to gauge in some languages than others (e.g., Romance versus tonal languages). "You translate a word to English and it's just—it doesn't have the same, almost a feeling," Rachel, a Latina attorney in her thirties, reflected. "Like it's [the] history and feeling of this word. That can be really difficult [to convey]."

At other times, cultural differences are embodied in communication, confusing and frustrating attorneys, interpreters, judges, and immigrants alike. Several attorneys pointed out, for example, that something as small as differences in house-numbering systems (e.g., the third house on Such-and-Such street versus 1234 Such-and-Such Street) can lead to communication breakdowns in immigration court. Similarly, varying cultural norms governing interaction with authority figures, such as judges, can also lead to serious communication breakdowns during immigration hearings.

For example, several attorneys pointed out that, although American culture generally dictates that one address authority figures directly as a sign of respect, in other cultures one is expected to avoid eye contact with those in authority, as well as to agree with whatever they say—even if it is not accurate. As Harry explains:

> You may say something that you think is sort of vague and [the court] will take it as something specific and, all the sudden, start asking you questions. . . . It doesn't make any sense, but you're just gonna say "yes, yes, yes," because . . . that's how you've been raised. So [clients] sometimes get in trouble because there are just certain cultural issues where you're not gonna say "no" to somebody in authority. You're gonna try to just agree with them. And you have to not agree with people obviously if . . . you give an answer and [they] repeat it back in a way that's wrong. Some clients just go with that. And then, all the sudden, they're going down a bad path.

This, in turn, may lead judges and ICE attorneys to believe that respondents are lying. Credibility is crucial to most deportation hearings because, as many attorneys stressed, discretionary relief often rests upon credibility.

Communication issues posed by country and dialect variations, as well as the provision of interpretation in immigrants' secondary languages, were also frequently mentioned. For example, Diane, who started her own immigration firm in the mid-2000s, recalled a case being "ground to a halt" because an interpreter did not speak the same dialect as her client. Another explained that many of his Indigenous clients were not provided interpretation in their primary language. Instead, they were typically offered interpretation in a secondary (colonizing) language more commonly associated with their countries of origin.[79]

Attorneys noted that inappropriate interpretation occurred not only when clients spoke uncommon dialects or languages but also when clients spoke popular languages. Spanish interpretation was most common in the courts under study, reflecting both the large Spanish-speaking immigrant communities in the area and the fact that Latin American immigrants make up the majority of immigrants placed in deportation proceedings each year. Spanish varies greatly across—and within—the countries where it is spoken, and speakers from each country have distinctly different accents and vocabularies. As one attorney reflected, Spanish-speaking immigrant communities in the region are predominantly Central American, but most of the Spanish-speaking interpreters working in immigration court are Colombian, Cuban, or Puerto Rican. This linguistic disconnect was said to cause miscommunications with potentially grave consequences. Many attorneys noted that, although some interpreters were aware of and attempted to account for such differences, many neither acknowledged nor attempted to address this reality.

Complicating matters further, unlike in other court settings, interpreters are not required to interpret all statements made during immigration proceedings, often rendering only those statements *made by* and *directed to* immigrants.[80] Immigration courts also permit both consecutive and simultaneous interpretation but lack guidelines regarding when one form of interpretation should be used over the other.

The difference between these two interpretation styles is significant. Consecutive interpretation is the rendering of one language to another "spoken in brief sound bites successively, without omissions or embellishments, so that the parties can understand each other slowly and deliberately."[81] Simultaneous interpretation is the rendering "of one spoken language into another when running renditions are needed at the same time as the English language communication."[82] Consecutive and simultaneous interpretation methods are thus quite distinct, and the use of one or the other may lead to disparate courtroom experiences.

Indeed, the National Association of Judiciary Interpreters and Translators (NAJIT) advises that consecutive interpretation be used when LEP individuals play an "active role" in court, or "when they must speak or respond," and that simultaneous interpretation be used when participants play a "passive role."[83] This recommendation, however, is not always observed in immigration court. Instead, technological constraints and other aspects of the hearing (e.g., physical presence of the immigrant in the courtroom as opposed to appearing remotely from detention, or physical presence of the interpreter in the courtroom as opposed to participating via teleconferencing) tend to dictate the use of consecutive versus simultaneous interpretation.

Many attorneys pointed out that interpreters often provide shortened, summary-style interpretations of courtroom dialogue. At other times, they simply fail to interpret dialogue not directed at immigrants altogether. These interpretation practices not only have implications for the accuracy of what is being communicated between individuals during a deportation hearing; they can also have a negative effect on immigrants and attorneys alike. Charles remarked that shortened interpretations are downright "nerve-racking." "If you don't know the other language, then you're sort of on pins and needles like, 'What in the heck is [the interpreter] saying?' It's huge. . . . You're speaking your native language and the interpreter comes back in English—and you were going on for a long time—and the interpreter says, 'She said yes.' It can play a huge role . . . [with regard to] the psychological impact. It'd be great if we could do it all in a language we all understood."

Given the frequency of shortened interpretations, some attorneys said that they prepped clients to provide testimony in "bite-sized speech" with deliberate pauses that allow—and can prompt—interpreters to produce word-for-word interpretations. Still, they stressed that this was an inadequate means of addressing a larger problem.

Laura Abel, senior policy counsel at the Lawyers Alliance for New York and former deputy director of the National Center for Access to Justice at Cardozo Law School, has criticized immigration court for the routine provision of partial interpretation, in which interpretation is limited to dialogue spoken by, or directed toward, immigrant respondents.[84] As a result, "LEP individuals may not be able to comprehend the testimony of English-speaking witnesses and exchanges between the Immigration Judge and Trial Attorney and defense counsel."[85] Furthermore, when immigrants are acting pro se, they cannot count on a lawyer to summarize uninterpreted dialogue and "may leave the proceeding with no idea what has just occurred . . . [and] unable to respond to testimony provided by other witnesses."[86]

Beyond questions of adequate or appropriate interpretation, attorneys also highlighted the occasional interpreter error. Recognizing—and challenging—interpreter mistakes requires at least some second language competency. Although many of the attorneys I interviewed spoke a second language, most acknowledged that they weren't in an ideal position to judge interpreter accuracy.

Attorneys also expressed frustration over what they perceived to be the court's bias in favor of "official interpretation." They agreed that interpreters, when challenged, stand by what they have said and that judges side with interpreters. As such, only about half the attorneys interviewed said that they challenge interpreter errors, but only when such errors are "egregious" enough to be detrimental to a case.

For example, Marco, a young attorney of Latin American descent, recounted objecting to an interpretation of the Spanish slang term *maricón* as "fairy." The attorney explained that, in the context it was uttered, the original connotation of the word was derogatory and was more appropriately translated as "faggot." Because he felt the case outcome hinged in part on the correct interpretation of this single word, it necessitated an objection. Limiting objections to serious errors such as this can be difficult for attorneys. Another attorney elaborates, "[W]hen something's off and you're representing someone, you do kind of take it a little bit personally. [This happened to me recently,] so I was kind of biting my tongue and punching my fist, but I didn't say anything."

Videoconferencing

Immigration court is further complicated by the use of telephonic and videoconference technology. Attorneys I interviewed associated the use of these technologies during hearings with a number of technical difficulties, from poor connections and inaudible audio to dropped calls and frozen images—all of which were disruptions I frequently witnessed during my court observations. Just as attorneys repeatedly stressed a preference for in-person interpretation over telephonic interpretation, they preferred that their clients be physically present in the courtroom as opposed to appearing via videoconferencing.

Immigrants do not have a right to an in-person hearing in immigration courts where videoconferencing equipment is used. Videoconference technology is generally used in place of physically transporting detained immigrants to immigration court for their hearings under the auspices of efficiency, safety, and cost savings. It is also used to facilitate judge substitutions and remote attorney appearances when needed.

The use of videoconferencing in court settings has been widely criticized as having the potential to "greatly change the dynamic of a [court] proceeding."[87] Videoconferencing depersonalizes contact between courtroom actors[88] and impedes defense attorneys' ability to provide zealous representation to their clients.[89] It may impair defendants' audio and visual perceptions of hearings and deprive them of spontaneous interjections, opportunities to address the court, and the ability to seek clarification.[90] It may also negatively influence the court's perspective, the defendant's experience, and process fairness.[91] Because it is frequently used in place of transporting detained or jailed individuals to court, videoconferencing disproportionately impacts those who cannot afford—or are not eligible for—bond.[92]

The Fourth Circuit U.S. Court of Appeals has recognized that videoconference testimony fails to convey emotion with the same power of in-person testimony, and both the Fourth and Seventh Circuits have acknowledged that appearing via videoconference is *not* the same as appearing physically and that it may be detrimental to an individual's case.[93] However, the circuit courts have yet to find that videoconferencing deprives immigrants of a full or fair opportunity to present their cases in immigration court.[94]

It is difficult to discern how widespread the use of videoconferencing is within immigration court because official records on the use of such technology are not generally released to the public. Still, the availability of videoconferencing technology in immigration courts across the country, the increase in matters received by the immigration court in recent decades,[95] and the increasing use of detention[96] have led some to predict that videoconferencing may become the dominant method of deportation adjudication.[97]

Videoconferencing technology was first used in immigration court in 1995.[98] The passage of IIRIRA in 1996 formalized its use in immigration court.[99] By the mid-2000s, most immigration courts had been outfitted with videoconference technology.[100] By 2010, 12 percent of all immigration court hearings were conducted via videoconference.[101] Today, videoconferencing is used in place of physically transporting detained immigrants to court for their deportation hearings in about one-third of all detained cases.[102] It is also used to permit judge substitutions and remote attorney appearances.

Videoconferencing was consistently flagged as problematic by attorneys. Charles lamented that videoconferencing is "choppy" and often accompanied by a time lag. Another attorney remarked on how "annoying" videoconferencing can be, adding that they have "a lot of trouble with the TVs and sound going out and the screens freezing." Mitch, a former ICE trial attorney in his forties, characterized the court's videoconference technology as "somewhat antiquated," noting that the picture quality can be "degraded so much that you can only see a form [instead of a human being]." Attorneys also told stories of judges losing their temper over videoconferencing malfunctions. Emily, a private immigration attorney, noted that "it's obviously a problem when [immigrants] start talking and you can't hear them."

Given these technological issues, it is no surprise that attorneys flagged any combination of interpretation and telephonic appearances or videoconferencing as potentially detrimental to their cases. For example, many highlighted the negative cumulative effects of the transmission of sound across multiple devices, locations, and people. As Charles, whose take was characteristic of those I interviewed, summarizes: "If efficiency is an issue with live interpreters, individuals in the same room, it's more of an issue [with videoconferencing]."

Audiovisual difficulties were also said to exacerbate problems of interpreter accuracy. Like many, Emily stressed that interpreters are "not just supposed to be saying the words, but conveying emotion as well." This is much harder to do, attorneys said, when interpreters cannot see or hear the person speaking very well—or, in some cases, at all. Moreover, interpreters generally performed consecutive interpretation when conducted via telephonic appearance or videoconferencing, which attorneys found problematic.

Videoconferencing was also associated with limited interpretation more generally. Attorneys recalled entire stretches of courtroom dialogue during videoconference hearings that were not interpreted for clients—instead, only communication directed to or spoken by clients was interpreted. Although attorneys acknowledged that interpretation of *all* hearing dialogue would likely double the length of hearings, for a minority it was a matter of due process. Alex, who had an established private practice and staff of several attorneys, recounts:

> [Videoconferencing is] really awful. I had a [complicated case representing a drug trafficker in a deportation proceeding where] the government was really, really fighting the case. We started out with his ex-partner testifying, so it was Spanish and my client could understand that. But then we had an expert testify for three hours. And we didn't have simultaneous translation. We had no translation. My client couldn't understand anything that was being said. And the court thought that was fine. And I actually suggested having the translator step out, we get [the respondent] a phone in the room, and [the translator] just uses my cell phone and translates in the back of the courtroom. No. That wasn't allowed. It ended up we had about nine hours in just English testimony that we ultimately needed. I went to [the detention facility] with my laptop and I translated it for him. . . . [The court] didn't care. They didn't care at all. You know I tried to argue due process and everything, and "we don't have the capability" was their response.

Court observations corroborated how often long stretches of English courtroom dialogue between judges and attorneys were not interpreted for immigrants—whether they were represented by attorneys or appeared pro se. In such instances, immigrants were not provided summary explanations of what was being said and were not invited to pose questions or request clarification.

Scholars have highlighted the ways in which problems with videoconferencing are exacerbated in the context of immigration court, where credibility assessments and interpretation play a central role in adjudication.[103] Nonlinguistic and paralinguistic cues, including intonation and physical gestures, are fundamental aspects of communication.[104] Telephone and video equipment lacks the technical capabilities court interpretation requires, compromising the quality of interpretation.[105] Telephonic interpretation eliminates visual cues and impedes sound cues that interpreters rely on "to determine the meaning, style and tone of the speech to be translated."[106] As telephonic interpretation is provided via speakerphone, it is accompanied by the "additional drawback of poor sound quality."[107]

Similarly, videoconferencing inhibits the accurate transmission of communication and immigrants' comprehension of dialogue, altering voice tones and changing the meaning of words, making some words inaudible, and impairing immigrants' abilities to accurately interpret nonverbal cues from interpreters and others.[108] Videoconferencing exacerbates cultural differences in communication and reduces mutual trust and understanding, carrying serious implications given the multicultural interactions inherent to immigration court.[109] Moreover, videoconferencing inadequately captures body language and eye contact, dehumanizing individuals, which "fundamentally alters the way a judge perceives an asylum applicant's testimony . . . [thereby making] an applicant seem less trustworthy" and negatively impacting fact finder decisions.[110] For these reasons, Abel has called for the curtailment of both telephonic and videoconferencing when interpretation is used in immigration court.[111]

More generally, videoconferencing has been associated with litigant disengagement and may "interfere with meaningful participation in the adversarial process."[112] Ingrid Eagly, professor of law at UCLA Law School, finds that immigrants with televideo trials are significantly less likely to apply for relief from deportation and voluntary departure, or obtain lawyers, than similarly situated immigrants with in-person trials.[113] Eagly argues that videoconferencing confuses and discourages immigrants; impedes confidential attorney-immigrant communication; reduces immigrants' ability to understand and assert their rights and harms judges' ability to advise immigrants of their rights (something they are legally required to do); and prevents family, community members, and the public from attending hearings in remote locations.[114]

Given such issues, most attorneys I interviewed felt that courtroom technology negatively impacts judges' evaluations and decisions. Attorneys frequently pointed out that discretionary relief from deportation rests heavily upon credibility, which is determined as much by *how* one is perceived as *what* one says. "When you have live people in court," Emily reasons, "it's much easier for . . . the judge to evaluate demeanor." Charles confirms, "it's very impactful to see someone there [in the courtroom] and crying" as opposed to watching someone give testimony on a TV screen. One attorney claimed that judges rarely look at respondents when they appeared via videoconferencing. Mauricio, a midcareer attorney who spent several years as a public defender in the 1990s before going into immigration law, summarizes that "it's a very difficult thing, [videoconferencing]. Your client cannot see you unless the judge moves the camera. Your client, if he [doesn't speak English], can only hear the translator . . . [and is] looking down at this screen and not at the judge. . . . The problem is, there's no real sense of being here." Ultimately, attorneys overwhelmingly agreed that interpretation, telephonic conferencing, and videoconferencing technology—on their own—pose numerous due process issues, and these problems only intensify when interpretation and technology combine.

ICE Trial Attorneys

As mentioned above, it is the ICE trial attorney's burden to establish an immigrant's alienage and deportability during a deportation hearing.[115] As such, the ICE trial attorney functions in a parallel role to the prosecutor in a criminal hearing and is considered to be the adversary of attorneys who represent immigrants facing deportation.

Immigration attorneys I interviewed painted complicated and often contradictory pictures of ICE attorneys. Some ICE attorneys were said to be "compassionate," "patient," "reasonable," and "smart," and others were characterized as "aggressive," "dumb," "ruthless," and "tricky." "Well, you have those who are like the judges and are patient and try to give the benefit of the doubt," Mauricio says, "and then you have those who think that they're running for prosecutor of the year! 'We oppose! We oppose! We oppose!'" Some attorneys "contest everything just to do it," sighed another attorney.

Still, most attorneys stressed that ICE attorneys aren't all "bad people." Even those who come off as very "stone-faced" or engage in "accusatory" questioning are usually "courteous and professional." "Some [ICE attorneys] deserve to be talked about rudely," another attorney remarked, though stressing that most are "pretty good" and "overall very reasonable."

Many immigration attorneys pointed out that ICE attorneys' behavior and demeanor are influenced by age, experience, and the local ICE office culture.[116] They generally agreed that younger, less experienced ICE attorneys are typically more "gung-ho" than older, more seasoned attorneys. Still, a handful of attorneys argued that, although the "baby" ICE attorneys are generally tougher, ICE attorneys can also become "hardened" or, like judges, "jaded" over time.

Immigration Judges

In the face of unreliable interpretation and technology, ICE attorney Russian roulette, and possibly from within the walls of a detention facility, the deportation hearing proceeds, presided over by an immigration judge. Immigration judges are Administrative Law Judges (ALJs) and part of the executive branch of government, as opposed to judicial branch.[117] All immigration judges are appointed by the U.S. Attorney General. Immigration judges are technically classified by the Department of Justice as "attorney employees"[118] and must be attorneys in order to sit on the immigration bench.

Given their classification, immigration judges lack the job security and independence afforded to judges in the judicial branch, as well as the power of contempt authority, making it difficult for them to sanction attorneys appearing before them.[119] They do, however, have ample discretion to adjudicate immigration cases, and their decisions are considered final. Although decisions can be appealed, successful appeals are limited and rare. Taken together, these factors have caused scholars such as Fatma Marouf, professor of law and director of the Immigrant Rights Clinic at Texas A&M University School of Law,[120] and Gerald L. Neuman, J. Sinclair Armstrong Professor of International, Foreign, and Comparative Law and codirector of the Human Rights Program at Harvard Law School,[121] to question the presence of outside influence and personal bias in immigration judge decision-making.[122]

The attorneys I interviewed expressed mixed feelings toward immigration judges. Most agreed that, in their experiences, immigration judges tend to be pleasant, professional, and unbiased. For example, a few attorneys characterized several judges in the courts under study as being "the best." As one attorney elaborated, "God knows, the judges [in the court here] are just superb. . . . They have such respect for the lawyers that they will sometimes accommodate you to death. . . . I don't know how they can be so patient. But then there are other courts that are very similar . . . [that are] excellent, wonderful."

Elizabeth, a midcareer attorney working at a small practice, states that "I really like the judges [here]. I like all of them. I think they're all really fair. Some of them are a little tougher than others but, in general, they're pretty fair." She highlighted one judge who comes off "strict and by the book" but who actually "takes the time to read your argument and will research it on his own," and another who was particularly "great with kids," making a clear effort to put them at ease. "Each have their quirks that make them relatable," she concludes, "and it shows that they really care and they're not out to just deport people and get them off their docket."

These sentiments were shared by most of the attorneys with whom I spoke, who described most judges as "fair," "impartial," and "concerned" not only with immigrants' comfort in the courtroom but also with their comprehension of the law. Some attorneys pointed out that many immigration judges come from ICE backgrounds—as opposed to the private bar or nonprofit realm—but are not inherently biased.[123] Charles summarizes how "[some judges here] take the approach that the government never loses. If someone is deported for whatever reason or some criminal thing, then they've done their job. And if someone is granted asylum, then they've also done their job. So it's not like a loss. They're not trying to deport everyone." Still, a handful of attorneys pointed out that some judges are "more generous with their interpretation of the law than others."

Many attorneys acknowledged that judges' behavior can be rather disconcerting to attorneys and their immigrant clients. Attorneys agreed that some judges are "friendlier" while others are "a little more intimidating." As one attorney put it, some judges are "less patient, much more likely to . . . be aggressive and hostile in questioning the client, be rude to the attorney, [and] be too deferent to the government [attorney]." Still others framed this as a matter of being more direct. Elizabeth states simply that "[there are some judges who] don't want to hear your sob story. They don't want to get into anything with you. They want you to file your application, make your argument, [and] get out."

More attorneys, however, cast judges in a positive light, though they are sometimes odd. "I think some [judges] are more maybe prone to joke, to be more 'familiar' with people, which can be off-putting," one attorney explained, "but it's never, never anything rude. . . . It gives [the hearing] sort of a human touch." Indeed, several attorneys characterized judges' behavior as perhaps surprising at times but mostly benign. A few judges were specifically known among the immigration bar for being "jokesters." This was something Elizabeth highlighted. She explained that she warns her clients in advance in case the jokes wind up lost in translation. Attorneys did acknowledge, however, that a minority of judges made remarks in court that they found troubling.

Attorneys pointed out that some judges make statements—whether the judges realize it or not—indicating bias against immigrants of certain genders or sexual orientations[124] or nationalities. Many recounted stories in which judges were said to have made remarks such as "this guy doesn't look gay to me" or "she's not lesbian because she's way too pretty." Attorneys noted that some judges hold biases against Central American, Chinese, and Nigerian asylum seekers specifically, assuming that they are most likely to bring forth fraudulent asylum claims. However, the majority of attorneys emphasized that explicitly biased or derogatory comments are rarely uttered by judges. And yet generalizations about certain countries or certain immigration claims were said to be relatively frequent.

Still, many attorneys had been exposed to particularly troubling commentary from the bench at one point or another. One attorney recounted an instance he found especially offensive, noting that a judge commented on an African client's tardiness by saying, "Well you're late. And I'm Tarzan—you Jane." While acknowledging that this did not prove outright bias, the attorney stressed that he often feels forced not only to defend his clients but also to defend entire countries and cultures. As he put it, "I've seen some bad judges. . . . [You don't have to] just defend somebody from deportation, but to defend the entire atmosphere. Where they come from, what the country is like—things that really [should be irrelevant]. . . . We're dealing with the law here. Let's get to [the law]. . . . There's no need for extraneous things, which [is] how [judges] can just cover [up] their intent."

Some attorneys framed judges' bias, whether explicit or implicit, as being the product of judges becoming "jaded" over time. In fact, many said they thought this was inevitable. Rachel explains:

> Understandably, it gets really hard—when you're seeing the same thing day after day—to distinguish [individual cases from perceived patterns of fraud]. Okay this is another Chinese asylum claim. How do you make it that different in your mind when you've already been tainted by ten [Chinese asylum claimants] who you truly believe were lying? . . . How do you get off to a 100% fresh start at that point? Even for the most [fair] liberal person on the planet, if you truly believed and had come to the conclusion that those ten other people you had just seen last month were lying, and then you get your eleventh person, in your head you're just gonna think "Oh my god!" You're gonna come to the pre-conclusion that this person's probably lying, too. It's just impossible not to do that. . . . And I think the [immigration judges] do try their best to start off on a new slate with everybody, but, even me who's a bleeding heart liberal [laughs] working for [a nonprofit], I totally get it because [it's] just so hard after a while.

Similarly, Lara, who interned with the American Bar Association before taking a job with an immigration nonprofit, shared a case story wherein the judge revealed inherent biases against asylum seekers from Nigeria. As she recalls: "[The judge] was like, 'Oh yeah, yeah, yeah. Nigeria. There's the Christians, the Muslims, nobody gets along. Got it. Continue.'" Lara paused during our interview, then went on in an astonished tone of voice: "That's your worldview? That's what you've dumbed it down to? That's Nigeria? Okay, that's your bias then. I don't know how to get over that. I think that, in some ways, because [judges have] such high caseloads they sometimes adapt a very simplistic way of looking at the world, . . . as if almost everyone's trying to take advantage of the system. [As if they tell themselves], 'Everyone's out to commit fraud and I'm just a fraud locater. I'm just trying to read everyone's bullshit.'"

Indeed, every attorney I interviewed emphasized that the judges, along with other court actors, had become very overworked in recent years in light of mounting caseloads—caseloads that grew exponentially in the years following the completion of my interview research. As Mauricio laments, "I can see on the faces of some of the judges, they're getting tired. You know [the court] is so overwhelmed with cases, I don't know how they're gonna finish it because, see, as they finish one case here come twenty more. I don't know how they're gonna do it." Facing such pressures, several attorneys said that judges were bound to use shortcuts—including implicit biases—to help them move through cases more quickly. Others remarked that judges, given the caseload pressures, were doing their best with very limited resources. In particular, although federal district court judges may have several law clerks, immigration judges often share just one.[125]

Attorneys stressed that, when the courts have too many cases, judges' performance suffers. One attorney insisted that, although judges say that they read all the statements and case documents, she can tell "from the way judges ask questions and what they're asking, they really haven't read everything. They can't—they don't have time." Another attorney shared that she had witnessed judges fall asleep in court, which she linked to sheer exhaustion. She was not alone—multiple attorneys recounted stories of judges appearing to fall asleep during court.

Judges "are hearing a lot of traumatic things day in and day out and they're expected to just pump out the cases," Emily explains. Referencing a well-known analogy by the former head of the National Association of Immigrant Judges, Dana Marks,[126] she stressed that immigration court is "like handling death penalty cases in traffic court"—and this is even without the increased caseload. The immense emotional burden inherent in the nature of work, along with increased caseloads, adds to the everyday stress of the job. When asked if judges care what happens to immigrants at the end of their hearings, Dimitri sighs, then responds: "Nobody really cares," he says. "There are too many cases to handle. There are just so many cases."

Conclusion

As discussed in chapter 1, when people find that a legal process is fair, they are more likely to be satisfied with unwanted legal outcomes, to cooperate and comply, and to believe in the legal system's legitimacy.[127] Immigration court has long suffered from administrative and procedural shortcomings that threaten process fairness. Immigration attorneys noted numerous procedural injustices, from detention and interpreting practices to judicial behavior and videoconferencing technology.

Interpersonal treatment and perceptions of bias are both known to negatively impact evaluations of procedural justice.[128] Immigration attorneys framed the behavior, demeanor, and decision-making practices of judges and ICE trial attorneys as sometimes fair and sometimes unfair. Although attorneys characterized judges as "impartial" and "concerned," they also pointed to the implicit biases that shape judicial behavior and decisions. They also noted that some judges have quirky personalities that can at times be "off-putting" to those in the courtroom.

ICE trial attorneys' behavior and demeanor was said to run the gamut, from "compassionate," "patient," and "reasonable" to "aggressive," "ruthless," and "tricky." Attorneys also highlighted the increasing court backlog and accompanying pressure that judges and ICE attorneys faced when handling cases.[129] As they explained, the combination of "jaded" judges and ICE attorneys who were strapped for time and resources opened the door for implicit bias to manifest in the courtroom.

Attorneys also consistently flagged the use of detention, interpretation, and technology as deeply unfair. These were cast as problematic because they altered and inhibited communication and participation during hearings. This raises serious procedural justice concerns as opportunities for participation—having the chance to speak and to feel heard—are key components of fairness.[130]

According to the attorneys, reliance on interpreters greatly disadvantages immigrants. Given that immigrants have limited or no knowledge of English, it is difficult for them to follow along as judges, lawyers, and expert witnesses talk. In turn, they may be unable to ask questions or request clarification, either from their own attorneys—if they are represented—or from judges and other courtroom actors. As attorneys described, the inability to speak English risks relegating immigrants to the margins of their own hearings.

Technology itself also threatens immigrants' ability to communicate in the courtroom. Attorneys lamented the poor audio and video quality that often accompanies the use of tele- and videoconferencing. They pointed to the limits such technology places on nonverbal forms of communication and stressed its dehumanizing effects.[131] Attorneys also argued that the harmful effects of detention, interpretation, and tele- and videoconferencing worsen when combined, a common occurrence, as the use of one often necessitates the use of the other (e.g., detained immigrants appearing in court via videoconferencing, interpretation taking place via teleconferencing, etc.).

Ultimately, attorneys expressed doubt over the procedural fairness of key immigration court players and practices, calling into question the legitimacy of immigration courts altogether. Their words, along with the laws and rules that govern immigration courts and deportation, are certainly indicative of procedural *injustice*. Accordingly, one might assume that immigrants facing deportation would be deeply displeased with the hearing process. Yet when asked about their clients' perceptions of the court, attorneys agreed—often to their own confusion and surprise—that immigrants were generally pleased with the court and its employees.

Indeed, the immigrants I interviewed for the most part found their own and their family members' deportation hearings to be procedurally fair. Some highlighted the court's impartiality. Others enthusiastically praised the judges presiding over their hearings and the interpreters translating on their behalf. Some even had nice things to say about the ICE trial attorneys calling for their deportation. In chapter 3, I introduce the concept of *immigrant legal consciousness* to situate what immigrants know about the law in the United States and to foreground these positive procedural justice assessments. As I will assert, one cannot begin to understand the stark differences between attorneys' and immigrants' perceptions of the court, deportation, and the immigration system without first exploring immigrant legal consciousness.

3

Tracing Immigrant Legal Consciousness

What do Central Americans know about U.S. law prior to arriving in the United States? How do they navigate the immigration system once here? For Samuel, like most I interviewed, the path to understanding U.S. immigration law is not linear. Instead, it is filled with starts and stops, ups and downs, facts and fictions.

Samuel, a Salvadoran man in his late thirties, explains that he didn't know much about the U.S. immigration system before coming to the country. He left home at age 14 "to better [myself]," he says, explaining that he didn't want to spend the rest of his life as a farmer. "I worked in the mornings, studied in the afternoons, and earned what, in the United States, you would call a high school diploma." He soon enrolled in college, joining the Salvadoran national police force to cover his costs. But after trying to balance his studies and police work for about six months, he dropped out of school.

Samuel spent several years as a police officer, assigned to various units across El Salvador. "This was the late 1990s," he recalls, "and by then there were a lot of problems." He continues: "It was during this time that [the gangs] began killing police officers." Instead of the police patrolling the gangs, Samuel emphasizes, "now, the gangs were patrolling the police." After the sixth officer in his department was killed, he left the force.

That summer, Samuel journeyed to the United States. He was detained by Border Patrol in Texas, processed, and released. He would be given an immigration court date by mail and was told he needed to appear to "fight his case." However, the distant relatives who were supposed to receive Samuel never came to pick him up and stopped answering his calls. He managed to reconnect with some old friends and decided to move to the East Coast. Although he didn't forget about it, he never followed up regarding his immigration court hearing.

Samuel acknowledges that, as a former police officer, he had a general understanding of how law works. What's more, for a time he was stationed near El Salvador's border with Honduras, where he performed checks with border patrol agents, antitrafficking units, and customs officers. From his perspective, this afforded him a basic understanding of immigration systems. He used his previous training and experience to help make sense of U.S. law.

"Look, [the U.S. legal system] is like any system at the global level, the general level," Samuel explains. "If you [follow the rules], good. But if you go against the laws, against the established norms, you're going to have trouble. Right? Here, things are arranged by state laws, county laws, [and so on]. If you abide by all of these you'll be okay." As Samuel explains, he dropped the ball when he got to the United States. "I very well could have looked into [what happened to my hearing and my immigration status]," Samuel laments, "but sometimes for lack of information, for lack of having someone to guide you when you come here, everything is disorienting."

As time passed, Samuel's knowledge of U.S. immigration law grew. He talked about immigration with friends and family. He heard stories of people going to immigration court and of others being deported. He learned how to keep a low profile as someone without a valid legal status. It wasn't until he was watching television one night and saw an announcement about Temporary Protected Status (TPS) that he decided to hire an immigration attorney. Suddenly, he recalls, "there was an opportunity to apply [for legal status] because President [George W.] Bush had offered this sort of amnesty for Salvadorans affected by the earthquake." He applied for and received TPS and a work permit. He was able to get his driver's license and work legally. It seemed as if things were falling into place.

Upon attempting to renew his TPS for the third time—the first two renewals were successful—Samuel received a letter stating that his renewal was denied. As it turned out, he had a standing order of deportation from the initial immigration court hearing he missed that first year in the United States. "From your errors, you learn a lot," Samuel reflects. "I thought that my deportation order was canceled out by my TPS," he stresses, "because that's what many people say, but it's a lie."

Samuel's lawyer informed him that there was little he could do about his status without appearing before an immigration judge in another hearing. He consulted with several more attorneys, but they all told him the same thing. Samuel was in limbo, his future tied to whatever—or whoever—came first: the passage of comprehensive immigration reform or discovery by *la migra*. Unfortunately, the latter sealed his fate.

Samuel managed to spend almost a decade in the United States as an undocumented immigrant before he found himself, once again, facing deportation. To his surprise, it was not his traffic tickets or even the ticket he got for driving under the influence (DUI)—complete with court-mandated rehabilitation—that landed him in immigration custody. Instead, it was a case of mistaken identity. ICE knocked on Samuel's door looking for someone who had supposedly lived in his apartment at one point or another, and the next thing he knew he was being arrested.

Samuel was held in immigration detention without bond for several months while awaiting his hearing. While in detention (of all places, he points out) he learned a lot about immigration law—and not from lawyers or "know your rights" trainings but from other detained immigrants. "There are quite a lot of them [inside]," he says, laughing. "Some joke that they're defense attorneys, because for as long as they're there, with so many testimonies that people give about their cases, there are people who go around collecting [those testimonies]. They go around collecting so many experiences [based on] so many cases that a few things end up sticking!"

His immigration outcome on the horizon, and no longer in detention, Samuel now makes it a point to share his experiences with others. "Having been in immigration [court and detention]"—he pauses here—"well, one realizes many things. Sometimes, one is ignorant. Right?" But "sometimes one small mistake can lead to one big problem, you see? Simply due to a lack of guidance." Samuel doesn't want others to repeat his mistakes. So he advises family members about paying speeding tickets and gives testimony at his church. "Sometimes," he insists, "that's enough to help the rest."

Like most immigrants interviewed for this book, Samuel learned about the workings of U.S. immigration law primarily through an amalgamation of legal stories and experiences. Some of the sources of his legal information were informal—television programs, community gossip and rumors, and first-, second- and, thirdhand tales of others' immigration woes. Like many of the immigrants I interviewed—although not all—Samuel consulted with numerous immigration attorneys over the years, each imparting additional wisdom. He also had formal encounters with the criminal justice system, including being arrested and ticketed for traffic violations, a trip to traffic court, and mandatory participation in rehab. Moreover, unlike most immigrants I interviewed, Samuel managed to connect with law enforcement and correctional officers from time to time, drawing upon his formal exposure to criminal and immigration law during the time he was employed as a police officer.

Spending time in detention, Samuel found himself further enmeshed in the immigration system both literally and figuratively. Immigration law was all around him. It was in the rigorous daily routines of the facility and the commands of detention officers. It was also on the tongues of detainees with little else to do but discuss their cases, legal strategies, and recent appearances in court while passing the time. By the time he was released, Samuel exhibited a powerful grasp of U.S. immigration law, something that he felt obligated to share with others through telling his own migration story.

Samuel's story illuminates the way immigrants piece together a patchwork of legal knowledge from both official and unofficial sources in the United States and abroad. This includes what they absorb in school, from the media, through stories told by detainees, family, friends, and neighbors, time spent with lawyers, police officers, and social workers, and their own experiences with the law. The weight of unofficial knowledge, however, is amplified in the immigration context, as Central Americans often have limited U.S. exposure to formal sources of legal information (e.g., K–12 education) and communities are often insular, isolated from mainstream American society by choice, discrimination, structural inequalities, or all of the above.

This chapter begins with five migration stories capturing the myriad paths of legal socialization experienced by the immigrants I interviewed. Drawing upon what law and society scholars refer to as "legal consciousness," I highlight how immigrants' legal knowledge evolves and is shaped over time as immigrants ask questions, consult professionals, and tell stories. This, in turn, informs immigrants' perspectives on their own and others' migration experiences and on the U.S. immigration system. Immigrant legal consciousness is then situated among other legal consciousness scholarship. Interviews with immigrants and attorneys reveal that immigrant legal consciousness positions immigrants to assess their deportation hearings, immigration court, and the immigration system in somewhat surprising ways.

Asking Questions, Consulting Professionals, and Telling Stories

Immigrants I interviewed were in agreement: they knew very little about immigration law when they arrived in the United States. Yet whether intentionally, by happenstance, or via osmosis, immigrants eventually formed an understanding of the immigration system and American legal system more generally. This often occurred by asking questions, consulting professionals, and telling stories. Interview after interview, immigrants and attorneys pointed to numerous sources of formal and informal information—some said to be better than others—that immigrants relied upon to make sense of the law in the United States. Although details varied, immigrants frequently absorbed information about the immigration system from a combination of attorneys and *notarios*, the criminal justice system, friends and family, immigration detention, the media, neighbors, and various professionals.

Mejor que creer es investigar.
"It's better to investigate than to believe."—Gloria

Gloria was just 20 when she arrived in the United States to work as a nanny. "I was an ignorant person from a small rural town," she says, reflecting on how little she knew about her rights as an immigrant or worker when she accepted the nanny position with its accompanying work visa. The visa afforded her a legal pathway to the United States, but it bound her to her employer.

The job was difficult. Gloria worked long hours seven days a week and was paid just $150 a month. The family employing her was very controlling. "They didn't allow me to do anything," she recalls. "I couldn't have friends, couldn't leave the house, couldn't even talk to people on the phone." So Gloria took it upon herself to find a way out. She connected with a family willing to pay her $250 a month "under the table" and that agreed not restrict her movement or social life. Weighing her options, Gloria gave up her visa—and legal status in the United States—in exchange for improved working conditions.

"It's better to investigate than to believe," Gloria insists, explaining how she transitioned from uninformed girl to knowledgeable woman with a firm grasp of immigration law. She describes herself as someone with a "curious nature," someone who has always questioned things. She recounts learning about the U.S. immigration system on her own by doing her research and asking questions. "One can't just take things for granted or at face value." Particularly when it comes to immigration law, "you can't just rely on friends and family because they don't always know what they're talking about—[often] they'll make you more confused and nervous."

Instead, Gloria prefers to seek advice from the "most studied person" she can find. Running through lists of various professionals, she highlights clinic doctors, schoolteachers, and social workers as generally knowledgeable. When they can't help her, they are usually able to direct her to the "right people." Gloria prefers, however, to obtain information about the law from immigration attorneys. "But," she stresses, "there is a lot of fraud out there," continuing, "so if you're go to an immigration attorney you have to ask to see their credentials."

This is just what Gloria did when her husband faced deportation after receiving a ticket for driving under the influence. The couple met with and hired several immigration attorneys over next three years while fighting his case in immigration court. Because Gloria's husband had Temporary Protected Status and a clean record—apart from the DUI—it looked as though he might have a real shot at beating deportation. In the end, however, he was ordered deported. Yet he remained in the country in violation of his deportation order. At the time, the couple agreed that this was best for their family, including their two U.S. citizen children.

Gloria's husband managed to stay off the government's radar for several years. Then he was in a second drunk-driving accident. He was promptly taken into police custody and transferred to immigration detention. Gloria quickly consulted with several immigration attorneys. He was facing deportation for the second time, was unlawfully present in the United States, had violated his previous deportation order, and now had not one but two drunk-driving accidents on his record. Gloria was told that there was nothing to be done.

Gloria attended her husband's second deportation hearing, which was very brief. This time, she brought their two children along, now teenagers. She hoped they would have a chance to speak with him—they did not. She recalls sitting in the back of the courtroom and watching as her husband, hands cuffed behind his back, was ordered deported and barred from applying for a visa to return to the United States for five years. "And that was the last time my children saw their father," she says softly.

In light of her husband's deportation, Gloria feels increased pressure to "fix" her own immigration status. She continues consulting with lawyers, social workers, and any professional whom she believes might have some useful advice. For Gloria, immigration relief is not a question of faith or hope. "It's better to investigate than to believe," she says again.

Me aprendí mucho en las noticias . . . luego vas y encuentras
a alguien como un abogado quien te puede ayudar.
"I learned about things on the news . . . then you go and
find someone like an attorney to help you."—Simón and Eva

Simón and Eva met and married in the United States in the early 2000s. Simón, born in Honduras, says that he left because "you can't live with dignity there." Eva, originally from El Salvador, agrees with her husband. The two explain that both countries have "a lot of poverty and few opportunities," as well as a lot of crime. "You can't take care of a family [there]," Simón adds.

As we sit in the couple's kitchen, Simón does most of the talking while Eva nods along. Their eldest daughter, Nora, sits quietly nearby. Admittedly, neither Simón nor Eva knew much about immigration laws in the United States when they arrived. "In reality, we didn't know anything," says Simón. He points out that, prior to the terrorist attack on September 11, 2001, it was "easier to be undocumented . . . but even then you were taking a risk."

Despite a general awareness of tightening immigration enforcement in subsequent years, the couple did little to educate themselves about the laws in the United States. "I never learned much apart from what I learned from television," Eva reflects. "You learn about things on the news." For example, by watching the news the couple discovered that they might be eligible for TPS. "[You hear about something on TV] and then you go and find someone like an attorney to help you," Eva adds, her husband nodding.

After obtaining TPS, the couple's life stabilized for a time. When Simón lost his TPS, he did not seek out legal assistance. "Under what law would I have qualified for anything?" he offers up, his statement more explanation than question. It was not until the couple decided to bring Eva's biological daughter, Nora, to the United States that they began seeking legal advice.

Eva gave birth to Nora not long before she moved to the United States, leaving her in the care of parents. Nora was raised by her maternal grandparents in El Salvador until they, too, decided to move to the United States. Unsure what to do, Simón and Eva purchased a plane ticket for Nora. When she arrived in Miami without a visa, Nora was immediately taken into immigration custody. She was released to Eva but placed in deportation proceedings.

The couple had consultations with several attorneys before finding one who was willing to take Nora's case. "We heard about [our attorney] through a radio advertisement," Simón recounts. While working on Nora's case, their attorney inquired about Simón's status and took him on as a client, too. Although Simón and Eva have learned a great deal about the immigration system while working with their attorney for over several years, they explain that they still don't know much. "When you're [in court] with a good attorney," Simón insists, "you trust that your attorney will represent you well."

Le roban mas el dinero a uno que lo que ganan.
"They steal more money from you than they earn."—Aracely

"I didn't know anything about the laws in the United States when I arrived," Aracely begins. "I wanted nothing more than to come here to work." She recalls crossing the border with her then-husband and immediately looking for a job. "First I worked in a Chinese restaurant. Then I found work at an Italian restaurant, and that's where I've stayed."

A couple years into her job, Aracely asked her boss to help sponsor her work visa. "It was then that I began to learn about immigration in the United States," Aracely reflects. Her boss agreed and found an attorney willing to take the case. The attorney filed the application, which was approved by the Department of Labor. However, he disappeared, abandoning her case entirely. "I don't know what happened," Aracely explains. "I gave [my boss] the money [for the attorney] . . . and, like that, I lost the money."

Still hopeful, Aracely paid another attorney to take her case, only to have a similar experience. "I paid [him] and when he moved offices, he left the application behind. The office told me that my attorney had abandoned my application and no one was going to take it over." Eventually, Aracely managed to hire a lawyer who did help her obtain TPS. "It's the only thing that protects me," she insists.

Aracely points out that, although she has learned a lot about immigration law by watching television, she prefers something "a little more legal." As she explains, "I always like to talk to lawyers, but it always costs hundreds of dollars." Indeed, Aracely met with numerous attorneys over the span of two decades. Regardless of whom she met with, she always seemed to hit a wall. "All the lawyers have told me there is nothing they can do [for me], that the immigration laws are blocked," she sighs.

As a survivor of domestic violence, Aracely once inquired about the possibility of obtaining a U visa, a special immigrant visa for victims of crime.[1] "I've heard a lot about the U visa, and I have a lot of reports from the police, photos of how [my ex-husband] left me," she says with frustration. "The lawyer just told me that the case happened many years ago and now it didn't matter."

Today, Aracely characterizes many of her own experiences with attorneys as fraudulent. "I have heard about many [cases of fraud], but it [has also] personally happened to me," she asserts. "Money is money. You pay, and you want someone to continue with your case. To me, that's fraud. At a minimum, have the manners to say, 'Okay, I'm not going to continue with your case [for this reason] and so I'm going to give your case to [another attorney].'" Summarizing her thoughts, she says bluntly: "To me, [attorneys] steal more money from you than what they earn."

Situating Immigrant Legal Consciousness

The migration narratives of Samuel, Gloria, Simón and Eva, and Aracely explored in this chapter highlight the dynamic role that legal socialization plays in immigrants' lives as they navigate the immigration system in the United States. Through these narratives, immigrants recount how they come to learn about the law and also outline what they expect from the law. They demonstrate how they adapt to, challenge, and harness the law in the face of immigration problems. What's more, they shine a spotlight on immigrant legal consciousness.

In her classic work *Getting Justice and Getting Even: Legal Consciousness among Working-Class Americans*, the anthropologist and sociolegal scholar Sally Engel Merry defines "legal consciousness"[2] as the "ways people understand and use the law," including "the way people conceive of the 'natural' and normal way of doing things, their habitual patterns of talk and action, and their commonsense understanding of the world."[3] Over time, this definition grew to include people's expectations about the law and their sense of legal entitlements and rights,[4] as well as how they use this knowledge to respond to the law[5] and deal with problems.[6]

However, for the sociologists Patricia Ewick and Susan S. Silbey, legal consciousness is also about meaning-making. It is about defining the parameters of law from the bottom up through the everyday experiences of regular people. It is not just about legal attitudes but the *production* of such attitudes—even the production of law itself.[7] Ewick and Silbey elaborate:

> [L]egal consciousness [is] neither fixed, stable, unitary, nor consistent. Instead, [it is] something local, contextual, pluralistic, filled with conflict and contradiction. The ideas, interpretations, actions and ways of operating that collectively represent a person's legal consciousness may vary across time (to reflect learning and experience) or across interactions (to reflect different objects, relationships or purposes). To the extent that consciousness is emergent in social practice and forged in and around situated events and interactions (a dispute with a neighbor, a criminal case, a plumber who seemed to work few hours but charged for many), a person may express, through words or actions, a multi-faceted, contradictory, and variable consciousness.[8]

Thus, legal consciousness is a dynamic phenomenon evolving over time, affected by culture, identity,[9] and politics as well as direct and vicarious encounters with the law.[10]

Similarly, immigrant legal consciousness is grounded in an ever-expanding repertoire of lived experiences and stories that offer meaning and provide guidance in daily life. Like Samuel, Gloria, Simón and Eva, and Aracely, the majority of those I interviewed said they "didn't know much" (or, in some cases, anything) about immigration law before coming to the country. Recall, for instance, how Gloria referred to herself as an "ignorant person from a small rural town" and that even Samuel, a former police officer, described being "disoriented" by the U.S. legal system upon his arrival.

Many immigrants I interviewed stressed they realized how under-informed they were about U.S. immigration law only upon confronting the realities of their own or a family member's deportation. For example, as Angelica, a Salvadoran woman whose immigration court hearing will be reviewed in chapter 4, elaborates, "If I had the information [then] that I've now come to understand, I could've [legalized my status] much earlier because before there was a little more help." Echoing Samuel, she continues: "But when . . . someone like me comes to this country alone, you don't have anyone to help you. . . . It's hard." Similarly, Eduardo, who will be introduced in chapter 4, explains: "When we first came here, if we had known, we would've done things differently."

Yet just as the migration narratives highlighted in this chapter suggest, immigrants' understandings of the U.S. immigration system—and their place within it—grew over time. Many cited learning about immigration law on the internet or from radio and television. Again, Samuel and Simón and Eva described first hearing about TPS through television announcements and news programs. They were not alone.

For most, however, family, friends, and neighbors were primary sources of immigration information. Immigrants generally agreed that immigration fears, gossip, reforms, and rumors often crept into daily conversations whether at home, work, or elsewhere. Rita, a Honduran woman whose deportation hearing will be examined in chapter 4, stresses: "From the moment one begins the journey to the United States, one is always thinking about immigration."

Deportation stories, in particular, were frequently shared. Again, all of the immigrants I interviewed for this book came from mixed-status families—some family members residing in the United States without authorization, others who were American citizens by birth, and still others who fell somewhere in between. They also lived, worked, and socialized in mixed-status communities. Most could list a half-dozen people who had faced deportation in the past or who had pending cases, aside from themselves and their immediate family, when we spoke. Whether aunts and uncles, children, cousins, coworkers, friends and neighbors, partners and spouses, or siblings, there were many people with whom to discuss deportation in both the abstract and the concrete sense.

There were also many people to turn to for immigration advice, should it be needed. Angelica, for instance, described learning about both immigration and labor law from friends at work whenever she or someone else had an issue. "[They would say,] 'No, well, look at this. Look at that. You have rights here. You're not in your country,'" she explains. Others, like Freddy, whose migration story will be recounted in chapter 5, picked up bits and pieces of information about political asylum from people he met who avoided deportation.

Immigration stories are not bound by borders, traveling through networks of friends and families spread across vast distances. Many of those I interviewed discussed learning about deportation while still in Central America. For example, Sara, a Guatemalan woman whose migration story will be examined in chapter 5, sought advice from family and friends who had experienced deportation before she left for the United States. Whether through sought-after advice or the retelling of deportation stories of friends and family, immigrants picked up information about the U.S. immigration system.

Some immigrants I interviewed, like Gloria, were skeptical of advice from friends and family. They preferred to speak with attorneys and other professionals, including community organizers, doctors, social workers, and teachers, when immigration questions arose. Several immigrants noted seeking out or obtaining information from teachers and other professionals at their children's schools. This often took the form of targeted "know your rights" trainings. Angelica, for instance, had attended several talks hosted by a prominent local nonprofit. She explains, "They're having reunions, [they're organizing politically], . . . they're doing good things for the [Latino] community."

Although some I interviewed, like Gloria, sought professional advice from a variety of sources without prodding, others did not. For example, Sara contacted a nonprofit with immigration questions only after her friends urged her to do so. "'Go, go on and go there! Go on!' they told me," she recalls. Indeed, a number of immigrants were hesitant to discuss immigration issues outside their trusted circles.

Still others attempted to obtain professional advice and repeatedly hit dead ends. Immigrants noted numerous difficulties preventing them from connecting with immigration attorneys in particular. First and foremost, attorneys were often prohibitively expensive. Even a brief consultation could wind up costing several hundred dollars, as Aracely stressed. Second, immigrants struggled to find attorneys, especially free and low-cost attorneys, who were taking clients. "Lawyers are not cheap," says Eduardo, whose deportation hearing is highlighted in chapter 4. "I called every lawyer on the three-page referral list [provided by EOIR], starting with the free lawyers, then the ones [who offered consultations] for under $100," recalling how long it took him to find an attorney who would take his case. Language barriers further complicated matters. Many with whom I spoke for this book had limited English proficiency, and many attorneys in the practice area seemed unable to accommodate Spanish translation.

When immigrants did manage to connect with attorneys, their experiences were somewhat hit-or-miss. Many had gone to multiple consultations without ever receiving concrete legal assistance or information. They often left confused and frustrated. Like Aracely, a handful of those I interviewed self-identified as victims of attorney or *notario* fraud, having been misled, ripped off, or cheated by individuals claiming to be able to assist with immigration legal matters.[11]

Although immigration attorneys spoke about *notario* fraud at length, immigrants I interviewed did not. Instead, the majority of immigrants I interviewed whose family members had been represented by an immigration attorney, or who themselves had been represented by one, described positive attorney-client interactions. As will be discussed in chapter 4, they often praised their attorneys as knowledgeable and hardworking or explicitly mentioned their attorneys explaining the immigration system to them.

Setting the Record Straight?

Immigration attorneys I interviewed agreed that their Central American clients usually know people who have already gone to court or been deported. As one attorney put it, they "all talk to each other." Although attorneys often characterized their clients as "very confused" or "not very knowledgeable" about immigration law, they acknowledged that immigrants, through swapping stories, do pick up information about the law.

"It's word-of-mouth in terms of the court," Elizabeth, an attorney, points out, noting that her clients often repeat what they've heard about various judges or trial attorneys from friends, family members, and/or immigrant detainees. Again, this is consistent with what Samuel and the other immigrants with detention experience shared during our interviews.[12] For example, Alex, a young Salvadoran man whose deportation hearing is recounted in chapter 4, described the role that "jailhouse lawyers" play in detainees' legal socialization. "[This one detainee], he would help everyone to learn about the legal system," Alex recalls. "It's hard to imagine someone trying to hurt your case in detention. In detention [all the detainees] want to help your case." As one attorney summarizes, "People *talk* in detention. . . . There's a lot of sort of information-sharing."

And even though some attorneys felt that social networks and storytelling benefited their clients, many stressed that this is also how immigrants pick up a lot of misinformation. Even when clients had gone through legal proceedings before, such as facing criminal charges, attorneys were skeptical that this improved their understanding of the law. Attorneys frequently pointed out that the differences in due process rights, rules, and terminology between the criminal justice and immigration systems are often confusing for their clients.

"They all think they're eligible for bond," Elizabeth shares. "[They ask], 'Why can't I get a bond?' 'Well because you committed an aggravated felony.' 'It was a misdemeanor.' 'I know it was a misdemeanor [in the criminal system] but it's considered an aggravated felony [in the immigration context].' I wish they would change some of the terminology so that it was easier to explain to people." Similarly, another attorney with whom I spoke, Noah, insisted that most knowledge gained through criminal justice experiences is useless in the immigration context. "[Immigrants] who committed a crime and are now in [deportation] proceedings seem pretty clueless about the whole thing," he reflects. "In fact, the people who come out of criminal court often have really wrong ideas about what happens. They're like, 'Where's my court-appointed lawyer?' Like, 'Why can't we get the prosecutor's documents?'" He laughs. "Yeah, that's not happening."

An attorney named Harry points out that, "in terms of having had some prior [criminal] court experience . . . [clients] are kind of more familiar with what's going on and more comfortable in that sense probably." Yet as Harry and others saw it, this wasn't worth much. Harry elaborates: "I don't really ask [my clients] if they know [about immigration law] because it's just not worth it." "Whatever they know, half the time it's gonna be wrong anyway. Not to be condescending to my clients, but [they have] a lot of misperceptions. . . . My impression is that most of them have a relatively good idea about the system because they've had friends or other people who went through it. But they for sure don't have a full idea. There are definitely gaps, misperceptions, and myths."

Indeed, attorneys generally agreed that a large part of their job involved "setting clients straight" and managing—or attempting to manage—their expectations. They emphasized that clients frequently compare their own situations with those of other immigrants, exploring how they believe their cases could turn out based on what they've heard. "Information on immigration processes and outcomes is principally through friends and family," Diane explains. "That's even more so if a person isn't particularly sophisticated. . . . But even [highly educated] folks, sometimes they'll tell me things it's like . . . 'well my friend got this and that relief,' and it doesn't matter how much you try to explain [that their friend's outcome is irrelevant to their case]. . . . I always joke if I had a *dollar* for each one of these I'd be a *multimillionaire*."

When clients are not bringing up immigration stories about friends, family, or other detainees, some attorneys noted, their clients frequently reference immigration information picked up from the media, a lot of which is incorrect. "A lot of the information that [immigrants] get is from Hispanic media, because the Hispanic media covers immigration news at the top of the hour, every hour, every single day," Rachel explains. "So, they're hearing a lot of information, but they don't necessarily know whether it applies to them, or people in their family, or what it means because the news is reporting stories to get attention. They're not reporting stories to give people legal information."

Like Rachel, Alex stressed that there is a lot of misleading and outright inaccurate information in the Spanish-language media regrading the U.S. immigration system. She was particularly frustrated with the popularity of Spanish-language radio shows that purport to offer legitimate legal information but are, in actuality, attorney advertising tactics:

> A lot of [immigrants] listen to the radio shows, which I think is detrimental actually. A lot of misinformation gets passed around on those radio shows. . . . [Here's] an example. Someone came in here and said, "This attorney said on her radio show that via TPS I can bring my children here legally." It's like uhhh no. . . . There's no program to bring your children here if you have TPS. So that's one example and it's perpetuating this around the community. . . . I kind of look down on [the radio shows] because you're paying for advertising. . . . All it is is advertising. If you're on these radio shows to get business there's a reason. They're not getting referrals. Everyone [at my firm] is word-of-mouth.

Many of the attorneys I interviewed shared Alex's skepticism over attorneys and others who advertise their immigration services,[13] linking advertising to both ineffective assistance of counsel and *notario* fraud. "[*Notario* fraud] is a huge problem," remarks Demitris, who, like others, shared several stories of clients' victimization. Approximately half of the attorneys interviewed for this book claimed that a substantial portion of their clients had been victimized by *notarios* or by their former attorneys. Harms ranged from overcharging clients for delivered services to charging them for work that was never done, did not need to be done, or did them irreparable harm.

"There's one [case] that stands out in my mind," Elizabeth begins, "because I think [the previous attorney] took like $20,000 from this guy. They filed a motion to reopen [the case] for him and then [administratively] closed the case and then requested that it be re-calendared for no reason." Frustrated, she explains how "[the attorney did this] just so that they could do a motion to [administratively] close [the case] again. So just kind of charging them for work that didn't need to be done." Anna, who at one pointed clerked for an immigration court judge, shared that numerous respondents wind up in deportation proceedings operating under false assumptions given to them by *notarios*.

Lara, particularly knowledgeable about *notario* fraud, stressed that the combination of confusion, hopefulness, and misinformation makes immigrants especially susceptible to being taken advantage of by unscrupulous attorneys and individuals posing as attorneys or legal consultants. As many attorneys explained, barred attorneys and *notarios* often "get away with" defrauding clients because many of their victims are here illegally and do not feel that they can file complaints or seek legal recourse. Harry, like a handful of other attorneys, stress that he has filed a number of bar complaints against people who "screwed up" for his clients.

Although some attorneys, like Mauricio, argued that the prevalence of *notarios* makes immigrants fearful that they have a bad lawyer and leads to "a lot of lawyer shopping," others, like Diane, disagrees. "I don't know what it is," exclaims Diane, "[but] folks who've had really bad lawyers then just go get other bad lawyers. And there'll be this sort of parade of horrors before [they get a good attorney]. . . . I've found that they're surprisingly not [skeptical] on the whole. . . . I think there's just this kind of understandable desire to have somebody fix it."

About half the attorneys with whom I spoke said that, in their experiences, ineffective assistance of counsel and *notario* fraud did not seem as prevalent as is often stated. For instance, like Rachel, several attorneys said their clients rarely bring up past problems with attorneys or *notarios*. Maura, who had never represented a victim of fraud, notes that most of her clients are recent arrivals, so they may not have yet had the chance to be victimized. A few others admit being somewhat skeptical when their clients express concerns over the work of their previous attorneys, emphasizing that many clients do not really understand what happened to them or what their attorneys had done in the past. In what was perhaps the most extreme opinion expressed by those I interviewed, Mauricio says that he did not understand why "lawyers point fingers" instead of protecting each other. "How do you, [the attorney], know what the facts are? You're listening to the client [who] lies anyway!"

As one attorney says bluntly, regardless of the source, "reeducating" clients after they've been misinformed is a lot of work. Mauricio summarizes: "I'm finding it harder and harder and harder for them to accept [what I explain to them]. They're busy listening to news that is probably wrong. . . . 'Oh, but [Mr. Mauricio], this is what happened to my friend. This is what happened to my friend! . . . He said that I should do this, this, and this.' Well, pay your friend. Ohhhh! Talk about frustrating.

Conclusion

As I have explored in this chapter, the legal socialization of immigrants like Samuel, Gloria, Simón and Eva, and Aracely is dynamic and varied. Immigrants claimed to know little about immigration law generally and to have known even less when newly arrived in the United States. Attorneys agreed, stressing that what little immigrants did know about the immigration system was typically wrong. At the same time, both immigrants and attorneys described a rich diversity of sources from which immigrants obtain legal information: attorneys and *notarios*, the criminal justice system, friends and family, immigration detention, the media, neighbors, and various professionals.

Of these myriad sources of information, immigrants prioritized what legal sociologists commonly refer to as "lawyer's law," or official understandings of state law.[14] When possible, they sought out legal information from attorneys or other professionals. Still, their access to formal sources of information—be it legal education and training or interactions with attorneys—was limited. Moreover, a number of immigrants I interviewed were somewhat leery of legal professionals, having either been burned in the past themselves or heard cautionary tales from others.

More often than not, immigrants assembled a patchwork of informal immigration knowledge vis-à-vis the stories they heard both before and after coming to the United States. Whether these stories provided immigrants *accurate* information is another matter. Indeed, many immigrants I interviewed acknowledged becoming more skeptical about the accuracy of immigration information they received from friends and family over time. Yet this was the information that was most readily accessible, freed from the constraints of English proficiency and income that was often needed in order to obtain professional legal knowledge.

Legal sociologists remind us not only that the law is everywhere[15] but also that informal understandings of law influence the way we think about and navigate legal processes and systems. Legal storytelling in particular plays an important role in legal socialization and the development of legal consciousness. As Merry explains: "[People] are constantly hearing stories about what the law is and what it can and cannot do. In these moments of talk, problems are defined in terms that the legal system recognizes as being either within or without its scope. In turn, this talk defines what law itself is and can do. Sometimes the media, neighbors, or friends provide this talk, but at other times judges, lawyers, and court officials play crucial roles in defining what law is and can do."[16]

Indeed, when making sense of their own migration stories, immigrants often recounted others' personal accounts, community gossip, and urban legends, engaging in a meta-storytelling of their own. In particular, they drew heavily on vicarious experiences with the immigration system when situating their own legal knowledge. Ample criminological and sociolegal literature demonstrates the important role vicarious experience plays in shaping people's perceptions of the law, legal systems, and legal actors. These vicarious experiences—and, at times, vicarious traumas—are passed along through social networks and social media as well as through intergenerational storytelling among families.[17]

This relationship between storytelling and legal consciousness may be more pronounced in the context of historically marginalized groups who have experienced social and legal exclusion. For example, Pryce and colleagues find that African Americans' attitudes toward the police are deeply influenced by the stories of police abuse and harassment told by their family and friends.[18] They note that these stories serve as a source of vicarious trauma and shape the way African Americans make sense of their own personal encounters with police.[19] Similarly, the Swedish criminologist Simon Wallengren and colleagues link the Roma community's distrust of the police to cultural socialization vis-à-vis "parental socialization, storytelling traditions, and the sharing of negative and discriminatory experiences relative to the authorities."[20]

Learning about the law through storytelling and vicarious experiences is not unique to immigrant communities residing in the United States. However, the role that storytelling plays in the development of immigrants' legal consciousness cannot be overlooked. Not only do immigrants lack access to formal sources of legal information; they hold a unique sociolegal position in the United States. Many exist in a state of "liminal legality," or a hyperawareness of the often precarious nature of their legal standing in the United States.[21] This is the case not only for undocumented immigrants but also for any immigrant without U.S. citizenship. Lacking citizenship, immigrants face legal and social exclusion from daily life, whether it be in attempting to access health care, drive one's children to school, find a job, or rent an apartment—the list goes on.[22] What's more, deportation is always a possibility for those lacking citizenship. Given this potential outcome, it is little surprise that immigration law was a frequent topic of conversation—and concern—among those I interviewed. The law is, in many ways, inescapable.

Ultimately, this amounts to a legal consciousness that is uniquely "immigrant."[23] Importantly, it is from this standpoint that immigrants navigate the immigration system and their experiences with it, including the deportation hearing. As chapter 4 makes clear, explorations of procedural justice in the immigration court context is not without a few unexpected surprises.

4

Who Says the Court Can't Be Fair?

Who says that immigration courts can't be fair? Certainly not Alex, whose deportation story is laden with positive procedural justice assessments.[1] According to Alex, never in his wildest dreams could he have imagined the ordeal he would go through in order to be granted asylum in the United States. Just 22 years old, Alex, a handyman, fled El Salvador when MS-13 gang members threatened to take his life. He reached the U.S. border after a monthlong journey, most of which was spent as a stowaway on one of the notorious cross-Mexico train routes known for narcotraffickers and migrant deaths.[2] Much to his dismay, Alex was quickly apprehended by U.S. Border Patrol. "We were hit with a spotlight, and within 15 seconds our group was surrounded," he recalls.

Alex was taken to a detention facility, where he had the good fortune of meeting a guard who spoke Spanish. "I explained [to him] that I hadn't come to work but to save my life," Alex shares. "When he asked me if I had proof of this, I showed him my gunshot wound." The guard told him how to apply for asylum but warned him that the process would be long and nearly impossible without a lawyer.

Alex applied for asylum on his own and spent several months awaiting his asylum interview while detained in a Texas jail with a contract to house ICE detainees. The days and weeks wore on him. To say that conditions at the facility were difficult would be an understatement. Facing what felt like indefinite detention, he began to reconsider taking his chances back in El Salvador. "I decided it would be better to be sent back to El Salvador than to die of hunger in that place," Alex remembers. He lied during his asylum interview, stating that he was not afraid to return, and asked for voluntary deportation.

Despite requesting deportation, Alex spent several more months detained, bouncing from jail to jail. He was eventually transferred to a detention facility on the East Coast. There, he met with a legal aid group that offers free basic assistance to detained immigrants and learned that he still had a viable asylum claim. Alex reevaluated his options. He had spent so much time already in detention, "which would have all been for nothing" if he went back to El Salvador. Plus, who knew how much longer he would have to wait to be deported.

Also weighing on his decision was the fact that he did, indeed, fear retuning to El Salvador. He was all too familiar with the stories of what happens to people like him when deported. His cousin, who was deported shortly prior, had been greeted by MS-13 the minute he stepped foot in the country at the El Salvador International Airport. Gang members detained him, took his clothing, and interrogated him—all this for someone with whom they hadn't had any previous issues. Alex wasn't sure he'd be so lucky. Once more, he decided to try for asylum.

In light of his decision, the legal aid group Alex met with connected him to an attorney who agreed to take his case pro bono (without a fee). He felt a sense of relief but knew his journey was not yet over. Alex had a good relationship with his attorney. He explains that his attorney treated him well. Knowing that some stories were difficult to discuss, the attorney never pushed him to do so; indeed, there were parts of Alex's story that I was never able to learn for similar reasons.

Despite appearing before an immigration judge during his deportation process on multiple occasions, Alex never stepped foot inside a courtroom. Instead, he attended his hearings via videoconferencing. On each of his scheduled court dates a guard led Alex, dressed in his standard-issue uniform, to a small private room in the detention center. Once there, Alex would sit down across from a television and camera and watch his hearing unfold via two-way livestream.

Alex describes the judge presiding over his case as "very respectful." The judge rarely addressed him directly, speaking primarily with his attorney, who was physically present in the courtroom. "The judge spoke like a school administrator, very quickly and without joking," Alex explains. Because most conversations took place in English with limited interpretation, he generally waited until after the end of each hearing to receive a recap of the day's events from his attorney.

At his final hearing, Alex was given the opportunity to speak directly with the judge and explain why he came to the United States. Alex did this through the assistance of a court interpreter. "He translated everything I wanted to say in the way I wanted to say it," Alex shares. "I couldn't understand anything he said in English," but he even "made the same gestures with his hands, the movements I was making," Alex exclaims, pleased with the interpreter's performance.

He points out that, although the government attorney seemed rather aggressive and behaved arrogantly at times, she was neither his "friend" nor his "enemy." "She wanted to make me nervous . . . [but] she didn't look at me with repulsion. She looked at me like a normal person," he recalls. "She was very direct [and] didn't ask me lots of questions, just attacked specific points that could damage my case. . . . She did all she could to fight against [my case, but] she treated me well."

Alex emphasizes that the judge in his case was "impartial." As he explains it: "He was not on my side nor that of [ICE]. He was simply dedicated to listening to what we were saying." Like the others in court, the judge "was always very respectful with me." When I asked Alex what he thinks, overall, about the court and its actors, he stated that "all the people in the court conducted themselves very professionally." In Alex's eyes, the deportation hearing process had been a fair one.

Indeed, like the vast majority of immigrants interviewed for this book, Alex had few procedural complaints about immigration court and those who work there. Yet very few of the immigration attorneys with whom I spoke shared this perspective. As explored in chapter 3, attorneys cited numerous procedural issues inherent to immigration court (e.g., bias, communication and cultural barriers, professionalism, etc.). It is likely that, were several immigration attorneys to review Alex's story, they, too, might find it riddled with procedural justice issues. This chapter, however, revolves around immigrants' experiences and assessments of deportation hearings—not those of attorneys.

Unlike attorneys, immigrants who find themselves in deportation proceedings, like most people, rarely have any formal legal training. In fact, attorneys that I interviewed explained that it is not uncommon for Central American clients facing deportation to have had little more than grade-school educations, let alone training in the vast complexities of immigration law. Unfamiliar with the legal and professional norms of deportation, how do immigrants evaluate the court and its actors on measures of process fairness?

Perhaps surprisingly, immigrants I interviewed generally held the immigration court—and those who work within its walls—in high regard.

Unaware of the many procedural problems posed by the deportation hearing process, immigrants' assessments of court experiences centered upon the professional character of attorneys, interpreters, and judges, whom they generally found respectful and unbiased and even helpful at times. Most had little to say about the technological aspects of the hearing, such as telephonic interpretation or court appearances via videoconferencing, and what was said was generally positive. A few individuals who experienced videoconferencing during a hearing, including Alex, actually preferred it to appearing in person.[3]

A pattern of procedural complaints did emerge, however, around matters of *time*. Interestingly, the notion of time and its potential impact on fairness has been overlooked in procedural justice studies. As discussed in chapter 1, these studies tend to focus on tangible interactions between individuals and legal actors, not abstract notions. Yet in the immigration context, time becomes a legal actor in its own right, wielding state power to dramatically alter individual experiences of the court and the deportation process. Immigrants face what can feel like endless backlogs, continuances, and rescheduled hearings—evidenced by the nearly 2 million backlogged cases in immigration court as of May 2022.[4] While awaiting their hearing outcomes, those (like Alex) who are detained may feel that there is no end in sight to their loss of freedom. Immigrants who have been released on bond confront a different conundrum, unable to drive, work, or travel, all the while beholden to various forms of supervision and mandatory check-ins.

That immigrants generally perceive immigration court as procedurally just—with a handful of exceptions—merits further discussion, but this is not where the story ends. As outlined in chapter 1, assessments of procedural justice are tied to outcome satisfaction. The importance of this fact in the context of immigration enforcement, and more specifically in regard to compliance with deportation orders, cannot be overstated. Yet unlike what is found in most procedural justice studies, immigrants' evaluations of fair process are not necessarily linked to outcome satisfaction. Instead, it is the *distribution* of justice—in this case *who* is ordered deported compared with *who* is allowed to stay in the United States—that weighs heavily on immigrant satisfaction with deportation hearings.

With this in mind, I begin this chapter with a discussion of immigrants' evaluations of attorneys, interpreters, and judges, highlighting issues of bias, demeanor, and quality of interpersonal treatment. Set against the backdrop of four distinct yet complementary court narratives, I call attention to immigrants' belief in the professionalism of the court, as well as their surprise at feeling listened to and treated with respect by those involved in the deportation hearing process. Issues of culture, communication, and time are also discussed, revealing nuances in immigrants' procedural justice evaluations. I conclude with a discussion of immigrant satisfaction with deportation hearing outcomes. Ultimately, in this chapter I highlight the complexities of procedural justice in the immigration context and reveal the beginnings of what immigrants can teach us about fairness and the law.

Demeanor, Interpersonal Treatment, and Participation

Immigrants I interviewed had no shortage of words to describe the court and its actors. They were referred to as everything from "calm," "friendly," and "nice" to "aggressive," "intimidating," and "tough." Such seemingly divergent characterizations aside, immigrants generally agreed on at least three things. First, most found courtroom actors, especially judges, to behave very professionally. Second, they were pleasantly surprised with the treatment they received from judges in particular. Finally, for the most part they felt that they had been listened to and respected during their hearings.

Yo me sentí caundo salí, "eso no estuvo tan mal!"
"I felt when I left, 'that wasn't so bad!'"—Rita

Rita, a Honduran woman in her late thirties, is no stranger to deportation. Her husband, a Mexican national, has been deported once; it wasn't long before he returned to the United States illegally. At the time of our interview, Rita's sister had recently been ordered deported and Rita's daughter had been placed in deportation proceedings. Rita herself was also in the midst of her own deportation. Making matters more complicated, she had a standing order of deportation from a previous Notice to Appear in immigration court that she had ignored. Family entanglements with deportation such as this are not uncommon. Rita's circumstances were not unique among those I interviewed—several participants had at least one family member currently or previously in deportation proceedings, and still others had lost family members to deportation.

Armed with the knowledge of both her husband's and sister's removal experiences, Rita visited several attorneys and secured a lawyer to represent her and her daughter. She hoped to fend off deportation by obtaining a U visa, awarded to individuals who, among other requirements, can prove that they have been victims of crime in the United States.

Rita was not held in detention during her deportation case, allowed to remain out on bond to care for her younger U.S. citizen child. She recalls being nervous the first time she encountered the unfamiliar federal building that houses the local immigration court. She moved slowly through the security line, accompanied by her children, unsure where to go next. "I had only spoken to my attorney over the phone, and he hadn't shown up yet," she recounts. After asking a guard for assistance, she was directed upstairs to the court. Eventually, her attorney showed up, which provided a small sense of relief.

Awaiting her first hearing, Rita tried to remember what her sister had shared with her. "Calm down . . . the judge will ask basic questions. And just as she told me it would happen," she states plainly, "it did." As she sat in the courtroom, Rita observed the other cases on the judge's master docket, which consisted of a litany of initial appearances packed into one session. She characterizes her judge as quite strict. Despite a stern demeanor, however, Rita stresses that the judge appeared to be "just" in trying the cases before him. "He was almost yelling each time he spoke. He was a very strong person, learned, prepared to ask questions, [but] not one who talks just to talk."

After Rita was sworn in, the judge began asking her a number of questions. "I was told that he was the toughest judge in the court, but he wasn't like that with me," she says. "When it was my turn, I thought he was the nicest guy on the planet Earth!" The interpreter, whom Rita describes as "very nice," translated the judge's questions into Spanish and returned Rita's responses to the judge in English. In the end, she believes that her fear of facing a judge in court was unfounded. As she summarizes, "I felt when I left, 'that wasn't so bad!'"

At the time of our interview, Rita's outcome was still pending. She was given a subsequent hearing date, but this was canceled and then continued twice. Her attorney told her this was likely due to her pending U visa application, which he believed would ultimately be decided in her favor. In the meantime, Rita describes feeling as if she "is floating, unsure what will happen in her case." Although she takes issue with the prolonged delay in her hearing outcome, Rita says that the process has so far been a fair one.

"He was willing to listen."—Eduardo

Eduardo, a young, openly gay Guatemalan man, was granted asylum shortly before our interview. He speaks to me entirely in English, noting that he is "proud" of his English. "I love my English!" he exclaims. Having spent the majority of his life in the United States, albeit undocumented, his English is impeccable.

Eduardo and his younger brother were brought to the United States by their mother in 1999. She fled their abusive father, her husband, three years earlier and managed to save enough money working in the United States to pay a coyote to bring two of her children into the country illegally. At the time of our interview, neither Eduardo's mother nor his brother had managed to legalize their status, although his brother had married a U.S. citizen, with whom he had two children.

Growing up in the United States as an undocumented teenager was difficult. "You go places and people look at you and think you don't speak English or that you're undocumented," he shares. "Luckily, I've learned the language," reflecting on his encounter with ICE that would eventually land him in immigration court and provide an opportunity to request asylum.

Recalling his transfer from police to ICE custody after being arrested on suspicion of a DUI, he insists that his language abilities are what saved him. "There is no help with translation [in ICE custody]. . . . They do not care." He continues: "It's like, 'Okay, we are going to deport you back to Guatemala,' and if you don't speak the language you don't even know [what's going on]!"

Eduardo was pressured by ICE agents to sign his own deportation order, but as he explains, he knew better. "So I said, 'I don't think it works that way," because I had [consulted an immigration attorney about asylum in the past]." Aware that he could file a defensive asylum claim if placed in deportation proceedings, he chose to challenge his deportation in court and, with no criminal record, was released on bond and placed under intensive supervision.

Eduardo waited eight months for his first hearing, which was delayed and rescheduled twice during this time. He recalls being extremely stressed, noting that "the system itself is not really friendly. Maybe [the employees] are desensitized by so many cases, and I can sympathize, but it was heartbreaking." He continues: "The process is so slow. You try to get information and they just say they'll let you know."

At his initial hearing, Eduardo felt "intimidated" and "scared." He says that he had "high expectations" of the court and that he was "all dressed up," but as it turns out, immigration court is "like traffic court—very casual." He recalls the court security "talk[ing] down to people [who don't speak English], . . . addressing them as less than and, at the same time, not being able to do anything about it, . . . a feeling [of being] powerless." He remembers everything at this first hearing as being very matter-of-fact. "[Everything is] so black-and-white. There is no information from your lawyer. Sometimes the lawyer doesn't even tell you what is going on," he emphasizes. "You feel vulnerable. Anyone can walk in and, sure, a lot of other people are there for the same reason, but you feel ashamed. It's embarrassing."

Although Eduardo does not speak highly of external court staff, he notes that his hearing experience was fair and unbiased. He explains that, prior to his hearing, he was quite nervous about how the various courtroom actors would treat him because his asylum application rested upon his sexuality. Yet "I was being treated and judged based on the whole picture, all the evidence," he insists. He says that he is "lucky" to have had such a "kind" judge. "[The judge] just seemed very willing to listen." "[I thought] when you go to court, it would be like Judge Judy, she's not going to let you speak," he elaborates, "but [my judge] let you speak and would listen and rephrase questions I didn't understand." Eduardo says that one of his biggest fears was that "the judge would say, 'You missed the [one-year asylum] bar. You didn't apply and you've been here for 16 years. Why should I listen to you?'" He pauses: "But he was willing to listen." In addition, his judge "would even make jokes," which he liked.

He describes the ICE trial attorney in his case as both considerate and compassionate regarding the sensitive nature of his claims and testimony, noting that "she did her job." "Before the actual hearing she said to me, 'I read your entire file,' which was embarrassing [because of the personal information it contained regarding sexuality and sexual assault] but amazing [as] . . . the trial attorney [in my friend's case] didn't even look at this file," he points out. She then told Eduardo that she would need to ask him a lot of questions in order to clarify some things, but she wanted him to "take his time," which he thought "was very sensitive on her part."

Reflecting on his case, Eduardo feels lucky to have received asylum. He knows that the odds were against him and, in spite of everything, believes that the deportation hearing process was fair. Still, he worries about the precariousness of his asylum decision, that it could be overturned with a change in policy. He won't be able to rest easy "without worrying that something's gonna happen" until he finally becomes a citizen.

Todos están hacienda su trabajo.
"They're just doing their jobs."—Walter

Sitting across from Walter at a local Guatemalan restaurant, I hear that he has been going to immigration court for his deportation proceedings for the previous four years. "I've witnessed numerous other cases before other various judges, and some have been very rude," he explains. It is on this basis that Walter believes his judge has treated him better than average.

Walter didn't plan on migrating to the United States. He quit school after completing the sixth grade to become a carpenter. When he was 35, his mother fell ill. Walter and his 10 siblings pooled their incomes to support her, but it just wasn't enough. It was decided that one of the siblings would have to go to the United States in order to send money home for their mother's medication. After no one volunteered, Walter agreed to go.

Walter's journey from Guatemala to the United States cost $11,000. As he puts it, this was the "cheap" option, consisting of a full month of travel, often on foot. His family sold a home and some land in order to cover the trip's cost, and Walter agreed to pay this loan back once he started earning an income in the United States. He was apprehended by Border Patrol agents and sent back to Mexico several times, but he remained determined. "It's a game of chance," he explains. "They'll send a bunch of guys running across to distract the [Border Patrol], and while they're dealing with someone over there, you get through over here unnoticed." Walter got through on his fourth try.

His deportation saga began after being stopped outside a liquor store on his way to a dinner party. Accused of trying to avoid a stoplight by cutting through a parking lot, the arresting police officer questioned Walter about his immigration status upon seeing his expired license. "I told him I wasn't going to say anything else because I knew that I didn't have to," Walter recalls. The officer "wrote up every [charge] he could think of," presumably disgruntled that Walter would dare assert his rights. All of the charges were dropped, with the exception of the charge for driving without a license. Walter spent two days in jail before being taken into ICE custody.

He was held in detention for three months while awaiting his first deportation hearing, all the while moving from facilities in Pennsylvania to Florida to Louisiana. He appeared for his initial hearing via videoconferencing from inside detention, at which point the judge reduced his bond from $28,000 to $7,500. "He said it was the lowest bond he could give me," Walter remembers. Fortunately, Walter had $3,000 in savings, which, combined with money he obtained from selling his car and calling in a favor from a friend, allowed him to post bond. For Walter, being placed in deportation proceedings would be extremely costly—by the time we spoke, he had paid an additional $7,000 in immigration fees alone. He had also paid $4,000 in legal fees to an attorney whom he likes but who sometimes gets "angry" from "the stresses of being a lawyer."

He describes the judge presiding over his case as "nice" and "a good person," something he had not expected in the least. Despite this, Walter is unable to look his judge in the eyes even though his lawyer told him that eye contact was important. "It's just that out of respect you don't do this in Guatemala," he explains, "look [authority figures] in the eyes." Instead, Walter looks in the judge's direction. "This way, it seems like I'm looking at the judge, but I'm really looking at the [judicial] seal behind him."

Walter is nearly fluent in English and says that he never bothers to listen to the interpreter assigned to his case. "[The interpreter] is Dominican, and she talks super fast. She also uses words that we don't use in Guatemala," all of which Walter says is very confusing. "I listen to the judge," he emphasizes.

Walter has little to say about the ICE trial attorney in his case. "Obviously, [they] don't want you to be here—they want you deported," he explains, his assessment moving beyond the attorney in his case to some amalgamation of attorneys he's witnessed over four years. "They can be jerks," he adds, "giving you a hard time over something insignificant." Reflecting on the court as a whole, Walter assesses that "they're all just doing their jobs."

When I ask Walter how he feels about his impending case outcome, he says he is extremely anxious. When we last spoke, Walter told me he would not leave if ordered deported. "What will I do in Guatemala?" he asks. "What kind of life can my son have in Guatemala?"

La verdad es que tu no sabes nada!
"The truth is, you don't know anything!"—Angelica

Angelica came to the United States in 2006, leaving her four children behind in El Salvador. She managed to acquire a series of cleaning jobs and was eventually granted Temporary Protected Status (TPS). Although TPS affords individuals the ability to live and work in the United States legally, it does not make them eligible for citizenship.[5] Instead, those with TPS must apply to renew their status every few years or risk becoming undocumented. What's more, as noncitizens, people with TPS are forever at risk of being deported. As Angelica explains, her TPS status was short-lived.

Losing her legal status was just one in a series of many hardships that Angelica would face as she tried to make a life for herself and her children in the United States, including an attempted sexual assault that left her homeless and without work. After several years apart from her children, and without a way to bring them to the United States legally, she returned to El Salvador, gathered her children, and attempted to sneak them—and herself—back across the United States–Mexico border, where they were promptly apprehended.

Angelica was placed in detention and separated from her children for eight days. The group was then reunited and moved to a family detention center for three months. She describes the detention facility as if it were a "military operation." "You get up at five in the morning. Everyone to the bathroom. Everyone gets ready. They take everyone out in a line. For breakfast, another line. Imagine, almost every fifteen minutes, another line." She adds, however, that "the kids get to play, which is nice."

A few family members helped pay Angelica's bond. She managed to hire an attorney to represent her, but, as she puts it, "not all attorneys are equal. . . . What he wanted most was to get his money—it was never to help people." She continues: "For him it was taking money and, if they send you back, 'I don't care.'" Angelica highlights the stories of friends and family with "good" attorneys who managed to obtain relief. "I don't know why I didn't find someone who helped me," she bemoans.

"The truth is, you don't know anything," Angelica exclaims when I ask her to describe her deportation hearing. She notes that she appeared before the immigration judge just twice before being ordered deported. She describes the judge in her case as "kind of intimidating," but like Walter she stresses that they are just "doing their job like everyone else." She notes that neither the judge nor the court interpreter allowed her to tell her story. "The judge just asks for documents," she says, and the interpreter did not appear to be on her side. "I practically felt like [the interpreter], instead of helping me, [hurt me]," including scolding her outside the courtroom for attempting to ask a question.

Upon being asked to sign her deportation order, Angelica's attorney said "practically nothing. He didn't have any words for me, just gave me the papers to sign." Despite being ordered deported, Angelica decided to stay, well aware of the fact that what she was doing was against the law. "I may not know a lot about immigration law," she remarks, "but if I had known [when I came here] what I've come to know now, I could've gotten my *permiso*[6] or my residency." She continues: "But when someone like me comes to this country alone, you don't have anyone to help you. You arrive here and you sleep in the street. It's hard."

Still, Angelica remains hopeful. Two of her children are DACA recipients, and her mother has become a U.S. resident and will soon be able to apply for citizenship. When we met, Angelica was exploring avenues to reopen her case and keeping her fingers crossed for immigration reform. "Back to my country? I do not want to go."

Evaluations of Procedural Justice

The court narratives of Alex, Rita, Eduardo, Walter, and Angelica represent the range of procedural justice evaluations that immigrants shared with me during our interviews. With the exception of a handful of individuals like Angelica, most people found court actors and the deportation hearing to be procedurally just. Although not always stating so explicitly, their characterizations of immigration court rested upon assessments of (1) behavior, demeanor, and impartiality, (2) quality of interpersonal treatment, and (3) opportunities for error correction and participation—including the ability to speak and be heard—all of which are linked to procedural justice.[7]

For instance, when legal authorities, be they police officers or courtroom personnel, treat people politely, respectfully, and in an unbiased manner, people are more likely to evaluate legal encounters as procedurally fair.[8] Recall that Alex characterizes his judge as "very respectful." Rita describes her judge as "stern" but "just" and her interpreter as "very nice." Eduardo refers to his judge as "kind" and the ICE trial attorney in his case as "sensitive." Similarly, Walter considers his judge to be "nice" and "a good person."

Others I interviewed used similar language to describe courtroom actors, calling them "educated," "very friendly," and "helpful." What's more, most immigrants I interviewed—even those who did not view immigration court actors in such a positive light—remarked that they were impressed with the overall professionalism of the court and its staff. They also emphasized that courtroom actors were simply "doing their jobs." Positive characterizations such as these are generally indicative of positive procedural justice assessments, which is what immigrants shared time and again.

Opportunities for error correction and participation, too, have been deemed crucial components of positive procedural justice assessments in courtroom contexts.[9] In immigration court, such issues are inextricably linked to English-language proficiency, a factor not typically explored in procedural justice literature. As noted in chapter 2, immigration attorneys emphasize that lack of English fluency leaves clients at a disadvantage in court. Under these circumstances, courtroom dialogue is mediated through the interpreter—if it is actually translated at all—the end result being that interpreters become de facto "gatekeepers" of the deportation process.[10]

Immigrants who were at least somewhat fluent in English, like Eduardo and Walter, made explicit remarks about the importance of language in the courtroom. Eduardo not only preferred to speak to me in English during our interview; he preferred to forgo interpretation at his deportation hearing. "I did not use an interpreter," he says. "I feel more comfortable speaking in English, especially talking about past childhood abuse that I went through. . . . In Spanish it felt really vulgar. . . . The word 'rape' in English does not sound as bad as the word for [rape] in Spanish. I didn't feel comfortable saying some things in Spanish." For Eduardo, speaking without the aid of interpreter was not only more comfortable; it gave him more control. Others, like Walter, accepted interpretation but simply ignored it and focused on the English-language dialogue dominating their hearings.

Interestingly, many immigrants I interviewed were very pleased with courtroom interpreters despite having limited English abilities. Unlike attorneys, who emphasized quality of translation in their assessments of interpreters, immigrants I interviewed focused their assessments on interpreter behavior and demeanor. These individuals, Alex among them, commonly described interpreters with such words as "competent," "good," and "friendly." Yet assessing one's interpreter without mastery over the original and interpreted languages can be quite tricky.

When I pressed Alex, for instance, about his evaluation of his interpreter, he said that he knew the interpreter was good because "[he] made the same gestures with his hands, the movements I [made]." Like others, he also found his interpreter to be impartial. "I don't think he was translating with the aim of helping or hurting my case, just translating." Whether or not Alex and others with little grasp of English are able to accurately assess interpreter quality, however, remains questionable.

It should be noted that, although not all interpretation assessments were as positive as that put forward by Alex, few were as damning as the critique leveled by Angelica. Indeed, Angelica was the only immigrant I interviewed who held a resolutely negative evaluation of her interpreter. Recall that Angelica's interpreter scolded her for attempting to ask a question outside the courtroom. Moreover, Angelica insists that, instead of "helping" her during her hearing, the interpreter actually "hurt" her.

Overall, she insists that her interpreter had a nasty demeanor, treated her poorly, and served as an impediment to Angelica's ability to participate in her own hearing.

Despite their divergent assessments, Alex and Angelica both highlight their interpreters' demeanors and the ways their interpreters treated them during their hearings. It seems reasonable that, in the face of communication barriers, demeanor and interpersonal treatment are especially salient to evaluations of procedural justice. Although legal arguments and lines of questioning may be "lost in translation," concrete actions such as facial expressions, physical touch, and tone of voice have the ability to transcend language.

Barriers to communication, such as a lack of fluency in English, impact more than individuals' comprehension of the deportation hearing. For many, interpersonal treatment, in conjunction with being afforded a space to speak and be heard, has important implications for assessments of impartiality. Recall that Alex connects issues of judicial bias with opportunities to participate in his deportation hearing, stressing that his judge listened to both his and the trial attorney's arguments as evidence of his impartiality. The perception of an impartial judge, as well as feeling listened to, greatly influenced Alex's positive evaluation of the deportation hearing process. Similarly, Eduardo was heavily swayed by what he perceived as his judge's willingness to explain things, listen, and "let [him] speak." He was also deeply impacted by the impartiality and compassion on the part of the ICE trial attorney in his case when it came time for him to discuss the crux of his asylum claim—the persecution he had experienced due to his sexuality.

Again, even when immigrants evaluated courtroom actors negatively, most still found the deportation process to be fair. For example, recall that Rita characterizes her judge as a "very tough person" who yelled several times in court and was not one to chit-chat. Yet despite the judge's stern demeanor, Rita characterizes him as fair and did not find his behavior or demeanor problematic. Even Angelica, who finds the deportation hearing process to be problematic and who assessed the judge, interpreter, and her own attorney negatively, feels that these individuals are simply "doing their jobs like the rest of the world." Indeed, as will be discussed in chapter 5, Angelica's central complaint about her experience had more to do with the substantive fairness and morality of immigration law than the court and its actors. Ultimately, interviews revealed very few process-related complaints about the deportation hearing in particular or immigration court more broadly.

A Waiting Game

The most glaring exception to immigrants' positive assessments of the court centers upon issues of *time*. By far the most frequent procedural complaint leveled by immigrants was the length of time the deportation process takes. As detailed in chapter 2, immigration court is incredibly backlogged, with nearly 2 million cases pending in the court by the summer of 2022.[11] Although the backlog of cases in the court was not as bad when I began my research in 2014 as it is today, it was still already at several hundred thousands cases.[12] It is little surprise, then, that nearly every immigrant interviewed for this book cited long wait times, cancellations, delays, and continuances. For many, the deportation hearing process had been ongoing not for weeks or months but for years. In fact, several people whom I intended to interview were in the end unable to participate, their hearings pushed back so many times that they never made it to court in the nearly two years during which I collected data.

While in deportation proceedings, immigrants who have been released on bond are often forced to comply with ICE's Intensive Supervision Appearance Program (ISAP).[13] As part of the program, individuals complete weekly or biweekly check-ins with a case manager, accept home visits, perform telephonic check-ins, or even wear electronic monitoring bracelets with GPS tracking.[14] For those in detention, the wait is generally not as long and the delays and continuances are not as many, but it is still agonizing. Even in the best cases, being held in immigration detention is like being held in jail. In some cases, immigrants are detained in actual jails—at times mixed in with the general population—that have contracts with ICE. In the worst cases, being held in immigration detention is akin to being held in a prison camp.[15]

Like most jails and prisons, detention facilities are often located in remote areas, making it difficult to receive visits from family and, as noted in chapter 2, from lawyers. Complicating matters, it is nearly impossible for those without legal status to visit detention facilities even if they have a way to get to them. As one interviewee recalls, "[My six-year-old] told me that, if I go away again, her heart will break," adding—through a steady stream of tears—that in addition to being away from his family for six months, he missed the birth of his second child while detained.

Yet it is not the intensive supervision or the detention that makes waiting difficult; it is the wait itself. Recall that, at the time of our interview, Walter was not only awaiting his hearing outcome; he was also awaiting a confirmation of his final court date. He explains that the fact that his lawyer believes in his case does not lessen the daily anxiety he experiences. "The wait is the hardest part," he shares. "I just want a decision whether I go or stay. It's on your mind every day—it never goes away."

In Eduardo's eyes, the wait begins before the deportation hearing starts. He notes feelings of frustration and stress as well as a sense of being in a never-ending legal and social limbo. Like Walter, he, says that "the most frustrating [part of the deportation process] is the time." He elaborates:

> I've been in proceedings since 2013 . . . [and] was granted asylum two and a half years later. From there, it's another year before I can apply for residency, . . . [and] not only that, I have to wait four more years to apply for citizenship. So my process will finally be done in 2021. . . . That is if everything goes well, and that's not counting [the fact] that I've been in this country since 1999. That's 21 years. That's a lifetime and I don't understand why. . . . This is a puzzle I can't put together. . . . The reality is that is a very long time . . . to really feel like a citizen, like this is my home, that they can't kick me out, that I can dream big . . . without worrying that something's gonna happen. . . . So that's where the system is failing me, is failing us.

Although their circumstances are quite different, the complaints leveled by both Walter and Eduardo are similar at their core. Not only does a prolonged deportation hearing process amplify the stress, fear, and frustrations of being deportable; it leaves one unable to make plans for the future. In such cases, it is not only the deportation outcome that is pending but also one's entire life that is on hold.

Interestingly, although length of process greatly influenced immigrants' procedural justice evaluations, it has been largely ignored in procedural justice literature. Yet it is not far-fetched to imagine that evaluations of process could hinge on matters of time. Imagine two police stop scenarios. In one, a driver is made to pull over to the side of the road and waits about five minutes before the officer returns with her license and registration. Perhaps she gets a speeding ticket, perhaps she does not. In an alternative scenario, the driver is required to wait fifteen minutes for the officer to return—with or without a speeding ticket. While she waits, she becomes increasingly anxious, unsure what is going on and why it is taking so long for the officer to return. Whether she receives a ticket or not, she may find the wait alone may make the legal encounter seem less fair.

Similarly, when immigration court dates are repeatedly postponed or rescheduled, individuals become increasingly anxious. They may feel that their hearings are deemed unimportant, even if the consequences could be life-altering. For those who are detained, postponements and rescheduling can make the deportation process feel "indefinite." In some cases, it may even persuade people to forgo their hearings and accept deportation, as was almost the case with Alex. Overall, immigrants stressed that the time spent dealing with rescheduled court dates, attending hearings, and waiting for final deportation decisions is confusing, frustrating, and ultimately unfair, as immigrants are forced to put their lives "on hold."

It is possible that complaints about waiting times such as these may actually tap into underlying procedural justice concepts such as process control,[16] representation/opportunities for participation,[17] or voice[18] as they may be driven by feelings of being "in the dark" about one's case or simply "at the whim of the court." However, immigrants and attorneys interviewed for this book reported having lengthy discussions about the time the deportation process takes with their attorneys and clients, respectively. Thus even when immigrants understand and are forewarned about delays and waits, they still find them procedurally problematic.

Distributive Justice

As discussed in chapter 2, procedural justice and distributive justice are two distinct concepts. "Procedural justice" refers to the "fairness" of a given process. "Distributive justice" refers to the fairness of the allocation of outcomes across individuals or encounters. Notably, both procedural and distributive justice should be distinguished from outcome satisfaction.

The vast majority of scholarship addressing questions of procedural justice have demonstrated that it outweighs distributive justice in outcome satisfaction equations.[19] People generally care more about fair process than equitable outcomes when it comes to determining how satisfied they are with their own legal outcomes in a given police encounter or court hearing. Yet there are some important exceptions.

For example, Casper and colleagues[20] find that assessments of procedural justice *and* distributive justice impact criminal defendants' satisfaction with case outcomes. Pillai et al.[21] find that distributive justice actually outweighs procedural justice in relation to job satisfaction and organizational commitment in both India and China, suggesting that, in certain cultural contexts, fairness of distribution matters more than that of process. Recent scholarship has also demonstrated that, in postcolonial settings, procedural justice—in conjunction with distributive justice and efficacy—impact perceptions of police legitimacy.[22]

Findings described in this chapter lend further support to the value of examining distributive justice assessments when concerned with matters of fairness and the law, at least in the immigration context. If procedural justice theory is taken at face value, one would expect evaluations of fair process to be tied to outcome satisfaction, even in instances when outcomes were not desirable. In this context, then, positive evaluations of the deportation hearing process should make outcomes of deportation a bit easier to swallow. However, not a single immigrant interviewed for this project found their own or their family members' deportation orders acceptable. Moreover, those I interviewed who had been ordered deported had failed to comply and were residing in the United States illegally; several had violated their deportation orders more than once.

In part this is due to immigrants' perceptions of state legitimacy, coupled with understandings of the substantive fairness of immigration law, which will be explored in chapter 5. In part, however, this is due to immigrants' concern with the equity of deportation hearing outcomes or the distribution of justice. What immigrants lack in formal legal training they make up for through the legal storytelling of family, friends, neighbors, and cellmates. The deportation cases of others come to serve as reference points for immigrants' own experiences with immigration court.[23]

Indeed, immigrants I interviewed often cited deportation stories, as well as the media, when explaining why they initially expect poor treatment in immigration court, followed by swift deportations. Many fear immigration judges prior to meeting an actual judge in person. Others are unsure if they will be provided with interpretation or how much (if any) of the deportation hearing process or relevant immigration law will be explained to them. Still others brace themselves for attacks from ICE trial attorneys.

Although some immigrants were still awaiting deportation decisions when we spoke, others had final deportation decisions in hand. In these instances, immigrants framed outcome satisfaction in relation to the real and imagined case outcomes of others. Those who had received relief from deportation felt fortunate, explaining that most immigrants are not so lucky. Those who had been ordered deported stressed that their outcomes were unfair when one considers the outcomes of others in deportation.

Recall the way Angelica pins her deportation order to an assessment of her attorney not in his own right but in relation to other attorneys. "Not all attorneys are equal. . . . I don't know why I didn't find someone who helped me," she remarks, blaming her attorney for her deportation order. She went on to recount several stories—including the cases of two of her children—in which deportation hearings, aided by "good" attorneys, ended in relief from deportation. Others emphasized the types of people who are able to obtain relief from deportation, including "people with misdemeanors, serious crimes, [like] robbery and things, and . . . sometimes they [get to stay here] without deportation. . . . That frustrates you like you have no idea. It kills you. To see that, it kills you."

In reality, it is nearly impossible for immigrants who have been convicted of crime to avoid deportation; however, it does happen. Moreover, the mere perception that immigrants with criminal convictions are sometimes granted relief from deportation while those with no criminal records are ordered deported is enough to weigh heavily on assessments of outcome satisfaction. Ultimately, whether or not they were awaiting final deportation decisions, most immigrants I interviewed cared deeply about equity in the distribution of deportation hearing outcomes.

Although these findings run counter to most procedural justice re-search, they are not without any precedent. In a classic article on how citizens assess process fairness, Tyler[24] pays close attention to the con-nection between consistency of treatment and outcomes—essentially, distributive justice—with process fairness and outcome satisfaction. Tyler finds that consistency with (1) past experiences, (2) prior expecta-tions, (3) what is believed to generally happen to others, and (4) recent experiences of friends, family, and neighbors have no effect on proce-dural justice assessments or outcome satisfaction. He suggests that this lack of a consistency effect may be due to population characteristics and legal knowledge acquisition:

> Perhaps the most striking deviation from the predictions is the failure to find strong consistency effects in citizen judgments of fairness. In this study citizens are not basing their judgments on a comparison of their outcomes or treatment with other experiences, either their own or of oth-ers'. . . . There are several possible explanations. . . . Citizens may thus lack the knowledge necessary for judging whether their outcomes or treat-ment were better or worse than those of others. . . . [However, it] may be that the lack of awareness of others' experiences is characteristic of only some populations. Special groups may have greater knowledge about oth-ers and rely more on others' experiences when evaluating their own. . . . If citizens lack the information needed to rely on consistency, that is, on cross-situational comparisons, their alternative is to rely on judgments that can be made with the information they do have . . . [such as] the be-havior of the officials, . . . their honesty [and] whether the official followed general ethical standards of conduct.[25]

As Tyler explains, some populations may lack the information needed to judge consistency across treatment or outcomes. In such instances, individuals rely on information they do have, such as officials' behavior and formal legal knowledge like standards of conduct.

Yet the immigration context is indicative of an alternative scenario to that described by Tyler. Indeed, immigrants appear to comprise the type of "special group" Tyler casually mentions. Again, as discussed in chap-ter 3, immigrants lack formal legal knowledge, such as awareness of their rights in immigration court or an understanding of ethical standards of conduct. Under these circumstances, assessments of distributive justice, along with evaluations of behavior and demeanor, play a crucial role in evaluations of fairness and immigration court.

Conclusion

The procedural justice evaluations I highlight throughout this chapter raise as many questions as they provide answers. Why do immigrants find the deportation hearing procedurally just, while attorneys do not? Why is it that some procedural justice factors appear to matter less in the immigration context, while factors that are typically excluded from procedural justice studies appear so important? Moreover, if procedural justice operates differently in the immigration context than it does in traditional criminal justice settings, how might this impact immigrant perceptions of state legitimacy and compliance with deportation orders?

I address these questions in the chapters that follow. Drawing upon narratives of government corruption in Central America, I link perceptions of legitimacy to the unique lens through which immigrants relate to the law, as well as notions of ethics and morality. I draw connections between legitimacy and compliance, as apparent incongruities—immigrants believing in the state's power to deport (some) immigrants yet refusing to comply with their own deportation orders—are explored. Compliance with immigration law is thus not a question of fair process but a question of the *substantive* fairness of immigration law.

5

Deportation Hearings, Legitimacy, and the Rule of Law

Might the desire for rule of law ever become so strong that one is willing to break the law in order to find it? For Sara and many other Central Americans I interviewed, the answer is a resounding "yes." As she tells it, Sara had no choice but to flee to the United States. "Life is very different [in Central America]," she explains. "People [in the United States] don't know what it's like there—sometimes you don't even have food to give to your children." Yet it was not poverty that led Sara to illegally cross the United States–Mexico border with two small children in tow; it was rampant gang violence and impunity for criminals.

Sara's journey to the United States was not her first experience migrating in search of a better life. Sara was born in Honduras in the 1970s. Life in Honduras was difficult. "There isn't any work," she stresses, "so there is a lot of delinquency." Eventually, Sara moved to Guatemala, got married, normalized her immigration status, and had two children. But life in Guatemala proved difficult too. Sara was forced to separate from her husband and later discovered that she did not actually have legal status in Guatemala—she had been cheated by an attorney. Still, returning to Honduras was not an option.

On her own, Sara struggled to provide for her sons and ensure that they could afford to stay in school. Keeping her children in school was about more than an education—it was a matter of security. "I've been both father and mother for my children," she explains, recounting the obstacles she has faced as a single parent. "Here it's different," she began, "but [in Guatemala] school is very expensive. You have to pay for [everything]. . . . When they're in elementary school it's easier. They can walk to school or ride a bike. But by the time they're in secondary school, you have to pay for them to take the bus." However, Sara feared the alternatives. "When they're stuck at home they become restless" or, worse, "their friends pressure them to sell drugs—there are a lot of distractions out there."

Despite her best efforts, keeping her children safe from trouble in Guatemala would prove nearly impossible. A local gang began targeting her older son when he reached his early teens. Over time, harassment transitioned from verbal to physical. On one occasion, Sara's son was nearly beaten to death outside his school. "He came home to me from school and he had been beaten. His face was very badly beaten, horrible," Sara recalls with a pained expression. When she asked him what happened he replied, "Just because I was wearing my shoes, at school. Just because they were so nice. Look, mama, what they did to me. It's because you bought me these nice shoes, mama, that they did this. . . . They told me that they were going to kill me. . . . I don't want to study anymore." Sara continues: "Thank god for a [security guard]. He saw him and intervened. If not"—Sara pauses—"they would've killed him." School was no longer safe.

Sara's son dropped out, but the harassment continued. He was being pressured to sell drugs, and the gang wouldn't take no for an answer. Sara felt helpless. Unable to turn to the local authorities, whom she viewed as incapable, Sara sent her son to the United States illegally. He managed to cross the border undetected and moved in with relatives.

Shortly thereafter, Sara followed with her toddler and a young nephew. However, she was not as lucky. Caught at the border, Sara and the children were held in a family detention facility for four days. There were no beds and very little food—she gave hers to the children. Tears well in her eyes as she recalls her six-year-old nephew, cold and hungry, asking, "But aunt, why can't we leave this place?" Upon release, Sara was placed under ICE supervision. She was given a deportation hearing date and told to appear.

Sara wears an electronic monitoring device on her ankle as we speak. She disdainfully laments her regular probation-style check-ins with ICE—visits that cost her $120 round-trip in taxi fare—and her inability to legally work while awaiting her next deportation hearing, which has been postponed multiple times. Recently, ICE showed up for a home visit only to discover that Sara wasn't home, having taken a job under the table. They required her to attend an additional check-in.

When an ICE employee began to lecture Sara about her transgression, she simply couldn't stand it. "I took advantage of the fact that somebody was listening to me," she explains. She started to yell. "I said, 'Take this stupid bracelet off of me! Put me in handcuffs! Put me in jail! Deport me! You have to let me work! If you don't let me work [I won't be able to afford to come here]. I'll miss my appointments, and then if I miss my appointments, you'll deport me! This whole thing is ridiculous!'" The employee, rather taken aback according to Sara, began to console her. She offered to cut Sara some slack and said she wouldn't "get her in trouble this time." Still, she warned Sara to "be patient" and "try to do things the right way."

Frustrated with what she considers a lack of options, Sara breaks down, crying. "We come here with dreams. We leave our families behind, our parents. . . . We leave our children. But why? Why don't they let us work? Nobody comes here to cause harm. Nobody comes here to hurt anyone. . . . We only come here to try to help our families." As Sara sees it, "to have papers, a visa, would be so nice," but things don't always work out as planned. She sighs. "That's life."

Sara's experience captures the desperation driving many Central American immigrants to migrate to the United States, especially in recent years. As I introduced in chapter 1, Northern Triangle countries are often paralyzed by corruption, gang violence, and what many perceive as an absence of law and order. Confronted with this reality, Sara chose to break the law and move her family to the United States without authorization, convinced they would be safe. She desperately wants to follow the rules of her immigration supervision and comply with her court hearings, but she doesn't see how this is possible given her status as sole supporter of her family. The law and order she so desperately sought has become a web within which she is trapped. She sees little recourse apart from continuing to break the law.

Appreciation for the rule of law, a belief in the legitimacy of the U.S. government, and the search for security and opportunity attracted many of the immigrants I interviewed to the United States. As with Sara, it is also what led many to violate the law initially, entering the United States without authorization or overstaying their visas. Moreover, it led many to violate their deportation orders—or plan on violating said orders should they materialize—in the face of procedurally just treatment, either refusing to leave the United States or returning illegally, in some cases more than once.

Perhaps ironically, the deportation hearing itself serves as further proof for many of the immigrants I interviewed that the rule of law not only exists but actually functions in the United States. As I revealed in chapter 4, the deportation hearing, governed by established rules and carried out by intelligent and impartial judges, attorneys, and interpreters who adhere to the law in order to do their jobs, is viewed as procedurally just. As I will explore in this chapter, immigrants generally believed in the state's power to deport and greatly appreciated the U.S. government's approach to crime control. Ultimately, the deportation hearing, the immigration court, and the U.S. government writ large are all seen as legitimate in the eyes of these immigrants.

Still, there are several glaring contradictions present, at least when examined through the lens of procedural justice. Immigrants find the deportation hearing to be procedurally fair, yet they are not, nor will they ever be, satisfied with a deportation order. They find the state to be legitimate, yet they refuse to comply with orders of deportation. Traditional conceptions of procedural justice that link process fairness to outcome satisfaction, outcome satisfaction to perceptions of state legitimacy, and state legitimacy to compliance simply do not apply in this context. Instead, immigrants frame compliance with deportation and, more broadly, the U.S. immigration system in relation to evaluations of the ethics and morality. In this context, compliance is predicated upon the existence of viable pathways to legalization for "deserving" (i.e., noncriminal) immigrants.

I begin this chapter with a discussion of immigrants' evaluations of state legitimacy. Drawing upon five crime control narratives that are characteristic of those repeatedly shared during interviews, I call attention to the frequent juxtapositions of illegitimate and legitimate authority in Central America and the United States, respectively. I draw connections between legitimacy and compliance, as apparent incongruities—immigrants believing in the state's power to deport (some) immigrants yet refusing to comply with their own deportation orders—are explored. Immigrants reveal that, at times, compliance is a matter of the *substantive* fairness of law, something that no amount of fair process can alter.

Corruption, Impunity, and Security

Corruption, impunity, and security were among the most prominent themes emerging from immigrants' stories of their countries of origin. These were also among the principal reasons immigrants cited when asked what brought them to the United States. Whether the threats were abstract or tangible, vicarious or firsthand, immigrants generally described feeling forced to flee from or unable to return to Central America, fearing for their lives. Governments and their actors—be they politicians or police, judges or prosecutors—were typically described as corrupt, dishonest, and for sale. Criminal justice institutions were characterized as incapable of controlling, or even responding to, rampant criminality. Ultimately, when reflecting on crime, justice, and victimization, immigrants produce characterizations of Central American governments ranging from inept and ineffective to wholly illegitimate.

If the Northern Triangle was cast as the heart of unrestrained harm and violence, for many the United States was said to hold the promise of salvation. A place of safety and security, it was generally praised for its "tough on crime" policies and strict law enforcement. American judges were believed to be impartial, American police were said to protect the community, and American politicians, it was contended, would not accept bribes. Importantly, criminals were actually punished and sometimes rightfully deported. Ultimately, the state was considered to be both effective and legitimate, which—again—is what attracted many of those I interviewed to the United States in the first place.

El que no paga se muere.
"He who doesn't pay dies."—Freddy

"The United States is a country of opportunity," repeats Freddy, a Salvadoran man in his late thirties. "I've always said it and the whole world knows it." Still, Freddy did not leave El Salvador entirely of his own accord. Indeed, both of his illegal journeys across the United States–Mexico border were prompted by violent threats to his life.

The first time Freddy came to the United States without authorization was in 2004. His mother and brother, already living in the States, regularly encouraged him to make the move. At the time, Freddy was married and had a young child. He and his father owned a small public transportation business in San Salvador, El Salvador's capitol. He was committed to building a life in his native home. However, this was not easy.

As Freddy explains, when the gangs started getting involved in the transportation sector, "[our] business completely fell apart." He reflects, "I go to work and this guy shows up and says, 'If you don't pay me, you're not going to work.' And this is what happens in my country—he who doesn't pay dies." He continues: "It's worrisome. To this day everyone says that the police and government are trying to do something [about the gangs], but they never—," his voice trails off momentarily. "I'm not saying that they don't do *anything*. There are good people, but there are also people involved in bad things. There is always money being made. The mafia is a money-making machine."

Like many small business owners in El Salvador,[1] Freddy was caught in a difficult situation. "I've never been a person who was okay with that sort of thing," he reflects. In the end, he closed his business and headed to the United States. "If I hadn't come here, I'd probably be dead."

Yet after a trip to traffic court landed him in deportation proceedings just four years later, Freddy found himself back where he started. He didn't fight his deportation; neither did he turn around and head for the United States. Instead, he decided to begin anew in El Salvador, planning to return to the United States one day. He found a job delivering newspapers. Shortly thereafter, a local gang began extorting him.

He lets out an exasperated sigh as he recalls his first encounter with the gang. "They told me, 'If you're going to [deliver papers in] my neighborhood, you're going to give me $1,000 or you have to go—if you don't want to die.'" Having saved some money while working in the United States, this time Freddy decided to pay the gang and hoped that they would leave him alone.

Instead, the gang continued demanding payment. "I went to the police, but they didn't do anything," Freddy exclaims.

The third time I even went to [the special unit] that supposedly handles extortion. They kept telling me, "Don't worry. We're going to get them! We're going to put those guys in jail!" Supposedly, they did something. They did arrest a few guys, but I don't know what happened because I had to come back [to the United States]. I was afraid. [The gang] said to me, "We know where you live. I know your family, your brother, where they live, what car they drive." Everything! They tell you everything—every little detail! "Wow," I thought to myself, "I have to go. Of course, I have to go." And maybe three days later, my brother-in-law was assaulted leaving work. . . . Look, if they take your phone, steal your wallet, let them take it. You're okay. But thank God that's all. It's truly ugly.

Fearing for his life for the second time, Freddy decided to return to the United States illegally.

Freddy wishes that things were different. He misses his family and is nostalgic for everything from El Salvador's "beautiful beaches" to the weather to simply enjoying himself on the weekends with friends. Adapting to life in the United States has been challenging, even with the support of his family, some of whom live here. He is frustrated with the Salvadoran police and government, which he finds corrupt and wholly ineffective at controlling the country's gang problem. "You go through *this* neighborhood, you have to pay *this* gang. You go through *another* neighborhood, you have to pay *another* gang!" He sighs again. "Everyone in El Salvador has to pay their 'tax,' *Jesus.* . . ."

La situacion es muy difícil.
"The situation is very difficult."—Graciela

Graciela came to the United States illegally more than a decade before we spoke. She didn't plan to stay. She dreamed of saving enough money to be able to return to El Salvador and open her own restaurant. "People used to think, 'Okay, I'll go to the United States for three or four years. I'll work hard, save money, and return to my country to open a business,'" she reflects. "Now, nobody is thinking about doing this because of [the gangs]."

Graciela found stable work in the United States and later had a daughter. As time passed, she was joined by her two younger brothers, both of whom were harassed, threatened, and attacked by the gangs, eventually escaping to the United States. "My father and [one of my] brother[s], they bought a bus with the money I sent them," she begins, her voice dropping to a whisper. "Then, the [gang] started charging them 'rent.'"

Barely audible now, she continues in a hushed tone: "'You have to pay,' said the [gang]. 'If not, we won't let you pass.' And so then, you're working for [the gangs]."

Despite acquiescing to the gang's demands, her brother was subsequently attacked twice. On one occasion, while driving his bus, members of the gang cut off her brother's long hair. On another occasion, he was attacked while on his motorcycle. Graciela recalls the events in rapid sequence: "[My brother] had a motorcycle. He went out on his motorcycle. They wanted to take it. The gang members set it on fire and threw a car on top of it. They left him beaten." He was afraid, she adds, so he fled the country.

The gang also tried to recruit Graciela's youngest brother, who now lives with her. "[The gang was] very rough with him," she explains. "They did everything they could to make him join. They 'jumped' him, as they say. And that's why he came here." In light of her own family's experiences with the gangs, Graciela is deeply afraid of going back to El Salvador—especially as a parent. She is convinced that neither she nor her daughter would be safe. "And my daughter? She would end up joining the gang too. There, they force people to join the gang—*force*. . . . The situation is very difficult."

The biggest challenge, as Graciela sees it, is corruption. "There is a big difference [between the United States and El Salvador] with regard to impunity," she explains. Although the police, judges, and other government actors generally "do the same job" in both countries, corruption is not an issue in the United States. "The police do their job the same here as in [El Salvador]. The judges, the same. The only thing is that in [El Salvador] they're more corrupt. They're for sale. [Whereas in the United States], I think if a judge or someone else tries to [take a bribe], they'll be put [him] in jail very quickly."

Graciela is not optimistic that things will improve in El Salvador. Indeed, she believes that gang violence is beyond control. "It's very ugly. The gangs are kicking people out of their homes, out of their *own homes*," she emphasizes, continuing in a hushed tone. "They're doing this so that they can live in other people's houses. The violence has reached a point that is unlivable. . . . [They] are charging everyone what they call 'rent,' . . . and the rent is more than people earn, so you are working just to lose money maintaining [the gang]." She laments, "I don't know what this country is going to do to eradicate [the gang problem]."

Las autoridades aquí, ellos no andan con juegos.
"The authorities [in the United States], they don't play games." —Luis

Growing up in postwar El Salvador was difficult. Like many Salvadorans who came of age during the late 1990s, Luis was raised by relatives. His mother left for the United States during the war, normalized her immigration status, and eventually sent for his sister and one of his brothers. "My mother is a citizen now," he says, "and my siblings have green cards." Luis's mother hoped to bring him to the United States with a visa. "When she tried to see if she could arrange something for me," he explains, "she couldn't because I already had a criminal record [in El Salvador]."

Luis doesn't share many details but mentions that he got caught up in drugs and later a gang. "When I remember my youth," he reflects, "it was a totally foolish life, an environment of drug addiction and alcoholism." He continues: "When I remember my youth, it's something very painful for me—all of the scars, all of the wounds." Realizing this was not the life he wanted, Luis "set [his] sights on the United States." To him, it was the only way out.

Luis was caught at the United States–Mexico border and given a deportation hearing date, which he did not attend. Instead, he reunited with his family and attempted to start over as an undocumented immigrant. Although he managed to escape gang life, Luis struggled to overcome his addictions. He alternated between sobriety and relapse for years, even spending some time in rehab. "There's a blindfold that prevents us from seeing clearly because we're totally [caught] in a world of addiction," he surmises, his voice breaking.

Despite being cautious, Luis was arrested for possession of marijuana. He had been in the United States for nearly a decade. He was placed in a county jail to face criminal charges. Although a judge wound up throwing out his drug charge, Luis was not released. He was transferred to immigration custody because his arrest had triggered deportation.

Unlike most of the immigrants I interviewed, Luis has had extensive firsthand experience with the legal systems in both his country of origin and the United States, which he says are "totally different." Luis points out that El Salvador has had a serious problem with gangs, corruption, and impunity "for a long time. . . . This is nothing new." He elaborates:

> The way things have evolved, the gangs have been able to obtain very powerful contacts in high positions in [El Salvador]. [The parallel would be] if a gang or gang members here were able to [influence] Congress. . . . [In the United States] the authorities are too strict to allow this. Here you have the FBI! The authorities here, they don't play games. When they catch someone, they truly apply [the law] to them and they put them in jail in accordance with the crime they have committed. . . . [In El Salvador], yes [criminals] are incarcerated, but it's as if they're out in the street because there is no seriousness, there is no order. . . . And since they see that there is no order, they do whatever they want.[2] On the contrary, [in the United States] either you compose yourself or they make you.

Reflecting further, Luis reiterates the importance of enforcing the law. "Appropriate enforcement . . . creates order," which, he argues, is something the United States has and El Salvador lacks.

Luis, however, holds no illusions about the justice system in the United States. "With time, you realize that [there exists both] justice and the injustice [in the United States]," he explains. He explains that "there are people in prison for serious things, but there are also people in prison for trivial things," including immigrants who are detained or deported for minor violations. Ultimately, though, Luis finds the absence of the rule of law in El Salvador much more troubling than the occasional overextension of the rule of law in the United States.

Este país . . . le abre sus puertas, pero tiene que portarse bien.
"This country . . . opens its doors to you, but you have
to behave yourself."—Elena

"I never dreamed of coming to the United States," explains Elena, a Salvadoran woman in her forties. Elena grew up near El Salvador's border with Guatemala. Like her four siblings, she moved to the capital, San

Salvador, to attend university. She was pursuing a degree in communications and marketing when an older brother, already in the United States on a graduate scholarship, convinced her to move north. "I visited the United States four times with a tourist visa, and on the fourth trip I stayed," she says.

Although Elena's brother eventually obtained his U.S. citizenship, Elena never managed to legalize her status. She has lived as an undocumented immigrant in the United States for over twenty years. For a time, she cleaned houses. Then she worked at a manufacturing plant. "The pay was better, but the job was hard," she adds. Eventually, Elena took a job at a restaurant. Although the pay is "low," she has a flexible schedule and enjoys engaging with customers. "I walk to and from work every day," she says. "People ask me if I'm afraid of the police and I'm not. I like the police because they protect the community."

Elena is adamant about feelings for the United States. "I always say that I love this country," she shares. She appreciates the United States because "it's a well-organized country." "I like that there is more security here." By contrast, she stresses that El Salvador is "a poor country" that experienced civil war for 12 years and is now confronting "extreme gang violence." She continues: "On the news they say that El Salvador is losing its professional workers to the United States, like me and my brother, who had a good job as an engineer."

Elena admits that life is still difficult in the United States. Although not in deportation proceedings herself, she is no stranger to deportation and its effects. When I interviewed her, Elena's partner, a legal permanent resident, had just narrowly avoided deportation after a long journey through the criminal justice and immigration systems. "This country welcomes you. . . . It opens its doors to you, but you have to behave yourself."

When I ask Elena what she would do if she ever found herself facing deportation, she doesn't miss a beat. "God brought me here many times. . . . God won't let this happen to me because I love this country. My daughter was born here. I support this country."

Legitimacy in Central America and the United States

Narratives of violence, victimization, and the rule of law shared by Sara, Freddy, Graciela, Luis, and Elena explored in this chapter highlight the state's real and perceived inability to control crime in Central America and its ability to control crime in the United States. Throughout interviews, immigrants repeatedly recounted violent episodes that triggered their own and their family members' migration, situating such episodes in the broader sociopolitical climates of their countries of origin. Although details varied, these stories typically included implicit and explicit assessments of (1) corruption, (2) impunity, and (3) security, shedding light on immigrants' perceptions of state legitimacy. With few exceptions, immigrants I interviewed found Central American governments, institutions, and actors to lack legitimate authority.

When immigrants reflected on the law in Central America, they generally painted a picture of widespread violence that was deeply embedded in the fabric of everyday life. Much of this violence was described as gang-related. State actors such as police, and state institutions such as courts and prisons, were either left out of these reflections or deemed incapable of providing assistance due to ineptitude, corruption, or both.

For example, recall that Freddy said the police "didn't do anything" when he reported being extorted by a gang. This is particularly interesting, as the police did eventually make several arrests in the case. However, as Freddy explained, the arrests led to gang retaliation, spurring his migration to the United States. Others, like Freddy, who turned to the police for help received little support; many didn't bother. From their perspective, violence was something you tolerated, succumbed to, or fled.

A subset of those I interviewed said that they feared the police in their countries of origin as much as they feared the gangs. For example, as Rita, introduced in chapter 4, shares: "[In Honduras] you fear the police. You don't have faith in them—to the point that you believe they might hurt you." Participants also noted that even when those said to deserve punishment were apprehended by the police, facing trial, or sentenced to time in jail or prison, the effects on crime and justice were slim. Crime seemed to continue unabated, becoming more extreme as time passed.

Interview participants explained that worsening violence was facilitated by corruption and impunity, which were said to go hand in hand. They stressed that this was a problem among police, judges, and lawyers. Recall that Graciela framed police and judges in the United States and El Salvador as similar, with the exception that "in [El Salvador] they're more corrupt. They're for sale." Similarly, Angelica, introduced in chapter 4, laments: "Sadly, [in my country] it is the police themselves who are complicit with the gangs. It is the judges themselves who are for sale, the lawyers themselves who are for sale." Samuel, introduced in chapter 3, puts it more bluntly: "If you commit a crime and you have money, you can avoid punishment."

Corruption and impunity were often said to run from the streets to the most powerful seats in government. Recall that both Freddy and Luis framed corruption as endemic, with Luis stressing that criminal actors had managed to gain "very powerful contacts in high positions in [El Salvador]" and Freddy emphasizing that many police and government actors "are involved in bad things," as "there is always money being made." Similar sentiments were echoed by many.

Ultimately, in the eyes of the vast majority of immigrants I interviewed, corruption and impunity have resulted in an untenable lack of security in Central America—the palpable absence of the rule of law. Recall that Sara and Freddy fled to the United States fearing for their lives. They were not alone. Samuel, Alex, and Jessica's son Eddie all came to the United States fleeing concrete threats of gang violence or assaults they managed to survive. Even those who had not initially come to the United States out of fear were concerned about being forced to return to countries that were now much more violent than when they left. As Angelica states simply: "[In my home country] there isn't law. . . . The laws no longer exist. And the government does nothing."

And yet most immigrants expressed strong beliefs in the legitimacy of the U.S. government. They exhibited a deep appreciation for the state's ability to enforce the law and hold police officers, judges, and other legal actors accountable. In the United States, participants stressed, the law not only "exists" but is "applied," "enforced," and "obeyed." In the United States, the law is *effective*.

Immigrants generally favored what criminologists refer to as "tough on crime" approaches to lawbreaking, particularly for individuals who have committed violent offenses.[3] They frequently stressed that "laws exist for a reason" and liked that laws were "strictly" enforced against "criminals," whether poor or rich, civilian or official. Recall that Luis appreciated that U.S. "authorities . . . don't play games, . . . truly apply[ing] the law" to anyone who commits a crime. He was not alone. Immigrants praised the United States for what they perceived as an overall lack of corruption and impunity. Police, judges, lawyers, and other government actors were framed as upholding the law, not violating it. Like Graciela, many remarked that if a U.S. police officer, judge, or other authority figure attempted to take a bribe, they would promptly "be put in jail."

In turn, immigrants felt much safer in the United States than in their countries of origin. Rita explains: "Here, people obey the laws. . . . The laws in the United States, I don't know much about them, but I like that they're strict. . . . Maybe not everywhere, but in most places [in the United States] you are listened to and protected [by the government]. . . . It feels very good to know [this]." Rita's remarks were not unique. For example, Elena notes that she "isn't afraid of the police." "Some people say the police are racist," she continues, "but I haven't seen this. I like the police because they protect the community." She adds: "I like [the United States] because it is much safer than El Salvador. I love this country." Similarly, Luis captured the perspectives of most interviewees when he insisted that one of the United States' greatest strengths is that "either you compose yourself or [the authorities] make you."

The appeal of tough-on-crime approaches extended to the immigration system. Many participants cited immigration enforcement as being integral to law enforcement in the United States. Most agreed that immigrants who commit frequent or serious crime deserve deportation. As Samuel explains, "Without an immigration system, it would affect everything in the [United States]. . . . The system gives people opportunities. This country gives people opportunities. It's us immigrants who sometimes abuse this. Sometimes we don't respect [the law]."

Similarly, Angelica expressed a strong appreciation for the U.S. government's ability to enforce the law against those who break it, including immigrants. As she reasons, "I support immigration enforcement against those who are killing, sexually abusing children [and] all of that, that they stop them. . . . People should follow the law. I believe that people should face the consequences of their actions." This perspective was echoed by many like Samuel and Angelica, who supported immigration enforcement actions against "criminal immigrants."

Most immigrants were quick to distinguish between "serious crimes" and "minor infractions." Like Angelica, several participants pointed out that "of course people make mistakes" like driving without a license or driving drunk. In those instances, they argued, the punishment should fit the crime, such as losing a driver's license or paying fines as opposed to deportation. At the end of the day, as Elena summarized: "This country welcomes you. . . . It opens its doors to you, but you have to behave yourself."

Mention of factors associated with procedural justice—such as bias, interpersonal treatment, and opportunities for error correction or participation—were strikingly absent from immigrant discussions of state legitimacy in both Central America and the United States. Instead, immigrants were primarily concerned with questions of efficacy, such as whether or not police prevent crime, whether or not criminals are held accountable, and whether or not criminal justice is for sale and government officials are on the take.

The importance of this should not be overlooked. As noted in chapter 1, when a legal process is deemed fair, people are more likely to be satisfied with its outcome, believe in the legitimacy of the authorities and system involved, and comply with authorities and their decisions.[4] Indeed, it has been argued that fair process is perhaps *the* determining factor with regard to assessments of outcome satisfaction and legitimacy. However, recall that this is not always the case. For example, in some contexts, both outcome satisfaction and legal authorities' perceived legitimacy are influenced by procedural *and* distributive justice, as in the case of criminal defendants.[5] Similarly, procedural justice may matter less than distributive justice in some cultural and sociopolitical settings.[6]

Indeed, many immigrants I interviewed framed their own satisfaction with immigration court outcomes in relation to the outcomes of others, both real and imagined. For example, Samuel was very pleased to have received relief from deportation, noting that he had fared better than the typical immigrant. Freddy, in contrast, expressed deep frustration over the fact that some immigrants manage to obtain relief from deportation in the face of "serious" convictions, while he was ordered deported for what he considered to be a minor criminal infraction. "To see that," he exclaims, "it kills you, it [just] kills you." This view was shared by most.

Still, assessments of neither procedural justice nor distributive fairness weighed heavily on immigrants' beliefs in the legitimacy of the U.S. government. Furthermore, as will be discussed shortly, these assessments had little effect on immigrants' compliance with deportation orders. Such findings are indicative of those noted by the handful of criminologists who have examined the relationship between compliance, fairness, and legitimacy in postcolonial[7] and post-Soviet[8] contexts, where the legacies of police and judicial corruption, as well as state repression, are still palpable if not ongoing. Given widespread corruption, impunity, and insecurity throughout Central America, coupled with the not-so-distant memories of civil war and state crime reviewed in chapter 1, it is not surprising that the immigrants I interviewed would give primacy to instrumental concerns over fair treatment when evaluating legal authorities, institutions, and systems.

Compliance, Fairness, and Legitimacy

Most immigrants I interviewed were deeply disillusioned with the justice systems in their countries of origin. For many, the promise of the rule of law was in part what brought them to the United States. It is also what fueled their desire to stay. Compared with the perceived lawlessness of Central America, strict adherence to and enforcement of the law were welcomed by many, with one glaring exception: their own deportation orders.

Again, nearly all the immigrants I interviewed were either in violation of an existing deportation order when we spoke or planned to violate the law if ordered deported in the future. Indeed, immigrants were wholly unsatisfied with outcomes of deportation for themselves and their family members regardless of how procedurally fair they found their immigration court experiences or how much they appreciated the rule of law in the United States. Many explained that, although they prided themselves on abiding by the law generally, this was not an option in the context of immigration law, which is simply not compatible with most immigrants' needs.

In explaining this apparent contradiction, most immigrants ultimately questioned the substantive fairness of U.S. immigration law overall. For example, recall Gloria from chapter 3, herself an undocumented
immigrant. Gloria and her husband fought his deportation case in immigration court for three years, at which point he was ordered deported.
Fully aware of the consequences, Gloria's husband chose to remain in
the United States illegally. Years later, after getting into a car accident, he
was subsequently arrested, detained, and forcibly deported. Reflecting
on both deportations, Gloria spoke highly of all those involved. As she
explains: "Well, [judges and attorneys] study the laws. They study what's
right. They're just following what's right, so you have to respect their
decisions." Although her husband's deportations were correct in a legal
sense, Gloria felt they were not right in a moral sense or what was best
for their family. When we spoke, Gloria's husband was in the process of
planning his illegal return to the United States.

Like Gloria, Rita characterized her deportation hearing as rather fair.
She noted that her judge was stern but that he treated her much better
than she had expected. Yet Rita said that she could not handle even the
mere thought of deportation. If she were to comply with such an order,
she would have to leave her husband, an undocumented Mexican immigrant, and her two children, one of whom was a U.S. citizen, behind. "If
I am ordered deported," she shares, "I'll die." For individuals like Gloria
and Rita, the deportation of immigrants without serious criminal convictions is substantively unfair and always will be.

So what does substantively fair immigration law look like? Although
the specifics varied, immigrants unanimously agreed that it involves
the ability to live and work in the United States. As Freddy comments,
"There are fair things and unfair things about the [U.S. immigration
system]." He explained that substantively fair immigration law would
include permanent relief from deportation for families, noting that
"thousands of people have been separated from their children." Rita
echoed Freddy's remarks, stressing that permanent immigration relief
should be available, at a minimum, to parents. Aracely sums it up: "I
want more humanity, more humanity [from the immigration system].
Legalize people a little. At least give them permission [to be here] so that
they can stop living in fear."

Many participants described migration as a "human right," drawing upon religious discourse to argue for a rights-based claim to a life in the United States. For example, Graciela insists that "this territory is mine [too]. God made the world for all of us, and they shouldn't deport people for being here legally or illegally." Similarly, Wendi, a Salvadoran woman whose brother was deported, contends that "[the immigration system] is unjust because, in the eyes of God, we're all equal. . . . There should be some freedom, something that allows one to have more time [in the United States], that we would have more benefits like citizens. . . . [Our] only crime is to not have been born in this country." However, like Freddy, Rita, and others, Wendi limited the extension of such benefits to immigrants who had spent several years in the United States and who had U.S.-born children.

A smaller number of participants argued for broader immigration reforms. For instance, Angelica emphasized that if she could change just one thing about the immigration system, she would create more opportunities for immigrants who "simply want to make better lives for themselves and their families" in the United States. Similarly, in discussing his mother's lack of immigration options under existing law, Eduardo, whose own brush with deportation was highlighted in chapter 4, stressed that legalization should be an option for all immigrants without criminal convictions. He elaborates: "My mother, who is undocumented, has no options for relief. My father [who was abusive] still says that if she ever comes back [to Guatemala], he will kill her. . . . I wish the laws would make it a little more fair for everybody to get relief or adjust their status."

Walter, whose deportation hearing was recounted in chapter 4, concluded that meaningful immigration reform would have to address the entire system, creating pathways to legalization for undocumented immigrants and those with temporary status, like DACA or TPS. Simón and Eva, who were introduced in chapter 3, echoed Walter. The couple's daughter and Simón went through simultaneous deportation proceedings, ultimately receiving DACA and TPS, respectively. Despite finding their immigration court experiences to be procedurally just, the family was still disappointed with their outcome. As Eva explained, temporary relief from deportation was better than nothing but still far short of a pathway to citizenship. Simón captures the sentiments of many participants in summarizing his family's migration experience: "You come here to create a better life for your family, and there are risks [involved], and that's just what it is."

Conclusion

Examined through this lens, the positive procedural justice assessments of immigration court revealed in chapter 4 take on another layer of complexity. Traditional procedural justice theory holds that fair processes support outcome satisfaction, compliance with the law, and beliefs in state legitimacy. Yet in the immigration context, fair process does not appear to lead to outcome satisfaction or compliance.

As I describe in this chapter, immigrants' perceptions of the law, enforcement, and the state in the United States are deeply influenced by negative perceptions of the law and legal actors in Central America. Furthermore, as discussed elsewhere, most immigrants did not expect that they or their family members would be treated fairly in immigration court. Lacking formal knowledge of immigration law, many expected that noncitizens would have few, if any, rights in immigration court. They had also been frequently exposed to negative stories about deportation from friends, family, neighbors, and the media. Yet most were pleasantly surprised by their deportation hearings. Outcomes of deportation, however, were deemed wholly unsatisfactory regardless of the perceived fairness of immigration court employees and procedures.

Even when dissatisfied with hearing outcomes, immigrants held strongly to a belief in the legitimacy of the U.S. government, which they cast in stark opposition to the lack of legitimate authority in their countries of origin. Again, participants praised the United States for effective crime management, low levels of corruption and impunity, and the general sense of security afforded to those residing within U.S. borders. They stressed that the absence of law and order in Central America was largely what brought them to the United States in the first place—or what was keeping them here. Thus, immigrants granted legitimacy to the U.S. government in exchange for its perceived ability to address instrumental concerns about crime, impunity, and security, not because it upheld due process rights or treated people fairly in court.

Most immigrants also agreed that the U.S. government has both the authority and the obligation to enforce immigration law. Still, they took issue with the broad application of immigration enforcement to those who had not committed criminal offenses. They agreed that deportation should be reserved for "criminals," not "hardworking" immigrants who simply want to "provide a better life," generally one of safety and security, for their families. Drawing upon human rights and religious discourse, immigrants argued for the right to migrate and the right to live and work freely in the United States. In this context, the stakes are too high. The deportation orders of immigrants and their family members—both in the past and on the horizon—were almost unanimously cast as substantively unfair.

In the end, neither fair processes nor legitimate authority could make the realities of deportation any more tolerable for those I interviewed. As the immigrant narratives explored throughout this book demonstrate, compliance with deportation, and more broadly with immigration law, is not a question of procedural justice or a matter of state legitimacy. Instead, it rests upon the substantive (un)fairness of deportation and the (im)morality of the immigration system.

In chapter 6, I synthesize the relationship between procedural justice and legal consciousness to offer a robust critique of dominant procedural justice framings and call for a postmodern revitalization of procedural justice theory. Exploring America's obsession with procedural protections in the criminal justice system, as well as culturally, I challenge the value of procedural fairness and due process protections in the immigration system. Demands for enhanced due process and procedural fairness within immigration court are framed as little more than "criminal justice creep," a gentler form of *crimmigration*. Ultimately, I contend that, without a sincere and intentional reimagining of procedural justice, we risk its weaponization.

6

The Case for Substantive Justice

As explored in chapter 1, procedural justice is grounded in the premise that perceptions of fair treatment by legal authorities confer legitimacy to legal processes, outcomes, and systems. Perceptions of fair treatment can counteract feelings of marginalization and stigmatization,[1] make uncertainty more tolerable,[2] and signal that the law is legitimate and moral.[3] However, as I make clear throughout this book, perceptions of fair treatment are just that—perceptions. These perceptions are not only subjective; they are superficial. Just because a process appears to be fair, or even is fair, does not mean that its outcome will be fair. Neither does fair process necessarily make for a fair system.

Jerald Greenberg, known for his work on justice in the workplace, argues that organizational justice, which encompasses procedural justice, is sometimes nothing more than "hollow justice."[4] As he explains it, "any mere 'veneer of fairness' may function as effectively as any more deeply-rooted concern for moral righteousness as long as it is not perceived to be manipulative."[5] In short, procedural justice has the power to mask injustice, at times making it palatable even to those most deeply and directly affected by its reach.

Despite this—or perhaps because of it—procedural justice is an increasingly popular topic of academic inquiry, particularly among criminologists and especially among those who study policing. Procedural justice is seductive. The idea that procedural justice matters as much, if not more, than distributive justice, substantive justice, or legal outcomes is tempting. It may even be comforting to academics, practitioners, and policy makers. It suggests that as long as people believe a process is fair they will accept their fate, be it a criminal sentence, traffic ticket, or summary judgment—whether or not it is appropriate or desirable. It also suggests that as long as people believe a process is fair they will accept the legal system as legitimate—whether or not it should be viewed as such. Certainly, this speaks to utilitarian goals of obedience to the law and affords a possible shortcut to compliance and legitimacy. It also affords an out, a way of overlooking the substantive injustices upon which many legal systems rest and that are, admittedly, rather difficult to address.

Yet the draw to procedural justice runs deeper than this. It taps into understandings of justice that are built into the fabric of American legal consciousness and the U.S. legal system.[6] Procedure is sacrosanct in U.S. law. Violations of procedure warrant correction in the civil and criminal justice systems. In the absence of a procedural misstep, however, little can be done to address substantive miscarriages of justice. One of the most glaring examples of the American conflation of procedural and substantive justice can be found in the grounds for appealing criminal convictions, nearly all of which are procedural (e.g., improperly admitted evidence, ineffective assistance of counsel, prosecutorial misconduct). Within this context, it should be of little surprise that the wrongfully convicted often face nearly insurmountable challenges to exoneration even when exculpatory DNA evidence becomes available. From constitutional protections and case precedent to depictions of Miranda warnings in popular television series like *Law and Order*, American legal culture promotes the idea that playing by the rules—be it during a police search, a criminal trial, or a parole hearing—inevitably leads to just outcomes.

And what is procedural justice if not playing by the rules? Recall that perceptions of fair treatment are tied to factors such as authorities' behavior and motivations, decision quality, opportunities for error correction, and opportunities for participation and representation. Although these factors are undeniably linked to interpersonal treatment (e.g., the demeanor of legal authorities when engaging with laypeople), they are also undeniably linked to due process.

For example, rights to equal protection and freedom from discrimination, indigent defense, and appeals all contain elements of procedural justice. Such rights guarantee protection from biased legal authorities and decisions. They formalize oversight and the expectation that mistakes, if made, can and will be addressed. They ensure that legal proceedings are inclusive and that those confronted with the power of the state have a voice, a chance to challenge, contest, and present their side of the story. What's more, they prioritize procedure over substance, perpetuating the idea that fair process leads to justice.

Calls to reform immigration court often rest upon the idea that fair process facilitates justice. Like the immigration attorneys interviewed for this book, academics, practitioners, and activists frequently point to flaws in immigration court practice and procedure, as well as its lack of sufficient due process. This likely stems from the fact that immigration is a civil matter and thus that most constitutional protections afforded to criminal defendants are not granted to immigrants facing deportation, regardless of their documentation status. It cannot be denied that immigration court—and the immigration system, for that matter—lack the due process found in the criminal justice system. However, as the immigrants I spoke with and whose stories I recount herein make very clear, the problem with deportation is not procedural.

American Legal Consciousness and the Myth of Rights

The belief that injustices in the U.S. immigration system can or should be resolved through enhanced processes and the allocation of procedural protections stems from a "politics of rights" that pervades American legal consciousness and has come to dominate grievances and disputes related to discrimination, inequality, and injustice.[7] Within this mindset, immigration activists, practitioners, and scholars alike have advocated for enhanced due process rights in immigration court. Such calls include demands for the right to appointed counsel for indigent immigrants and the elimination of mandatory detention among other reforms. Yet emphasis on rights mobilization—especially when modeled after the criminal justice system—is misguided.

Published in 1974, Stuart Scheingold's *The Politics of Rights: Lawyers, Public Policy, and Political Change* sparked a vibrant discussion on the value of rights and legal mobilization that remains current to this day. In the book, Scheingold presents the "myth of rights," a conceptual framing that reduces legal rights to little more than political ideology and discourse.[8]

As Scheingold explains, Americans generally believe that litigation can evoke a declaration of rights from the court and be used to assure the realization of these rights, which is considered "tantamount to meaningful change."[9] Scheingold argues that this belief reflects American constitutionality—rights consciousness is codified into the United

States Constitution and the Bill of Rights. From this rhetoric of rights the myth of rights is born, nurtured, and sustained. It fosters a politics of rights that places precedent on litigation and the use of judicial channels to resolve social problems.

Although the belief in rights shapes Americans' behaviors in nearly all contexts, it is especially salient in the case of grievances and disputes related to discrimination, inequality, and injustice. Such grievances and disputes become politicized in the hopes of achieving what the myth of rights promises: the realization of a desired social change. Thus a *demand for* housing becomes a *right to* housing, which in turn is equated with acquiring housing. This channels grievances away from other, potentially viable forms of social action and into the judicial system for remedy.

Were the myth of rights to bear the fruit it promises, there would be no problem; however, Scheingold argues that litigation is often unsuccessful in eliciting rights declarations. He stresses that litigation, even when successful, lacks the ability to assure the realization of such rights through any oversight or enforcement mechanism. For example, *Brown v. Board of Education*, one of several groundbreaking civil rights cases in the twentieth century, is often credited with desegregating education in the United States. What is less often discussed, however, is the fact that it took multiple lawsuits and decades of continued mobilization efforts before schools were finally integrated.

Similarly, in 1973, *Roe v. Wade* famously established the right to an abortion, yet this decision has been relentlessly challenged by activists, legislators, and politicians. Indeed, more than half of U.S. states currently have laws on the books that severely restrict women's access to abortion. Of the 1,338 abortion restrictions passed since *Roe v. Wade*, approximately 44% were passed between 2011 and 2021.[10] In 2021 alone, 19 states enacted over 100 abortion restrictions, which, as the Guttmacher Institute highlights, is the highest number since 1973.[11] In 2021, the Supreme Court allowed Texas's six-week abortion ban to stand. The following year, the Supreme Court issued a decision in *Dobbs v. Jackson Women's Health Organization*,[12] overturning *Roe v. Wade* and effectively eliminating a constitutional right to abortion.

Like Scheingold, the political scientist and legal scholar Gerald N. Rosenberg presents a startlingly strong argument against the commonly held assumption that the courts can bring about social change. Exploring the aftermath of several prominent Supreme Court decisions typically believed to have brought about, or at least contributed to, significant social change (e.g., *Brown*, *Roe*, and others) in a myriad of ways, Rosenberg uncovers a number of substantial constraints that often prevent the Court from making an impact.[13] He points out that, although there exist several ways to overcome such constraints, in general Supreme Court decisions have played a role in bringing about social change only when such change was already occurring and had a combination of popular and elite support, as well as support from those with the power to implement such change.

Other federally protected rights, such as the minimum wage and various occupational health and safety standards, are systematically violated in the United States with little recourse. This is especially common when those whose rights are being violated are members of one or more marginalized groups, such as those with disabilities,[14] undocumented immigrants,[15] and women of color.[16] The state's inability—or unwillingness—to enforce and uphold legally protected rights calls the meaning of rights into question and poses a serious threat to the legitimacy of the legal system writ large.

Scheingold does acknowledge that the *notion* of rights is powerful, even if at times only symbolic. The mere act of claiming rights can itself be empowering and serve as a functional mobilization tool.[17] Through litigation, rights claims call the public's attention to injustices. They also have the ability to grant—or at least temporarily lend—legitimacy to the grievances of dispossessed groups and, in many cases, the groups themselves.[18] Most important, such rights claims galvanize individuals to collective action. As Scheingold summarizes this issue, "litigation is more useful in fomenting change when used as an agent of political mobilization than when it is employed in the more conventional manner—that for asserting and realizing rights."[19] Through such mobilization, voters and political coalitions are reorganized, as with political priorities, potentially leading to both legislative and social change.

Still, a rights declaration—by the courts or the legislature—is *not* tantamount to meaningful change. Rights require awareness. Rights cannot be demanded if their existence is unknown. Rights require respect. Rights cannot be upheld if those responsible for doing so do not see their value. Rights require resources. Rights cannot be asserted without enforcement mechanisms—and funding. Finally, rights are only as powerful as is permitted by the legal system within which they operate. Indeed, Scheingold contends that rights declarations are unlikely to be the most optimal means of ensuring tangible social change. Rights-based approaches to social change may lead down a fruitless path, resulting in rights that are difficult to enforce or, worse, that mask continued inequity and injustice.

Due Process and the Myth of (Immigrant) Rights

Although the United States Constitution affords the same protections to citizens and immigrants, regardless of immigration status, the Supreme Court has held that immigration matters are civil in character and do not benefit from the due process protections guaranteed in criminal proceedings. Despite being guaranteed the right to a "fundamentally fair" deportation hearing,[20] immigrants lack many of the procedural protections one might associate with a "fundamentally fair" hearing. Immigrants facing deportation are not guaranteed constitutional protections such as the right against self-incrimination, the right to a trial by jury, the prohibition on ex post facto laws, or the ban on cruel and unusual punishment.[21] Similarly, the formal rules of evidence in the criminal justice system generally do not apply in deportation hearings.[22] In practice, this means that evidence obtained without a proper warrant or in violation of *Miranda v. Arizona* can be admitted in immigration hearings, with the exception of egregious Fourth Amendment violations.[23]

Perhaps most egregiously, immigrants facing deportation are not guaranteed a right to indigent defense.[24] Universal representation in immigration court has garnered much support from activists, lawyers, and politicians in recent years.[25] In 2013, the New York Immigrant Family Unity Project, which provides immigrants with free court-appointed New York City public defenders, was the first to pilot an indigent defense system for immigrants facing deportation.[26] The Alameda County Public Defender followed suit, launching California's first immigrant public defender project in 2014.[27] Similar public defender projects have been piloted across the country, including independently established projects along with projects in 11 states that, together, make up the Vera Institute of Justice's SAFE Cities Network.[28]

Attempts have also been made to alter detention practices, but they have largely failed. Since the late 2010s, the Supreme Court rejected challenges to both the use of indefinite detention in *Jennings v. Rodriguez*[29] and the use of mandatory detention to hold certain categories of immigrants facing deportation who have been convicted of crimes, including those who are clearly eligible for relief from deportation, in *Nielsen v. Preap*.[30] In 2017, in its *Hernandez v. Sessions* decision,[31] the Ninth Circuit Court of Appeals upheld a preliminary injunction by a lower court in a class-action lawsuit filed by the American Civil Liberties Union requiring that immigration judges consider immigrants' financial circumstances when setting bond amounts. This decision, however, only applies to immigration judges working under jurisdiction of the Ninth Circuit, which includes the states of Alaska, Arizona, California, Hawaii, Idaho, Montana, Nevada, Oregon, and Washington. The *Jennings* and *Nielsen* decisions, along with several other recent Supreme Court decisions, have established a clear antiimmigrant sentiment among the Court's current majority. It is unlikely, for example, that the Ninth Circuit's ruling in *Hernandez v. Sessions*, which requires immigration judges to consider an immigrant's finances when setting bond, would withstand a Supreme Court challenge.

Certainly, persuasive arguments abound as to why immigrants merit additional due process protections within the immigration system, including the right to indigent defense. That immigrants who cannot afford an attorney are made to represent themselves in immigration court demonstrates just what a farce the U.S. immigration system really is. Immigrants are expected to navigate a legal system that is foreign to them in a language that is often also foreign (albeit with a right to interpretation). There are no special provisions for the representation of minors. Although uncommon, children as young as two and three years old have been made to represent themselves in immigration court.[32] Again, as discussed in chapter 2, it is not surprising that immigrants tend to fare better in immigration court when represented by an attorney than when representing themselves pro se.

The mandatory detention of individuals for civil matters is equally problematic. Immigration detention facilities are generally modeled after U.S. jails. In many cases, detention facilities, jails, and prisons are, indeed, one and the same, as the federal government frequently contracts with state and for-profit correctional facilities to house immigrant detainees.[33] Under some such arrangements, immigrant detainees are housed with the general population and thus treated as convicted criminals who are incarcerated as a form of punishment. Abuses, health and safety issues, and other rights violations have long been documented in U.S. immigration detention facilities.[34] Moreover, contrary to the U.S. government's position, ample research demonstrates that most immigrants do not pose a flight risk and appear in immigration court for their deportation hearings when released on bond under community supervision.[35] Immigration detention practices, as well as the conditions found in U.S. detention facilities, are often used to argue in favor of strengthening immigrants' procedural rights in the immigration system.

Indeed, the procedurally inclined might gravitate toward any number of relatively simple, apolitical changes to immigration court practice and procedure upon reading this book. Many such reforms could be implemented by immigration court leadership,[36] which would certainly address the concerns expressed by immigration attorneys I interviewed. For example, the use of telephonic conferencing and videoconferencing in immigration court could be eliminated in all but the most extreme circumstances (e.g., personal needs, public health, rare languages). Instead, in-person hearings wherein all parties—including immigrants, interpreters, judges, and lawyers—are physically present could be the norm. This would be facilitated by establishment of a right to in-person deportation hearings, the elimination of mandatory detention,[37] and the use of community supervision[38] for those with pending hearings.[39]

In lieu of in-person hearings, courtroom technology could be modernized. Courtrooms would be outfitted with multiple cameras so that detained immigrants can more closely watch speakers, aiding in the comprehension of nonverbal communication. Technology could be reviewed to ensure that it accurately captures speakers' faces[40] and what is being said. Reasonable accommodations would be provided to immigrants with disabilities that impair their use of technology.

The immigration court could also end its widespread reliance on interpreters working on private contract and return to hiring staff interpreters at each court. At a minimum, standards for immigration court interpreters could match those found in criminal courts. Preferably, these standards should also match or exceed professional norms.[41] These professional norms—not insufficient staffing or technology—could guide decisions on the appropriate use of consecutive and simultaneous interpretation. Minimally, attorneys, judges, and interpreters could be provided with basic training on the potential biases and challenges of interpretation and technology in immigration courts.

Although modest, such practical reforms would likely have huge impacts on both the functioning of the court and the experiences and perceptions of those who face deportation and those who work in and for the court. The creation of a federally funded immigration public defender system, as well as the elimination of mandatory immigration detention, are two other significant reforms that could also address some of the procedural issues raised in this book. The difficulties of obtaining immigration representation, let alone quality representation, are well documented.[42] These difficulties are exacerbated in the case of detained immigrants.[43] This is significant, as immigrants with legal representation are far more likely to obtain relief from deportation than those without representation.[44]

More relevant to the discussions with immigrants and attorneys highlighted in this book, however, is the assumption that legal representation would afford immigrants protection against procedural injustices in the courtroom. Yet the assumption that legal representation, or any other procedural protections, can stave off the harms of deportation, immigration court, or the immigration system writ large rests upon the myth of rights and America's obsession with procedure.

Procedural protections in the criminal justice system may afford an air of fairness and legitimacy—and this may be replicable in the immigration system—but such protections do not guarantee justice. Undeniably, due process rights such as criminal defendants' rights to evidentiary discovery, legal representation, and a speedy trial help to level the playing field when individuals come up against the power of the state. Still, they do little to address the substantive injustices inherent in the American criminal justice system.

The U.S. criminal justice is built upon the legacies of slavery and legalized racial discrimination.[45] It is deeply influenced by neoliberal capitalism.[46] From policing to courts to corrections, rights violations have been well documented. Constitutionally enshrined due process protections have failed to safeguard communities of color and other marginalized groups from disenfranchisement,[47] mass incarceration,[48] overpolicing,[49] and wrongful convictions.[50]

The right to counsel in the criminal justice system rests upon protections afforded by the Sixth and Fourteenth Amendments, as interpreted in several key Supreme Court decisions. *Gideon v. Wainwright*[51] is arguably the most notable such Supreme Court decision, in which the Court established the right to a state-appointed lawyer in the event that a criminal defendant cannot afford to hire one. Today, this generally happens in one of two ways: either through established public defender offices or through court appointments paid for by the state.

Indigent defense systems, however, are notoriously underfunded and underresourced, and public defenders often have excessive caseloads.[52] As the American Civil Liberties Union explains it, "access to an attorney means little if they lack the time, resources, or skills to be an effective advocate." What's more, it is not uncommon for individuals to waive their right to an attorney upon being arrested and interrogated by police.[53] Juveniles, those with mental health issues, those who lack experience with the criminal justice system, and those who are factually innocent are more susceptible to waiving their right to an attorney due to failures to fully comprehend their rights, leading to false confessions and plea deals that are less than desirable.[54]

Bail practices in the criminal justice system, like indigent defense, are also fraught with issues. Although there is no constitutional right to pretrial release or bail for individuals charged with criminal offenses, the Eighth Amendment protects criminal defendants from "excessive bail," or bail in an amount exceeding that which is deemed necessary to compel a defendant to appear for a criminal hearing. Prior the 1980s, this was broadly understood to imply a right to bail.[55] However, this changed with the passage of federal legislation mandating the pretrial detention of criminal defendants charged with serious felonies who pose a threat to the community.[56] In *United States v. Salerno*,[57] the Supreme Court upheld the constitutionality of such pretrial detention practices, noting that they neither violated the Fifth Amendment's due process guarantee nor the Eighth Amendment's protections against excessive bail.

Still, given that the vast majority of criminal charges in the United States are for less serious offenses, bail is frequently used in place of pretrial detention. One of the most criticized aspects of the cash bail system is that it disproportionately impacts poor defendants and people of color.[58] Although bail is sometimes determined based upon a defendant's financial circumstances, it is often determined by fixed bail schedules in which bail amounts correspond to criminal charges.[59] When an individual cannot afford bail on their own, they may use the services of a bail bondsman, who pays the bail up front and charges the defendant a fee. As Samuel Wiseman, a Penn State professor of law, explains, "commercial bail bonding is among the oldest forms of privatization in criminal justice."[60] It is not surprising that commercial bail-bonding is a multibillion dollar industry.[61] Defendants who cannot afford bail and do not turn to a bondsman are forced to await trial in jail.

Similar approaches to pretrial detention and bail are used in the immigration system. While an increasingly large swath of immigrant respondents facing deportation hearings are subject to mandatory detention, the handful of groups falling outside this category may be released on bond.[62] However, bail amounts often exceed immigrants' financial resources. Moreover, as many immigrants facing deportation lack legal status in the United States and come from mixed-status families and communities, they may be unable to access bonds or loans (keeping in mind that many undocumented immigrants struggle to access bank accounts).

In light of these issues, some have advocated for the right to be monitored—that is, to be placed under some form of community supervision not tied to paying bail.[63] Such monitoring, currently used selectively in both the criminal justice and immigration systems, has come under increasing scrutiny of late. For example, this type of monitoring often involves individuals wearing GPS tracking bracelets, for which they may be charged a daily fee.[64] Under many such arrangements, falling behind on daily fees leads to mounting debt and jail time.[65] It follows that community supervision is considered to be an emerging—and very profitable—market in the world of corrections, attracting private corporations and lobbying dollars.[66] In addition to concerns over burdensome monetary costs and the financial exploitation of immigrants, GPS tracking bracelets used as part of Immigration and Customs Enforcement's community supervision program have been known to cause pain, discomfort, and injuries to wearers.[67] Notably, removing or tampering with a tracking bracelet, even in the event of device malfunction and health and safety risks, can result in immigrants being billed for damaging tracking devices.[68]

Even if procedural reforms—such as enhanced immigration court interpretation and technology practices—or explicit due process protections—such as indigent defense, relief from mandatory detention, and freedom from excessive bail—were to be adopted, enforced, and respected in the immigration system, it is unlikely that deportation outcomes would be significantly altered. Questions regarding the quality of representation and the resources allocated to immigration indigent defense systems would persist. Moreover, although it is true that immigrants generally fare better in the immigration system when represented by attorneys, emerging literature suggests that they may actually be worse off with poor-quality legal representation than if they were to represent themselves.[69]

Similarly, guaranteeing immigrants the right to a bond hearing as part of the deportation process would likely reduce the number of immigrants in dentition, but it would also pave the way for increased exploitation at the hands of private interests, including the bond and community supervision industries. Moreover, the provision of high-quality interpretation and the elimination of problematic telephonic and videoconferencing might make the deportation hearing run more smoothly, but it would not create new categories of relief from deportation or expand the criteria by which immigrants qualify for relief.

Ultimately, the myth of rights is pervasive, yet it is not difficult to unmask. There are nearly endless examples of the failures of rights in the U.S. criminal justice and immigration systems. Yet when it comes to immigration court more specifically, one need look no further than the Fifth Amendment to reveal the empty promise of rights. In some sort of cruel joke, the Fifth Amendment guarantees immigrants a constitutional right to a "fundamentally fair" deportation hearing. But deportation hearings are fundamentally unfair. Most immigrants who find themselves facing deportation have no legal recourse to stop it, attorney or not. The vast majority of immigrants who meet the criteria for deportation are not eligible for any form of relief. Neither the circumstances of one's hearing (e.g., detained versus nondetained, represented versus unrepresented) nor the treatment one receives in court (e.g., respectful versus disrespectful, biased versus unbiased) change this.

Procedural injustices within immigration court are not merely the result of insufficient due process; instead they are symptomatic of substantive structural inequalities and inadequacies with the immigration system writ large. The U.S. immigration system sets up immigrants to lose almost every time. From exclusionary policies restricting authorized immigration[70] and limiting immigrants' ability to participate in American society[71] to draconian policies that criminalize immigrants for even the most minor infractions,[72] immigrants are caught in an uphill battle. Due process protections govern the rules of the game, ensuring that everyone plays fairly. Yet what good are rights if the game is rigged?

Conclusion

Despite a rapidly expanding body of "second wave" literature, many scholars of procedural justice continue dedicating their time to debates over the validity of this or that variation on procedural justice constructs, operationalization, and models.[73] Such debates are valid—how we conceptualize, define, and operationalize procedural justice matters. Still, it is possible for this to become a trap, wherein researchers become so focused on conceptualizing and operationalizing a construct that they fail to see the forest for the trees.

As Mariana Valverde, professor of criminology at the University of Toronto's Faculty of Law, points out: "Today as in the past, much of our education consists not in gaining the skills needed to undertake innovative concrete and dynamic analyses but rather in learning how to classify and categorize, like entomologists."[74] She continues, "Our first commitment is not promoting the prestige or the theoretical rigour of our chosen disciplines or fields—much less our chosen neologisms—but rather understanding the world we live in."[75]

Procedural justice studies are intended to help us better understand how fairness operates in the world and what implications this holds for society. Yet much procedural justice literature offers a homogenized, utilitarian, whitewashed version of fairness. This version of fairness has been severed from culture, history, identity, politics, and people. It has been severed from the very things that rich and meaningful sociological inquiry demands. This version of fairness has the power to make entire groups of people invisible, to erase history and mask deep divisions, inequalities, and injustices.

Without a sincere and intentional reimagining of procedural justice, we risk its weaponization. We risk a world in which procedural justice is little more than a tool for compelling approval of and compliance with unjust legal systems—particularly with respect to systems that have been built to oppress historically marginalized groups, including communities of color, immigrants, and the justice-impacted.

As explorations of procedural justice in immigration court make clear, fair process matters, but fair laws, fair legal systems, and fair societies matter more. We must humanize procedural justice. We must ensure that procedural justice research is inclusive of diverse perspectives, participants, and scholars. Specifically, scholars of procedural justice must endeavor to "center the margins" or, as the critical criminologist Rita Shah explains, "to draw attention to those marginalized by social processes that reveal themselves based on dis/ability, gender identity, race, religion, sexual orientation, and socioeconomic status, among others, and the intersection of these identities."[76] More than this, however, we must interrogate arguments equating fair process with justice. We must challenge policies and practices that use procedural justice as a mechanism for social control. Ultimately, we must integrate substantive justice with procedural justice. In an era of growing inequality, social unrest, and political instability, we have little choice.

Conclusion

Reimagining Deportation

María never had the chance to reflect on her deportation outcome. She died of cancer before her final hearing materialized. As she was lying in a hospital bed, surrounded by family and friends in her final days, immigration court was far from her mind. Instead, her sister later told me, María spoke mostly of Honduras before she died.

I was introduced to María through an attorney from a prominent nonprofit with a strong presence in the local immigrant community. A powerhouse at the forefront of immigrant rights activism and legal aid in the area, the organization was also well connected to immigrant rights groups across the country and, without charging a fee, handled a great deal of immigration cases for low-income immigrants. The attorney representing María and her two children—minors at the time—in their ongoing deportation hearing thought that they had a strong case. This was largely due to María's failing health and her status as a single mother.

Although María's attorney said that María would likely be open to speaking with me, she was initially rather guarded. We spoke on the phone only briefly before she invited me to her home. María's large apartment complex was, like many I visited during my research, primarily inhabited by other immigrants. It was situated among similar apartment complexes and sprawling shopping plazas filled with laundromats, Salvadoran restaurants, convenience stores advertising money orders, wire transfers, and shipping services to Latin America, and, of course, the occasional Starbucks or Subway. Although it felt somewhat familiar, this dense suburban landscape was quite different from that of María's former life.

María was born in a small town in the Honduran countryside in the 1970s. From a large family, she was the oldest of several siblings. Over the years, many of these siblings moved to the United States, often cross-ing the United States–Mexico border illegally along the way. None of María's brothers or sisters managed to obtain valid immigration statuses, but they established comfortable lives relatively quickly. They acquired jobs, established businesses, found partners, and had children. As con-ditions in Honduras worsened throughout the 2000s, María's siblings often suggested that she should move to the United States. She repeat-edly declined. Honduras was María's home, and she had no desire to risk her life or the lives of her children in attempting the journey to the United States.

Then María was diagnosed with cancer. It was aggressive, and access-ing the medical treatment she needed would be nearly impossible in Honduras.[1] Her teenage son, Julián, traveled to the United States first in the hopes of earning money to send back for his mother's care. However, María's condition worsened. Karla, one of María's younger sisters, finally convinced her to come to the United States to seek treatment. It was, as she saw it, a matter of life and death.

Traveling with her seven-year-old daughter, Sofía, María made the dangerous trip from Honduras through Guatemala and Mexico to the U.S. border. As was the case when discussing several other difficult times in her life, María shared very few details about the trip. Sofía and María were apprehended by Border Patrol, detained for several days, given an immigration court date, and released under community supervision. As part of her supervision, María, like many immigrants with pending de-portation hearings, was made to wear an electronic monitoring bracelet on her ankle.[2] It occasionally peeked out from under one of her many ankle-length skirts. Later, she would describe how uncomfortable the tracking device became as her body swelled from cancer treatment.

Karla, María's sister, and her husband, a Salvadoran man with TPS, helped María secure an apartment and navigate the U.S. immigration and health care systems, both notoriously complicated. A network of extended family members residing in the area, all of whom were undoc-umented with the exception of the latest generation of young children born in the United States, provided additional support. They brought María home-cooked meals and watched Sofía when María was pulled away for doctors appointments, regular check-ins with ICE, and meet-ings with lawyers. Family residing outside the area visited often, some driving upward of 10 hours each way. Everyone chipped in to help María and her children feel at home.

By the time I met María, she had secured her pro bono attorney and attended an initial hearing in immigration court. Although this was only a short preliminary hearing, she was pleased with this initial experience. She had little to say about the judge presiding over her case, the interpreter translating for her, or the ICE attorney arguing in favor of her and her children's deportations. She did note, however, that they were all doing their jobs.

Instead of focusing on the behavior of immigration court judges and ICE attorneys, María was preoccupied with the postponement of her next hearing, which had been pushed out several months. She worried about her children's futures, especially were something to happen to her. If deported, María's cancer would most certainly progress to a point of no return. Her children would be orphaned, their fathers out of the picture. Moreover, although María's aging parents and some extended family remained in Honduras, most of the family lived in the United States. María now saw life in America, never part of her plan, as the only option.

Like many immigrants I interviewed, María agreed to update me on her case as it progressed. I doubt she ever suspected the case would drag on in immigration court for the next five years. I certainly didn't. Shortly after our first meeting, I received a call from María's sister, Karla, asking if I could join them at a doctor's appointment to translate. I was surprised to learn that most of María's doctors were unable to provide guaranteed translation at her appointments, and I agreed to come along.

I spent the next year and a half accompanying María and Karla to various clinics, doctor's offices, and hospitals for appointments, scans, and treatments as a backup interpreter. On the way home we often stopped for pupusas, a Salvadoran treat consisting of corn- or rice-flour tortillas filled with melted cheese or a mixture of shredded pork and beans. Sometimes Karla would invite me to join her and María for a cup of coffee and some cookies at Karla's house. Or they would insist I come by for a brief visit with Karla's new baby and any number of relatives who happened to be around that afternoon. The two women would then brief me on the latest news from María's lawyer, which usually wasn't much.

I had only ever known María to be a woman of few words, but Karla increasingly did most of the talking.

Despite nearly two years of treatment, María's health did not improve. She began to decline rapidly and was hospitalized. Although María's son, Julián, was now 18 and living with friends, Sofía was still just eight. She moved in with Karla and her husband, who had already taken on the role of managing the family's pending deportation case.

At this point, the deportation hearing María and her children awaited had been postponed several times over. It was unclear when, if at all, they would have the opportunity to make a case for relief before an immigration judge. As Karla led me through a maze of hospital corridors back toward the lobby after one of my last visits with María, she updated me on the family's deportation case yet again. With sadness in her voice, Karla recounted the takeaway from a recent meeting with the attorney. In a macabre turn of fate, María's children had a better chance of receiving relief from deportation—and building a life in the United States—were María to die.

Not long after, María passed away. Dozens of people attended her funeral, which was held at the evangelical church where the family belonged. They prayed, sang, and wept for hours. After the funeral, María's body was returned to Honduras for burial. Her children, Julián and Sofía, remained in the United States. Their lawyer was right. It took over five years, but both Julián and Sofía eventually obtained relief from deportation. Last we spoke, they were patiently awaiting the arrival of their green cards.[3]

Procedural Justice in Matters of Life and Death

It is unclear how many immigrants facing deportation each year find themselves in situations like María's. Undoubtedly, there are others who view deportation as a death sentence because it signifies the loss of life-saving medical treatment they require. In some cases, severe medical conditions and the absence of available treatment in one's home country are sufficient enough to justify relief from deportation, but the threshold is high.[4]

For many, however, deportation is considered a death sentence regardless of one's health. Those seeking refuge from gang violence, oppressive governments, or police corruption—like most of the Central Americans I interviewed for this book—often fear that they or their family members will wind up dead if deported. For others, deportation signifies social death, or the systematic prevention of engaging in social relations and denial of one's humanity.[5] It means being separated from children and partners, family and friends, and, in some cases, the only communities they have ever known—possibly *forever*.

What is the value of procedural justice under such circumstances? Does it matter if the ICE attorney fighting for your expulsion listens to you respectfully while you respond to their allegations of gang affiliation? Does it matter if the judge ordering your deportation does so in a kind and reassuring voice? Certainly, procedurally just treatment in immigration court is not worthless—at least, not to the immigrants whose stories I explore in this book. Yet these same stories are cause for questioning the role—and value—of procedural justice in immigration court, the immigration system, and encounters with the law more broadly.

As reiterated throughout this book, the social, historical, and political contexts of U.S. immigration policy and Central American migration cannot be overlooked when examining matters of fairness in immigration court. For example, in following Jessica's journey through the U.S. immigration system in chapter 1, it is clear that immigrants' migration experiences do not exist in a vacuum. Jessica's orientation toward the U.S. immigration system and the law cannot be separated from El Salvador's civil war or her mother's clandestine attempt to create a new life for the family in the United States. Neither can we understand Jessica's decision to hire a coyote to bring her son to the United States for a better life, a *safer* life, without viewing it in the context of countless other Central Americans who have done the same thing—including Jessica's own mother.

These are the histories that Central Americans bring to immigration court and that shape their evaluations of procedural justice. Just as Jessica's assessments of immigration court, the deportation hearing, and the U.S. immigration system are shaped by her lived experiences, legal knowledge, U.S. and foreign policy, gossip, myth, and storytelling, so, too, are the experiences and evaluations of all those I interviewed for this book. Immigrant identity and the collective immigrant experience cannot be untangled from the way immigrants make sense of their experiences with the law and assess fairness, be it in the immigration courtroom or on the street. In other words, immigrant evaluations of procedural justice cannot be separated from immigrant legal consciousness.

This realization helps explain the divergent procedural justice assessments of immigration attorneys and immigrants in chapters 2 and 4, respectively. Recall that (1) behavior, demeanor, and impartiality, (2) quality of interpersonal treatment, and (3) opportunities for error correction and participation—including the ability to speak and be heard—are integrally linked to assessments of procedural justice.[6] Despite my interviewing immigrants and immigration attorneys with experiences in the same two courts in front of the same pool of immigration judges, interpreters, and ICE attorneys, immigration attorneys found the court to be procedurally unjust on a number of counts, whereas immigrants held the opposite opinion.

Although immigration attorneys characterized most judges as "impartial" and "concerned," many stressed that implicit biases shape judicial behavior and decisions in the courtroom. ICE trial attorney behavior and demeanor, by contrast, was framed as everything from "compassionate," "patient," and "reasonable" to "aggressive," "ruthless," and "tricky." They noted that increasing court backlogs and accompanying pressure to clear cases left "jaded" judges and ICE attorneys even more susceptible to the influence of implicit bias.

Attorneys also flagged immigration detention, interpretation, and courtroom technology as procedurally problematic. Attorneys pointed out that detention restricts attorney-client communication, as facilities are often in remote locations, calls to and from facilities are costly, and detained immigrants are often transferred between facilities without warning. Reliance on interpreters was also said to disadvantage immigrants, limiting their ability to understand what was said during hearings and possibly altering both the content and style of their speech. They expressed frustration over poor audio and video quality associated with tele- and videoconferencing. They found that these technologies make it difficult for courtroom participants to see and hear each other, have dehumanizing effects, and influence credibility assessments. Attorneys also argued that the harmful effects of detention, interpretation, and tele- and videoconferencing worsen when combined. Ultimately, immigration attorneys found numerous procedural faults with the immigration court and its actors.

Unlike these attorneys, immigrants I interviewed had few procedural complaints about immigration court. Not only did most immigrants find their own or their family members' deportation hearings to be procedurally just; they repeatedly expressed appreciation for the treatment they and their family members received while in court.

The vast majority of immigrants with whom I spoke evaluated the immigration court and its key players positively in all three of these areas. They characterized judges, interpreters, and even trial attorneys as "educated," "friendly," "good," "helpful," "kind," "nice," "respectful," and "sensitive." They viewed these individuals as "impartial," "just," and "professional." They stressed that these court employees were simply "doing their jobs" and upholding the law. With few exceptions, even those with limited English proficiency said they were given the opportunity to speak during their hearings and felt that they were "listened to" by courtroom actors, particularly judges.

However, immigrants were bothered by the long wait times, cancellations, delays, and continuances they experienced as their deportation cases dragged on for months or even years. They explained that the prolonged deportation process amplified the stress, fear, and frustrations of being deportable. Many added that it left them unable to plan for the future, placing their own and their families' lives on hold. Of all the procedural matters explored in this book, such lengthy, indeterminate waits were among immigrants' top concerns.

Distributive justice also played a crucial role in immigrants' evaluations of fairness and immigration court. Immigrants often framed satisfaction with hearing outcomes in relation to the real and imagined case outcomes of others. Those who received relief from deportation felt fortunate, explaining that most immigrants were not so lucky. Those ordered deported stressed that their outcomes were unfair when considering the more favorable outcomes of others, particularly those who manage to evade deportation despite criminal convictions.

Whereas immigration attorneys' evaluations of immigration court and its actors were grounded in their professional education and legal socialization, immigrants' evaluations of immigration court and its actors were tied to the real and imagined experiences of other immigrants. As detailed in chapter 3, immigrants' understandings of the immigration system are informed by informal and formal knowledge drawn from a variety of sources, including attorneys and *notarios*, the criminal justice system, friends and family, immigration detention, the media, neighbors, and various professionals. Although most immigrants prioritized information gleaned from attorneys or other professionals, many faced barriers to accessing such formal sources of information. Some were also skeptical of legal professionals, either having been burned in the past by or hearing stories of unscrupulous attorneys.

As a result, immigrants relied heavily on a patchwork of informal knowledge drawn from immigration stories they heard both before and after coming to the United States when discussing their own and others' deportation hearings. Community gossip, urban legends, and vicarious experiences—and traumas—picked up from family, friends, and the media, among other sources, led most immigrants I interviewed to believe that they or their family members would be treated poorly in court. Similarly, their exposure to corruption, impunity, and violence in Central America shook their confidence in state authorities.

Through these stories and experiences, immigrants established baseline expectations of immigration court and its actors, illuminating the dynamic role legal socialization plays in immigrants' lives as they navigate the U.S. immigration system. Immigrants expected very little of immigration court. In the end, however, their experiences in court often greatly exceeded their expectations. Yet despite finding the court and its actors to be procedurally just overall, immigrants stressed that they could never be satisfied with a deportation order. Moreover, nearly every immigrant I interviewed explained that under no circumstances would they comply with deportation. In fact, most had already violated a deportation order—some had violated several. These findings run counter to much research on procedural justice, legitimacy, outcome satisfaction, and compliance, begging the question as to why this might be the case.

As recounted throughout this book, many immigrants I interviewed came to the United States in search of the rule of law and the safety it affords. Immigrants I interviewed praised the United States for effective crime management and low levels of corruption and impunity. They saw the U.S. government as legitimate due to its perceived ability to address instrumental concerns relating to crime control and safety as compared with Central American governments, not simply because it upheld due process rights or treated people fairly in court. Still, procedural justice mattered too.

Perceptions of procedurally just treatment by attorneys, interpreters, and judges reaffirmed immigrants' belief in state legitimacy and the power of the rule of law in the United States more generally. Most immigrants I interviewed said that the U.S. government has the legitimate authority and obligation to enforce the law—including immigration law. Yet despite finding immigration court procedurally fair and viewing the U.S. government as legitimate, immigrants still framed deportation as an illegitimate institution, at least when applied to immigrants without serious criminal convictions.

In explaining this position, immigrants drew on human rights and religious discourses. They argued for a universal right to migrate, as well as to live and work freely in the United States. Most held that deportation should be reserved for "criminals," not "hardworking" immigrants escaping economic turmoil, government corruption, or violence. Ultimately, neither fair process nor legitimate government authority could make the realities of deportation acceptable to those who would have to live it.

Looking Ahead

What do the experiences of immigrants facing deportation teach us about procedural justice? First and foremost, they teach us that mainstream understandings of procedural justice fail to capture the diversity of meaning and value that people attach to fairness. Immigrants' procedural justice evaluations cannot be separated from their unique sociolegal status. Neither can they be severed from individual and collective (im)migration experiences. Similarly, the importance immigrants give to both distributive and substantive justice must be understood in relation to immigrant identity, the social, political, and economic forces of migration, and storytelling about the law.

These findings run counter to mainstream procedural justice research, which too often frames understandings of justice as static and people as homogeneous. Immigrant experiences with deportation force us to reconcile with the normative assumptions inherent in most procedural justice scholarship. They also lead us to question the value of procedural justice in an increasingly diverse and global society that is increasingly steeped in inequality. As such, this book joins a growing cascade of "second wave" procedural justice literature that is attentive to culture, context, identity, and power.

What's more, this book reveals the ways in which the promotion of procedural justice and procedural rights in immigration court masks the structural barriers and systematic inequalities inherent in the U.S. immigration system. Procedural protections foster perceptions of justice while fortifying mechanisms of social control.[7] To overlook this reality is to overlook the substantive injustices of deportation and the immigration system writ large: families separated, communities upended, opportunities lost.

Modeling enhanced procedural rights within the immigration system after the rights afforded in the criminal justice system is problematic in its own right. Adapting criminal justice practices and protections to immigration court and the immigration system, even if intended to safeguard immigrants from state harms and state power, entails criminal justice creep. The promulgation of criminal justice–inspired procedural safeguards within immigration court is simply the continued expansion of the criminalization of the immigration system, albeit wrapped up in liberal rights discourse. It is, at the core, crimmigration[8] under the auspices of promoting and protecting immigrant rights and well-being.[9]

Looking to the U.S. criminal justice system in hopes of improving the immigration system is misguided and dangerous. Procedural justice is no match for a criminal justice system built upon 250 years of entrenched colonialism, imperialism, racism, sexism, classism, and xenophobia, just as it is no match for an immigration system that rests upon the same. Instead, the lessons derived from the criminal justice system should center upon learning from past and, in many cases, ongoing mistakes: capital punishment, judicial bias, mass incarceration, police (and correctional officer) brutality, prosecutorial misconduct, privatization, solitary confinement, stop-and-frisk, and wrongful convictions.

Importantly, as evidenced by the assessments, opinions, and stories of immigrants interviewed for this book, Central American immigrants will not exchange substantive fairness for procedural niceties. Compliance with deportation orders is not predicated upon procedural justice or state legitimacy. Ironically, perceptions of procedural justice and state legitimacy only reify immigrants' desires to remain in the United States, even if this means that they must violate the law in order to do so.

Drawing inspiration from movements to abolish the death penalty and prison, meaningful immigration reforms should begin the process of dismantling the repressive U.S. immigration system: eliminate detention, end the practice of deportation, and reduce the need for an immigration court altogether. Reforms should also emphasize the decriminalization of immigrants and migration, remove the criminal penalties attached to unauthorized border crossings and unlawful presence, and expand authorized migration by removing visa quotas, eliminating rigid entrance qualifications, and shrinking exorbitant processing fees.

Problems with the immigration system, immigration court, and deportation cannot be addressed through the advancement of due process protections (e.g., right to indigent defense) and bureaucratic changes (e.g., hiring additional immigration judges). Continuing down the path of piecemeal immigration reforms that enhance due process rights will do little more than advance the illusion of rights in the immigration system and the myth of rights in the American mind. Moreover, as evidenced by this book, fair process will likely do little to enhance immigrants' compliance with deportation orders. There is little value to reform strategies aimed at fostering *perceptions* of justice in the service of social control, as opposed to fostering *real* justice in the service of collective well-being and human dignity.

Ultimately, immigrants teach us that perceptions of justice are subjective, that unjust laws are not deserving of compliance, and that a radical reimagining of deportation coupled with comprehensive immigration reform is required if we, as a society, are truly concerned with matters of immigration, fairness, and the law.

Epilogue

The story broke early in the summer of 2018. The U.S. government was separating immigrant children from their parents at the United States–Mexico border. Part of the Trump administration's new "zero tolerance" policy, family separation was a "byproduct" of a move to criminally prosecute migrants apprehended at the border without authorization.[1] As the Trump administration explained, the U.S. government had a history of placing migrant children in temporary custody when parents could not provide proper care. Indeed, separation was framed as being carried out in migrant children's best interests.[2]

"Separate." A relatively innocuous word. The reality, however, was anything but. Images of children in cages, now infamous, quickly surfaced. There were stories of eight- and nine-year-olds, not yet old enough to care for themselves, feeding and changing infants with whom they happened to be detained. Some children, it was said, cried uncontrollably. Others retreated inward. Parents were given no indication about their children's whereabouts. Some recounted being told that their children were being taken for a bath, only to learn hours later that they would not be coming back.[3] Others said that their children were "disappeared" while they were in court or receiving medical care.[4] Still others were ripped from their parents' arms.[5]

* * *

Around the same time that the Trump administration's "zero tolerance" family separation policy came to light, I had my first child. That summer, I sat in the safety of my own home and privilege as a U.S. citizen. A new mother with my newborn, I felt both a strong aversion to and a sickening pull toward family separation's injustices unfolding in the media. When my daughter cried, I imagined these separated children, some as young as four months old,[6] crying for their parents. When I traveled to Canada from Michigan across the Ambassador

Bridge that fall, I had nightmares about her being taken from me at the border.

Nearly two years had passed since I completed the interviews that would eventually serve as the basis for this book, yet I couldn't help but think back to the Central American mothers and fathers I met in the course of my research. I replayed my conversations with Angelica, who made multiple journeys across the United States–Mexico border, risking her life each time, to reunite with her children. I recalled the tears welling in Luis's eyes when he shared the pain he felt having missed his daughter's birth because, at the time, he was detained and awaiting deportation. I remembered the determination in Walter's voice when he swore that, if deported, he would find a way to return to the United States to be with his son. And I thought of Jessica, who had been separated from her mother as a child during El Salvador's Civil War, only to be separated from her own son years later in the hopes of building a better life for her family in the United States.

I thought, too, of the many more immigrant mothers, fathers, and children I had come to know in my years studying immigration and working with immigrant communities. Those I met at community ESL classes and "know your rights" trainings, in detention centers and jails, and at immigration court. Those I worked with, like Jasmine, who, barely old enough to drive, held down two jobs while finishing high school and raising her younger sister after their parents were deported. Or like Sylvia, who came to the United States as part of the Sanctuary Movement when she was just a girl after a death squad committed murder in her family's home and who spent years living in the shadows because, like several of the immigrants I spoke with for this project, the U.S. government did not recognize her as a refugee. Although each story was unique, when examined together clear patterns emerged: families torn apart, communities disrupted, and harms caused by a substantively unjust and inhumane U.S. immigration system. "Separated."

As I reflected on Trump's family separation policy in the face of growing public criticism, I naively thought that this was it, that the immigration system was finally headed for meaningful change. The violence of family separation was difficult to justify, excuse, or forgive. Who among even the most staunch antiimmigrant politicians or voters could bear witness to this and stand by in silence? Although the policy was challenged in court and officially ended by the administration just two moths after it began,[7] this was not the watershed moment for which I had hoped. Instead, the Trump administration continued its practice of family separation, albeit somewhat secretly, along with a more general attack on the U.S. immigration system that has yet to be repaired.

* * *

I have contended elsewhere that family separation as practiced by the Trump administration is best understood as criminal—specifically, a form of state-corporate crime.[8] This is because it involved the "systematic harm of thousands of migrant children and families predicated upon illegal and socially injurious actions at the intersection of the state and [nonprofit organizations]."[9] In just the two months during which Trump's "zero tolerance" policy was officially in effect, the government separated 2,654 children from their parents. However, it later became apparent that not only did the Trump administration begin separating children and parents as early as 2017; it continued this practice well into 2019.[10] All in all, it has been estimated that over 5,000 children were separated from their parents during this time.[11] Of these, at least 1,033 children were under the age of 10 and at least 103 children were younger than five.[12]

Separated children were held in state custody for months and in some cases years.[13] They were typically placed in short-term CBP and ICE holding facilities, including "temporary emergency influx shelters" and several criminal justice detention facilities.[14] They were then transferred to state-certified "shelters" run by nonprofit and private contractors with the Office of Refugee Resettlement.[15] Despite an elaborate web of procedures, rules, laws, and legal decisions and settlements governing the custody, care, treatment of migrant youth,[16] separated children experienced extreme and egregious emotional, physical, psychological, and sexual abuses and numerous rights violations while in state custody.[17]

Independent reviews carried out by journalists and politicians have since revealed that many facilities used to "shelter" immigrant children— essentially another form of detention—failed to meet basic health, hygiene, and safety requirements,[18] let alone provide proper adult care and supervision.[19] Reports of physical, psychological, and sexual abuse[20] of children by shelter employees—sometimes retaliatory[21]—have also surfaced. At least four separated children died while in, or shortly after being released from, state custody.[22] Notably, there was not a single child death in federal immigration custody in the decade leading up to the Trump administration's "zero tolerance" policy.[23]

Despite repeated court orders requiring the government to stop the practice of separating children from parents and reunite all separated children with their families, families remain separated nearly four years later. By mid-2022, as many as 1,200 families had yet to be reunited, and the parents of 237 children had not yet been located or contacted.[24] Citing inadequate recordkeeping, the government has stated on multiple occasions that it is unable to return all children to their families because it lost track of children in state custody and could not ascertain the identities of their parents.[25]

As Stephen Lee, professor of law and associate dean for faculty research and development at the University of California, Irvine, sums up, family separation under the Trump administration resulted in "spectacular violence."[26] It was a violence that, despite the administration's initial response, was undeniable. It was "hypervisible" and "immediately sensational."[27]

Although the spectacle of violence created by family separation was perceived as extreme and unprecedented by many in the public and the media, it was just another iteration of the status quo. Indeed, Lee contends that "our immigration system is pervasively organized around principles of family separation."[28] This reality is not immediately apparent, however, because such principles typically manifest as "slow violence" or "slow death." Such harms are "invisible" yet detrimental. They are difficult to identify precisely because they occur slowly, often compounding over time.[29] Masked in the mundane, these harms are easily overlooked, ignored, and excused.

For example, lead poisoning and other environmental harms caused by the Flint water crisis, the effects of which will last for decades,[30] constitute slow violence. So, too, does continued exposure to depleted uranium and other potentially toxic materials left by U.S. weapons used to wage war in Iraq (and elsewhere).[31] Slow violence is not limited to environmental or public health harms. Detroit's tax foreclosure crisis, in which the Wayne County Treasurer's Office foreclosed on over 100,000 homes after overtaxing homeowners and then sold those homes to investors and speculators at auction, can also be understood as slow violence.[32]

Slow violence is pervasive in both the criminal justice and immigration systems, even if rarely referred to by this name. The slow violence of overpolicing communities of color. The slow violence of mass incarceration, mass detention, and solitary confinement. The slow violence of living in fear of deportation. The slow violence of family separation.

Decades, if not centuries, of discriminatory, xenophobic, and substantively unjust immigration law, policy, and practice made family separation possible.[33] The Trump administration merely took advantage of the system it was handed, accelerating the slow violence that is built into the fabric of American (im)migration controls. Examined through this lens, family separation is not some abhorrent anomaly; it is the U.S. immigration system laid bare for the world to see.

* * *

During just four years in the White House, President Trump and his administration decimated the U.S. immigration system. Enforcement activities ramped up, while decades of policy, practice, and precedent were thrown out the window. Although only Congress has the power to rewrite federal immigration law, the executive branch has extensive authority over immigration funding, priorities, and protocol. Capitalizing on this power, the Trump administration made hundreds of changes—472 to be exact[34]—intended to cripple, disrupt, and damage the immigration system.

Within days of taking office, Trump signed the now-infamous "Muslim ban," the first of several executive orders in which Trump attempted to ban travelers and refugees from several Muslim-majority countries.[35] Indeed, the Trump administration moved swiftly to restrict immigrants' ability to come to and live in the United States legally. Trump announced an end to Deferred Action for Childhood Arrivals (DACA),[36] and Temporary Protected Status (TPS) was slated for elimination.[37] Legal protections for asylum seekers were severely narrowed.[38] The administration introduced the Migrant Protection Protocols, also known as the "Remain in Mexico" program, to deter and prevent people from legally seeking asylum at the border.[39] The Public Charge rule—along with a series of related policies—restricted green card eligibility for low-income immigrants.[40] Immigration filing fees were increased and related bureaucracy expanded, adding to the complexity, cost, and length of immigration processes more generally.[41] Visa denials increased, while rates of adjustment to permanent residency and refugee admissions decreased significantly.[42]

As legal pathways to the United States collapsed, immigration enforcement expanded. The Trump administration announced plans to hire thousands of new CBP and ICE officers—although it only added several hundred—and began constructing barriers along the United States–Mexico border.[43] Unlike the Obama administration, which officially prioritized the deportation of immigrants with criminal convictions and opposed breaking up families,[44] the Trump administration targeted immigrants for deportation indiscriminately. Furthermore, Prosecutorial Discretion (PD), which affords ICE the authority to decide when to pursue deportation against individuals believed to be in violation of the law, was restricted.[45]

The administration also instituted several "efficiency" reforms aimed at reducing the immigration courts' growing backlogs. The number of immigration judges nearly doubled.[46] Case-completion quotas and other court accelerators and performance measures were established.[47] Still, the influx of immigration cases outpaced the speed with which judges could complete them, and the courts' backlogs continued to grow.

In his last year in office, Trump capitalized on the emerging global pandemic in order to further an anti-immigrant agenda. COVID-19 served as a pretext to extend and expand exclusionary immigration practices, even when such practices were antithetical to the promotion of public health and justice, leaving immigrants, migrants, and refugees vulnerable to COVID-19 infection, among other harms.[48] In March 2020, the State Department shut down U.S. consulates and embassies and suspended routine visa processing; although permitted to reopen and resume operations in July, many sites did not resume processing.[49] A year later, dozens of visa processing sites around the globe remained out of commission.[50] Trump also issued a series of COVID-19 travel bans, restricting travel from China, Iran, Brazil, and over two dozen European countries, with additional bans on various categories of immigrant and nonimmigrant visas and numerous other restrictions.[51]

The administration of Joseph Biden has reversed *some* of the immigration policies and procedures established during the Trump administration both before and during the pandemic. For example, President Biden ended Trump's Muslim ban and eliminated the Public Charge rule.

The Biden administration also vacated several detrimental Trump-era legal decisions targeting protections for asylum seekers, increased refugee resettlement, and not only restored but extended TPS protections.

Yet the Biden administration has used the ongoing pandemic as a pretext to extend some Trump-era migration controls, including the Migration Protection Protocols. Most egregiously, the Biden administration continued using United States Code Title 42 to justify the automatic expulsion of migrants seeking entry at the border, which the Trump administration implemented in March 2020. Title 42, which became law under the 1944 Public Health Service Act, authorizes the director of the Centers for Disease Control and Prevention to prohibit the entry of individuals who might introduce a communicable disease into the United States. Title 42 also permits any customs officers, including Border Patrol officers, to implement the rule. The legality of this practice is questionable, as it circumvents migrants' legal rights to seek asylum or to contest their removal from the United States.[52] Despite opposition from public health experts[53] and several legal challenges, the Biden administration extended the use of Title 42 in December 2021.[54] Although the Biden administration announced plans to end the use of Title 42 in May 2022, this move was challenged by attorneys general from Arizona, Missouri, and Louisiana. On May 20, 2022, Judge Robert Summerhays, a U.S. District Court judge in Louisiana, issued an injunction ruling that the administration must continue expelling migrants under Title 42 until a full hearing on the merits.[55] To date, nearly 2 million migrants have been expelled under this policy, nearly 16,000 of them unaccompanied children.[56]

Whereas Trump and his senior officials demonstrated a blatant disregard for procedural justice and due process, the steps the Biden administration has taken to return the U.S. immigration system to a state of pre-Trump "normalcy" signal a return to procedural justice and due process. The overtly biased language of the Trump administration has been eliminated. The spectacle of violence has been sanitized. Yet many of the harmful policies and practices remain. Ultimately, these practices and policies were not unique Trumpian creations but instead reflect a legacy of substantively unjust immigration policy that has existed since America's founding.

* * *

In June 2018, a clandestine audio recording from inside a temporary "shelter" for migrant children in CBP custody was released.[57] On the recording, young children between the ages of four and 10 are heard crying for their parents. The children are inconsolable. From time to time, when my now-three-year-old daughter has a run-of-the-mill tantrum or breakdown and is seemingly inconsolable—as is often the case with three-year-olds—I can't help but think of that recording and the 5,000 separated children. When my daughter wakes in the middle of the night after having a bad dream and I am able to walk across the hall, sit by her side, and let her know that everything is going to be all right, I can't help but think of the thousands of immigrant parents who are unable to console their children, whether as a result of family separation, deportation, or other restrictive migration controls.

Family separation as practiced by the Trump administration may have been a case of "spectacular violence," but violence plays out on a daily basis in the U.S. immigration system. Although the harms of immigration court and deportation may appear mundane by comparison, they should not be tolerated. Deportation, veiled by the trappings of procedural justice and due process, is still deportation. It is slow death.

Although it is difficult to argue against procedural justice, it is not the answer. It sanitizes the spectacle of violence being carried out each day—legally—in U.S. immigration courts. Make no mistake: the deportation of hundreds of thousands of immigrants year in and year out, the systematic and sustained destruction of families, businesses, and communities—this *is* spectacular. At least, it should be.

Just as no amount of procedural justice or due process can assuage the pains of family separation, no amount of procedural justice or due process can make deportation humane. The substantive injustice of immigration court is neither mitigated nor excused by fair treatment or fair process. If anything, procedural justice furthers the state's ability to subject immigrants to slow death. Barring substantive reforms, the U.S. immigration system will continue to present immigrants on U.S. soil and around the globe with a nearly impossible choice, pitting human rights against the rule of law. The immigrants whose voices fill the pages of this book make this unshakably clear.

ACKNOWLEDGMENTS

This book could not exist were it not for the attorneys and immigrants whose words, experiences, and insights gave life to this project. To most of these individuals, I was little more than a passing stranger. Yet they chose to open up to me, in many cases revealing some of the most challenging and traumatic details of their lives. To these individuals I am grateful. I am also grateful to the dozens of attorneys, court staff, immigrants, interpreters, judges, and security guards whom I observed and interacted with over the course of this study, as well as the community members and stakeholders who supported this research.

I would also like to thank my wonderful editor, Ilene Kalish, at New York University Press. How fortunate I was to work with Ilene on this, my first solo-authored book. Ilene was enthusiastic about the project from day one. Having worked together on a previous project, I knew that, with her, the book would be in good hands. Little did I know just how lucky I was to be working with Ilene when I signed my book contract in February 2020, mere weeks before a global pandemic would upend the world. Offered without the slightest hint of annoyance or judgment, Ilene's kindness, patience, and positivity afforded me the space and encouragement needed to bring this book to fruition.

Ilene's talented colleagues at New York University Press were also quite indispensable. Yasemin Torfilli, an Editorial Assistant, thoughtfully supported project production, indulged my book cover ideas (leading to a cover inspired by the iconic artwork of Saul Bass), and kept me on track. Martin Coleman, Editing, Design, and Production Director, and his excellent team of talented editors helped to polish this manuscript, clarifying my arguments without ever inhibiting the voices of study participants or myself. I thank them all.

In actuality, this book was many years in the making. An outgrowth of my doctoral studies, I owe a warm thank-you to my dissertation chair, colleague, mentor, and friend, Jon Gould, who has helped me hone my academic voice and served as a model for the type of scholar I aim to be. I am also grateful to Eric Hershberg, Marjorie Zatz, Jayesh Rathod, and Raymond Michalowski, all of whom served on my dissertation committee and whom I am lucky to count among my colleagues and mentors. A great debt is owed to Ed Maguire, who not only pushed me to develop my qualitative research skills in the field but also is responsible for introducing me to the concept of procedural justice as a first-year PhD student in his proseminar. Robert Johnson, while not an official member of my dissertation committee, supported my research then and continues to serve as a cherished mentor to this day.

A great deal of gratitude is owed to Ian Robinson, who introduced me to Freire, the Border, and the world of community organizing through the Washtenaw County Workers Center, where I worked to support immigrant and labor rights. It was during this time that I first began to grasp the complexity of immigration law and the traumas of migration. It was also during this time that I started to question the fairness of deportation and the U.S. immigration system more broadly. Subsequent experiences with Justice for Our Neighbors (JFON), the Capitol Area Immigration Rights Coalition (CAIR Coalition), the Central American Resource Center (CARECEN), and Angie's Foundation further shaped my understanding of the politics and sociolegal realities of immigration in the United States.

Thanks as well to my former research assistants, Terrence Gourlay, Meagan Hebert, and Zeena Whayeb, who assisted with research for this book. Thanks are due also to the University of Michigan–Dearborn's College of Arts, Sciences, and Letters for providing research funds to support junior faculty during the COVID-19 pandemic. The completion of this book was also supported by my former teaching assistant, Tracy Maish, whose efforts in the classroom afforded me more time to focus on writing. Similarly, I appreciate the many engaging conversations on crimmigration and the cash bail system I had with former graduate students Audrea Dakho and Gina Telega. I am ultimately grateful to all my students. They keep me engaged, recharge my batteries, and help me interrogate my work through the eyes of others.

It should be stressed that I had the support of many wonderful coauthors, colleagues, friends, and family in Michigan and beyond throughout this project. This includes, but is not limited to, Katherine Abbott,

Mike Baney, Coquis Galvan-Santibanez, Lori and Todd Gardner, Rajeev Gundur, Cat Hadley, Brandon Hunter, Marisa Huston, Austin Kocher, K. Sebastian Leon, Maura Lynch, Clare Molnar, Pam Pennock, Jorge Gonzalez del Pozo, Anna Reytsman, Jessica Riviere, Ebony Sunday, Jacob Wilkinson, and Marcela Torres Wong. Through hours of conversation, both formal and informal, these folks pushed me to more critically contemplate the questions at the core of this book.

To my virtual writing crew, including Pam Aronson, Nick Iannarino, Olivia Lowrey, Belen Lowrey-Kinberg, Emily Luxon, Mike MacDonald, Margaret Murray, and Sarah Silverman, thank you for our regular writing sessions. These sessions helped hold me accountable and kept me motivated—especially on the days I thought I'd never finish this book. And a special thank-you to Hillary Mellinger and Watoii Rabii for the countless additional late-night writing sessions, drafts exchanged, and virtual hugs, all of which made the experience of writing this book much more enjoyable.

To Autumn Caines, thank you for opening my eyes to the weaponization of care. To Hector Fox, thank you for pushing me outside my disciplinary boundaries and continually reminding me of the role academics have to play in activism. To Kanika Mannan and Dave Caffrey, thank you for turning your lovely dining room into my own writer's retreat.

To Nataliya and my always thoughtful neighbors, Karen, Pam, Michelle, and Joshua and Jonathan, thank you for encouragement and support, for shoveling our sidewalks on snowy days, and backyard pandemic playdates and picnics. I would also be remiss not to thank my parents, Charlotte and Gregg. Without a doubt, these two people have forever left a mark on my writing—due, in large part, to my mother's unparalleled editing tutorials—and on my critical, intersectional approach to questions of power, inequality, and justice. Growing up with two professors for parents, I swore I would never go into academia. But as the old saying goes, apparently the apple doesn't fall far from the tree after all.

I am truly grateful to my thoughtful partner, Josh, who indulges my many research projects, this book included, and picks up my slack with a smile on his face. His reasoned wisdom and even-keeled approach to life helps to keep me grounded. To my daughter, Yves, I am thankful for every giggle and interruption. For every time I was forced to flee my computer as crocodiles approached, for all the times my desk began sinking because the floor was suddenly lava, and for the days that my chair magically became Mei's Catbus, thank you. Your effervescent spirit and mischievous wit are a welcome respite. And to Mr. D, the amazing pup who snoozed at my feet while I wrote most of this book—as he often did for the better part of 15 years—and who waited for me to send in my manuscript before leaving us. Thank you.

APPENDIX

Interview Protocols

1. I would like to begin by asking you a few general questions about your training and experience as a lawyer. Please tell me about your path to becoming a lawyer. What got you interested in law? (prompt: where and when did you go to law school, did you do anything between college and law school, what types of law have you practiced, what interested you in immigration law, how and why did you begin taking immigration cases)

2. Now I would like to discuss your current practice. Where do you work and what do you spend most of your time doing? (prompt: describe workplace, work alone versus team, average number of clients)

3. What aspect of immigration work do you enjoy most/least? Why? (prompt: also ask about obstacles/challenges)

4. I would like to learn more about your experiences as an immigration lawyer, but first I would like to hear a little bit about how the removal hearing process works. What happens in a removal hearing?

5. What is your role in the hearing? Who are the other key actors/players in the removal hearing and what are their roles? (prompt: be sure to ask about judge, attorneys, DHS, interpreters, court staff, respondents)

6. Now I would like to ask a few questions about your clients. How would you describe the demographics of your immigration clients (e.g., socioeconomic status, race, gender, age, education, etc.)? How if at all do these demographics impact removal hearing experiences and/or outcomes?

7. How would your clients describe you? Do you think that you relate to any of your immigration clients? If so, how?

8. What, if any, sorts of preferences do you have for specific types of clients or cases? Can you elaborate on this please? Are there any kinds of cases or clients that you would refuse to take? Why?

9. What level or amount of information regarding either the American legal system writ large or the immigration system more specifically do your clients tend to possess upon your first meeting?

10. Would you say your immigration clients generally understand or misunderstand the nature of the legal process when they first come to you?

11. If generally misunderstand: What kinds of misconceptions about removal proceedings, the immigration system, or even lawyers do they have and where do such misconceptions come from?

12. How common or uncommon is it for your immigration clients to have had negative prior experiences with immigration attorneys or individuals pretending or claiming to be immigration attorneys? What sorts of impediments do such negative experiences impose upon your relationship with your immigration clients?

13. What do the majority of your clients want from you and/or from their removal hearing experience?

14. How, if at all, does your identity (e.g., socioeconomic status, race, gender, age, education, etc.) impact your work as an immigration attorney and/or your relationship with your clients?

15. Now I would like to discuss the practice of immigration law. What skills do you see as important for effective immigration representation? What does ineffective immigration representation look like? Would you provide some examples? (prompt: legal information, counseling/support, language/interpretation issues)

16. Have you had to balance your advocacy with ethical concerns at some point? If so, how did you resolve this?

15. In general, would you say that removal hearings are fair or unfair? How so?

16. The following questions focus upon variations in the removal hearing experience and are concerned both with the perspective of the immigration attorney and the respondent, as well as the overall hearing experience and outcome.

17. How, if at all, would you say appearing via videoconferencing versus in court impacts a removal hearing?

18. How, if at all, would you say that language and/or interpretation impacts a removal hearing?

19. How, if at all, would you say that country of origin impacts a removal hearing?

20. How, if at all, would you say that immigration status impacts a removal hearing?

21. How, if at all, would you say that prior experience with the criminal justice system impacts a removal hearing?

22. How, if at all, would you say that prior experience with the immigration system impacts a removal hearing?

23. How, if at all, would you say that detention and/or bond impact a removal hearing?

24. How, if at all, would you say that having an immigration attorney impacts a removal hearing?

25. Now I would like to discuss other EOIR actors/players. In general, what are your thoughts on immigration judges? Can you please explain? (prompt: appear biased or unbiased, appear caring or uncaring, concerned with respondent understanding, listen to respondent, courteous to respondent and attorneys, etc.)

26. In general, what are your thoughts on DHS attorneys? Can you please explain? (prompt: appear biased or unbiased, appear caring or uncaring, concerned with respondent understanding, listen to respondent, courteous to respondent and attorneys, etc.)

27. In general, what are your thoughts on court interpreters? Can you please explain? (prompt: appear biased or unbiased, appear caring or uncaring, concerned with respondent understanding, listen to respondent, courteous to respondent and attorneys, concerned with clarity and accuracy, etc.)

28. In general, what are your thoughts on other EOIR staff? Can you please explain?

29. How, if at all, would you say that immigration work has impacted your personal life? Your psychological and mental well-being?

30. What are your current thoughts about the American immigration system? If you could change anything about the American immigration system, what would you change and why?

31. What are you current thoughts on the American legal system? If you could change anything about the American legal system, what would you change and why?

32. If you were not doing immigration work, what would you be doing?

33. Is there anything else you would like to add?

FAMILY OF IMMIGRANTS CURRENTLY OR PREVIOUSLY IN REMOVAL PROCEEDINGS

1. I would like to start by getting to know a little bit more about you and your family's immigration history. How and when did your family decide to immigrate to the United States? Could you please tell me a little bit about this decision? To clarify, where were you born? (prompt: why, when, how—type of visa/no visa, type of transportation, alone/with others)

2. What did [you/your family] do upon arrival to the United States (prompt: connect with family/friends, start working, study, etc.)?

3. What did [you/your] family know about the U.S. legal system before coming to the United States? (prompt: how did you/your family learn this?)

4. Did friends or family members help explain American laws to [you/your family] upon arriving in the United States? Have [you/your family] attended any legal rights training workshops, such as labor rights workshops, since coming to the United States?

5. How does the U.S. legal system compare with that in [home country]?

6. What did [you/your family] know about the U.S. immigration system/laws prior to coming to the United States? (prompt: how did you/your family learn this/where did you/your family get this information? family? friends?)

7. Did friends or family members help explain immigration laws to [you/your family] upon arriving in the United States? Have [you/your family] attended any immigration law or rights training workshops since coming to the United States?

8. You've told me that one or more of your family members have been to a removal hearing. I would like to discuss this, but first I would like to learn about your own experiences with the U.S.

immigration system prior to your [family member's/family members'] removal hearing(s). Could you tell me about this? (prompts: encounters/interactions with CBP, ICE, police, USCIS employees, Detention and Removal employees, EOIR employees—judges, DHS attorneys, office staff, etc.)

9. Now I would like to learn more about your family's experience with the removal hearing process. When did you find out that [your family member/family members] were being placed in removal proceedings? Could you please tell me about this moment— what were you thinking? Did you know why [he/she/they] were placed in removal proceedings? (adjust subsequent questions to reflect number of removal hearing procedures experienced—i.e., ordered removed more than once?)

10. [Was your family member/were your family members] held in detention leading up to and during the removal hearing? What, if anything, did [he/she/they] tell you about this experience? (prompt: facility conditions, detention officers, other detainees/inmates, contact with lawyers/legal rights organizations, contact with family)

11. What, if anything, did your family or family member(s) do to prepare for the removal hearing? (prompt: contact an attorney/legal aid, seek assistance from friends/family/church/community organizations)

12. Did you attend your family member(s) removal hearing? If so, could you tell me a little bit about the actual hearing? What was it like? If not, what, if anything, did your family member(s) tell you about the hearing? (prompt: attorney, DHS attorney, judge, other people in the courtroom, in the courtroom or appearing from detention on TV, an interpreter, family, contest removal versus seek relief)

13. Did your family, including the family member(s) having the hearing, understand what was going on during the hearing? (prompt: were the hearing procedures explained in advance or during the hearing, did a lawyer explain what happened after the hearing)

14. What did it feel like to be at the hearing(s)?

15. Do you believe [the/these hearing(s) was/were] fair? Why?

16. Did the judge appear biased or unbiased? Can you please explain?

17. Did the judge appear interested in [this/these case(s)] or concerned about what was going to happen to your family member(s) and the rest of your family in relation to the hearing?

18. What about the DHS attorney, did he or she appear biased or unbiased? Did he or she seem to care about what was happening to your family member(s) and the rest of your family in relation to the hearing?

19. What about your own attorney (if applicable), did he or she appear biased or unbiased? Did he or she seem to care about what was happening to your family member(s) and the rest of your family in relation to the hearing?

20. What about the interpreter (if applicable), did he or she appear biased or unbiased? Did he or she seem to care about what was happening to your family member(s) and the rest of your family in relation to the hearing?

21. Do you feel that your family member(s) or any other members of your family not undergoing the removal process were able to participate in the hearing? How so?

22. What was your and your family's reaction when you learned the outcome of the hearing? How did you and your family feel about this outcome?

23. What happened after the hearing? (prompt: where did you go, what did you do, who were you with, etc.)

24. How has [this/these] removal hearing(s) impacted you and your family?

25. If you could change anything about the hearing, what would you change and why?

26. What are your current thoughts about the American immigration system? Do you believe that having [a family member/# of family members] go through the removal hearing process changed the way you think about the American immigration system? How so?

27. If you could change anything about the American immigration system, what would you change and why?

28. What are you current thoughts on the American legal system? Do you believe that having [a family member/# of family members] go through the removal hearing process changed the way you think about the American legal system? How so?

29. If you could change anything about the American legal system, what would you change and why?
30. What are your plans for the future?
31. If outside the United States: Do you have plans to go to the United States? (prompt: why, how, concerns)
32. If inside the United States: Do you see yourself remaining in the United States? Do you have any concerns about your immigration status or future encounters with law enforcement or immigration enforcement?
33. Is there anything else you would like to add?

IMMIGRANTS CURRENTLY OR PREVIOUSLY IN
REMOVAL PROCEEDINGS

1. I would like to start by getting to know a little bit more about you and how you decided to immigrate to the United States. Could you please tell me a little bit about your decision to come to the United States? (prompt: why, when, how—type of visa/no visa, type of transportation, alone/with others)
2. What did you do when you got to the United States? (prompt: connect with family/friends, start working, study, etc.)
3. What did you know about the U.S. legal system before coming to the United States? (prompt: how did you learn this?)
4. Did friends or family members help explain American laws to you upon arriving in the United States? Have you attended any legal rights training workshops, such as labor rights workshops, since coming to the United States?
5. How does the U.S. legal system compare with that in [home country]?
6. What did you know about the U.S. immigration system/laws prior to coming to the United States? (prompt: how did you learn this/where did you get this information? family? friends?)
7. Did friends or family members help explain immigration laws to you upon arriving in the United States? Have you attended any immigration law or rights training workshops since coming to the United States?
8. I would like to learn about your experiences with the U.S. immigration system prior to your removal hearing. Could you tell me

about this? (prompts: encounters/interactions with CBP, ICE, police, USCIS employees, Detention and Removal employees, EOIR employees—judges, DHS attorneys, office staff, etc.)

9. I would also like to know more about your experience with the removal hearing process. When did you find out you were being placed in removal proceedings? Could you please tell me about this moment—what were you thinking? Did you know why were you placed in removal proceedings? (adjust subsequent questions to reflect number of removal hearing procedures experienced—i.e., ordered removed more than once?)

10. Were you held in detention leading up to and during your removal hearing? What was this like? (prompt: facility conditions, detention officers, other detainees/inmates, contact with lawyers/legal rights organizations, contact with family)

11. What, if anything, did you do to prepare for your removal hearing? (prompt: contact an attorney/legal aid, seek assistance from friends/family/church/community organizations)

12. Could you tell me a little bit about the actual hearing? What was it like? (prompt: your attorney, DHS attorney, judge, other people in the courtroom, were you in the courtroom or appearing from detention on TV, an interpreter, your family there, did you contest your removal/seek relief; how many times did you appear before a judge, was it always the same judge—adjust subsequent questions to reflect number of hearing appearances if applicable)

13. Did you understand what was going on during the hearing? (prompt: were the hearing procedures explained to you in advance or during the hearing, if you had a lawyer did s/he explain what happened after the hearing)

14. What did it feel like to be at the hearing?

15. Do you believe your hearing was fair? Why?

16. Did the judge appear biased or unbiased? Can you please explain?

17. Did the judge appear interested in your case or concerned about what was going to happen to you?

18. What about the DHS attorney, did he or she appear biased or unbiased? Did he or she seem to care about what was happening to you?

19. What about your own attorney (if applicable), did he or she appear biased or unbiased? Did he or she seem to care about what was happening to you?

20. What about the interpreter (if applicable), did he or she appear biased or unbiased? Did he or she seem to care about what was happening to you?

21. Do you feel that you were able to participate in your hearing? How so?

22. What was your reaction when you learned the outcome of your hearing? How did you feel about this outcome?

23. What happened after your hearing? (prompt: where did you go, what did you do, who were you with, etc.)

24. If you could change anything about your hearing, what would you change and why?

25. What are your current thoughts about the American immigration system? Do you believe that going through the removal hearing process changed the way you think about the American immigration system? How so?

26. If you could change anything about the American immigration system, what would you change and why?

27. What are you current thoughts on the American legal system? Do you believe that going through the removal hearing process changed the way you think about the American legal system? How so?

28. If you could change anything about the American legal system, what would you change and why?

29. What are you plans for the future?

30. If outside the United States (and applicable): Do you have plans to return to the United States? (prompt: why, how, concerns)

31. If inside the United States (and applicable): Why did you decide to remain in the United States? Do you have any concerns about your immigration status or future encounters with law enforcement or immigration enforcement?

32. If inside the United States (and applicable): Why did you decide to return to the United States? How did you return to the United States? Do you have any concerns about your immigration status or future encounters with law enforcement or immigration enforcement?

33. Is there anything else you would like to add?

NOTES

INTRODUCTION

1 Dana Leigh Marks, "Immigration Judge: Death Penalty Cases in a Traffic Court Setting," *CNN*, June 26, 2014, www.cnn.com.

2 Executive Office for Immigration Review, "EOIR Immigration Court Listing," U.S. Department of Justice, update June 21, 2021, www.justice.gov.

3 Both "deportation" and "exclusion" of noncitizens were replaced with "removal" by the 1996 Illegal Immigration Reform and Immigrant Responsibility Act (IIRIRA). The term "removal" applies to instances in which a noncitizen who was never properly admitted to the United States is being expelled, as well as instances in which a noncitizen who was properly admitted but violated one or more of the terms of admittance is being expelled. Kevin R. Johnson et al., *Understanding Immigration Law* (Newark, NJ: Matthew Bender & Company, Inc., 2009). "Removal" also includes those immigrants seeking admission to the United States who are being excluded (ibid.). Although individuals are no longer "deported" but rather "removed," I use the colloquial term "deportation" throughout this book.

4 TRAC Immigration, "Outcomes of Deportation Proceedings in Immigration Court," Immigration, data through May 2021, https://trac.syr.edu.

5 Executive Office of Immigration Review, *Statistics Yearbook Fiscal Year 2018*, U.S. Department of Justice, www.justice.gov; TRAC Immigration, "Immigration Court Processing Time by Outcome," data through May 2021, https://trac.syr.edu.

6 David J. Bier, "Mexico Deported More Central Americans Than the U.S. in 2018," CATO Institute, June 12, 2019, www.cato.org.

7 See Jacinta M. Gau and Rod K. Brunson, "Procedural Justice and Order Maintenance Policing: A Study of Inner-City Young Men's Perceptions of Police Legitimacy," *Justice Quarterly* 27 (April 2010): 255–79; Lyn Hinds, "Building Police-Youth Relationships: The Importance of Procedural Justice," *Youth Justice* 7 (December 2007): 195–209; Rebecca Hollander-Blumoff and Tom R. Tyler, "Procedural Justice in Negotiation: Procedural Fairness, Outcome Acceptance, and Integrative Potential," *Law & Social Inquiry* 33, no. 2 (2008): 473–500; Raymond Paternoster et al., "Do Fair Procedures Matter? The Effect of Procedural Justice on Spouse Assault," *Law & Society Review* 31, no. 1 (1997): 163–204; Jason Sunshine and Tom R. Tyler, "The Role of Procedural Justice and Legitimacy in Shaping Public Support for Policing," *Law & Society Review* 37, no. 3 (2003): 513–48; Tom

R. Tyler, "Procedural Justice, Legitimacy, and the Effective Rule of Law," *Crime and Justice* 30 (2003): 283–357.

8 See Matt Adams, "Advancing the Right to Counsel in Removal Proceedings," *Seattle Journal of Social Justice* 9, no. 1 (2010): 169–83; American Bar Association, *Reforming the Immigration System: Proposals to Promote Independence, Fairness, Efficiency, and Professionalism in the Adjudication of Removal Cases* (Washington, D.C.: American Bar Association, 2019); Peter L. Markowitz, "Barriers to Representation for Detained Immigrants Facing Deportation: Varick Street Detention Facility, A Case Study," *Fordham Law Review* 78 (2009): 1–31; Banks Miller, Linda Camp Keith, and Jennifer S. Holmes, "Leveling the Odds: The Effect of Quality Legal Representation in the Cases of Asymmetrical Capability," *Law & Society Review* 49, no. 1 (2015): 209–39; Marjorie Zatz and Nancy Rodriguez, *Dreams and Nightmares: Immigration Policy, Youth, and Families* (Berkeley: University of California Press, 2015).

9 I also gained access to a nonprofit's client database and was surprised by the ease with which I identified willing participants through cold-calling.

10 Convenience and snowball sampling are two commonly used nonprobability sampling techniques that are well suited for research involving difficult-to-access populations, such as immigrants. Earl Babbie, *The Practice of Social Research* (Belmont, CA: Thomson Higher Education, 2015); Mario Luis Small, "'How Many Cases Do I Need?': On Science and the Logic of Case Selection in Field-Based Research," *Ethnography* 10, no. 1 (2009): 5–38. Convenience sampling relies upon a researcher's preexisting social networks—or networks developed with the project in mind—to invite participants to take part in the study. Snowball sampling draws upon participants' social networks to recruit additional participants through referrals. This strategy facilitates trust between the researcher and recruits. Kay Standing, "Writing the Voices of the Less Powerful: Research on Lone Mothers," in J. Ribbens and R. Edwards, eds., *Feminist Dilemmas in Qualitative Research: Public Knowledge and Private Lives* (Thousand Oaks, CA: Sage Publications, 1998), 186–202.

11 It is well established that interviews are interactional events in which the positionalities and identities of the "researcher" and the "participant" can impact the resulting data. Maxine Birch and Tina Miller, "Encouraging Participation: Ethics and Responsibilities," in M. Mauthner, M. Birch, J. Jessop, and T. Miller, eds., *Ethics in Qualitative Research* (Thousand Oaks, CA: Sage Publications, 2002), 91–106; Roberta Villalón, *Violence Against Latina Immigrants: Citizenship, Inequality, and Community* (New York: New York University Press, 2010). With this in mind, I deliberately crafted my interview script to facilitate conversational exchanges that set participants at ease, reduced the power differential between researcher and participant, and afforded participants space for expression as well as silence. James A. Holstein and Jaber F. Gubrium, "Active Interviewing," in D. Silverman, ed., *Qualitative Research: Theory, Method, and Practice* (London: Sage Publica-

tions, 1997), 113–28; David A. Snow, Louis A. Zurcher, and Gideon Sjoberg, "Interviewing by Comment: An Adjunct to the Direct Question," *Qualitative Sociology* 5, no. 4 (1982): 285–311; Standing, "Writing the Voices."

12 Patricia Ewick and Susan S. Silbey, *The Common Place of Law: Stories from Everyday Life* (Chicago: University of Chicago Press, 1998).

13 Although interview data reveal important insights into participants' feelings about fair process, observations of procedural justice in "natural settings" by a "neutral" third party provide an "outside" referent regarding legal actors' behaviors and interactions between these actors and others during a legal encounter. Tal Jonathan-Zamir, Stephen D. Mastrofski, and Shomron Moyal, "Measuring Procedural Justice in Police-Citizen Encounters," *Justice Quarterly* 32, no. 5 (2015): 845–71.

14 Executive Office for Immigration Review, "FY 2014 Statistical YearBook," U.S. Department of Justice, 2015, www.justice.gov.

15 EOIR, "FY 2014 Statistical YearBook."

16 TRAC Immigration, "Outcomes of Deportation Proceedings in Immigration Court."

17 Several interpreters I interacted with during my court observations explicitly mentioned fear of reprisals for even being seen speaking to me given restrictions on speaking to the public as outlined in their employment contracts. This exploitative treatment of immigration court interpreters is well known among immigration and interpretation circles and has been the cause of several recent labor disputes over wages, employee classification, and union-busting. Nina Agrawal, "Judge Orders Compensation, Reclassification for Immigration Court Interpreters," *Los Angeles Times*, March 14, 2018, www.latimes.com; Maya P. Barak, "Can You Hear Me Now? Attorney Perceptions of Interpretation, Technology, and Power in Immigration Court," *Journal on Migration and Human Security* 9, no. 4 (2021): 207–23.

18 I was fortunate to receive a Tinker Field Research grant, allowing me to spend one month during spring 2014 conducting fieldwork in El Salvador and Guatemala. This trip provided additional historical, political, and social context with regard to migration from the region. As discussed in chapter 1, migration from these Northern Triangle countries has followed remarkably similar trajectories, in the case of El Salvador and Guatemala spurred primarily by civil war and state terrorism in the 1980s and 1990s and subsequently, in all three countries, by gang violence and state weakness. This has prompted various political and legal responses from the United States and resulted in differential opportunities and experiences for Central Americans who find themselves caught up in the American immigration system. As numbers of Central Americans fleeing violence—including an unprecedented number of child and teen migrants— have soared in recent years, numerous tensions and structural inequalities within the immigration system have been revealed. Although such tensions were made apparent in immigrant and attorney interviews I conducted in the

United States, they were also brought to light in conversations with academics, government officials, social justice activists, and deportees and their family members during Central American fieldwork.

19 Jon B. Gould and Maya P. Barak, *Capital Defense: Inside the Lives of America's Death Penalty Lawyers* (New York: New York University Press, 2019).

20 American Immigration Lawyers Association, *The 2016 AILA Marketplace Study: A National Reference on the Economics of Immigration Law Practice*, 2016.

21 Katherine Abbott, Maya Barak, and Austin Kocher, "Public Stakeholder Forum: Preliminary Findings from the National Immigration Lawyer Survey," Washington College of Law, American University, Washington, D.C., May 2019.

22 Kathleen Hull and Robert Nelson, "Assimilation, Choice, or Constraint: Testing Theories of Gender Differences in the Careers of Lawyers," *Social Forces* 79, no. 1 (2000): 229–64; Susan E. Martin and Nancy C. Jurik, *Doing Justice, Doing Gender: Women in Legal and Criminal Justice Occupations*, 2nd ed. (New York: Sage Publications, 2006).

23 John P. Heinz et al., *Urban Lawyers: The New Social Structure of the Bar* (Chicago: University of Chicago Press, 2005).

24 Silva Mathema, "Keeping Families Together," Center for American Progress, March 16, 2017, www.americanprogress.org.

25 Cecilia Menjívar, "Liminal Legality: Salvadoran and Guatemalan Immigrants' Lives in the United States," *American Journal of Sociology* 111, no. 4 (2006): 999–1037.

26 Department of Homeland Security, "Table 39. Aliens Removed or Returned: Fiscal Years 1892–2019," December 8, 2021, www.dhs.gov.

27 U.S. Immigration and Customs Enforcement, "Fiscal Year 2020 Enforcement and Removal Operations Report," www.ice.gov.

28 ERO-LESA Statistical Tracking Unit, "ICE Removals by Criminality FY2006–FY2017," www.ice.gov.

29 For discussions on how interview research mitigates some of the limitations of survey-based procedural justice research, see Rod K. Brunson and Jody Miller, "Young Black Men and Urban Policing in the United States," *British Journal of Criminology* 46, no. 4 (2006): 613–40; Patrick J. Carr, Laura Napolitano, and Jessica Keating, "We Never Call the Cops and Here Is Why: A Qualitative Examination of Legal Cynicism in Three Philadelphia Neighborhoods," *Criminology* 45, no. 2 (2007): 445–80; Irina Elliot, Stuart Thomas, and James Ogloff, "Procedural Justice in Victim-Police Interactions and Victims' Recovery from Victimisation Experiences," *Policing and Society* 25, no. 5 (2014): 588–601; Michael D. Reisig, Justice Tankebe, and Gorazd Meško, "Compliance with the Law in Slovenia: The Role of Procedural Justice and Police Legitimacy," *European Journal on Criminal Policy and Research* 20, no. 2 (2014): 259–76. For discussions on the benefits of observation-based procedural justice research, see Jonathan-Zamir et al., "Measuring Procedural Justice."

1. MODERN DAY DEPORTATION

1 Enrique Baloyra, *El Salvador in Transition* (Chapel Hill: University of North Carolina Press, 1982); Steve Hobden, "El Salvador: Civil War, Civil Society and the State," *Civil Wars* 3, no. 2 (2000): 106–20.

2 Hobden, "El Salvador."

3 Susan B. Coutin, *Legalizing Moves: Salvadoran Immigrants' Struggle for U.S. Residency* (Ann Arbor: University of Michigan Press, 2000).

4 Tom Barry, *Roots of Rebellion: Land and Hunger in Central America* (Boston: South End Press, 1987); Alex Segovia, *Transformación Estructural y Reforma Económica en El Salvador: El Funcionamiento Económico de los Noventa y Sus Efectos Sobre el Crecimiento, la Pobreza, y la Distribución del Ingreso* (Berkeley: University of California Press, 2002); Alex Segovia, "A Portrait of the Region's Large Economic Groups," *Revista Envío* 308 (2007), www.envio.org.ni; Robert G. Williams, *Export Agriculture and the Crisis in Central America* (Chapel Hill: University of North Carolina Press, 1986).

5 Rubiana Chamarbagwala and Hilcías E. Morán, "The Human Capital Consequences of Civil War: Evidence from Guatemala," *Journal of Development Economics* 94 (January 2011): 41–61; Randall Janzen, "From Less War to More Peace: Guatemala's Journey since 1996," *Peace Research* 40, no. 1 (2008): 55–75.

6 Chamarbagwala and Morán, "The Human Capital Consequences of Civil War"; Paula Godoy-Paiz, Brenda Toner, and Carolina Vidal, "'Something in Our Hearts': Challenges to Mental Health among Urban Mayan Women in Post-War Guatemala," *Ethnicity and Inequalities in Health and Social Care* 4, no. 3 (2011): 127–37; Nora Hamilton and Norma Stoltz Chinchilla, "Central American Migration: A Framework for Analysis," *Latin American Research Review* 26, no. 1 (1991): 75–110.

7 Michael P. Anastario et al., "Factors Driving Salvadoran Youth Migration: A Formative Assessment Focused on Salvadoran Repatriation Facilities," *Children and Youth Services Review* 59 (December 2015): 97–104.

8 Anastario et al., "Factors Driving Salvadoran Youth Migration"; Luis Noe-Bustamante, Antonio Flores, and Soon Shah, "Facts on Hispanics of Salvadoran Origin in the United States, 2017," Pew Research Center, September 16, 2019, www.pewresearch.org; D'Vera Cohn, Jeffrey S. Passel, and Ana Gonzalez-Barrera, "Rise in U.S. Immigrants from El Salvador, Guatemala and Honduras Outpaces Growth from Elsewhere," Pew Research Center, December 7, 2017, www.pewresearch.org.

9 Noe-Bustamante, Flores, and Shah, "Facts on Hispanics of Guatemalan Origin in the United States, 2017"; Cohn, Passel, and Gonzalez-Barrera, "Rise in U.S. Immigrants."

10 Bryan Baker, "Estimates of the Unauthorized Immigrant Population Residing in the United States: January 2015–January 2018," *Department of Homeland Security* (January 2021), www.dhs.gov.

11 Susan B. Coutin, *Nation of Emigrants: Shifting Boundaries of Citizenship in El Salvador and the United States* (Ithaca, NY: Cornell University Press, 2007); Susanne

Jonas, "Guatemalan Migration in Times of Civil War and Post-War Challenges," Migration Policy Institute, www.migrationpolicy.org; Cecilia Menjívar, "Liminal Legality: Salvadoran and Guatemalan Immigrants' Lives in the United States," *American Journal of Sociology* 111, no. 4 (2006): 999–1037.

12 J. Mark Ruhl, "Honduras Unravels," *Journal of Democracy* 21, no. 2 (2010): 93–107; Leah Schmalzbauer, "Family Divided: The Class Formation of Honduran Transnational Families," *Global Networks* 8, no. 3 (2008): 329–46.

13 Sean McKenzie and Cecilia Menjívar, "The Meanings of Migration, Remittances and Gifts: Views of Honduran Women Who Stay," *Global Networks* 11, no. 1 (2011): 63–81; Robert A. McLeman and Lori M. Hunter, "Migration in the Context of Vulnerability and Adaptation to Climate Change: Insights from Analogues," *Wiley Interdisciplinary Reviews: Climate Change* 1, no. 3 (2010): 450–61.

14 Ben Wisner, "Risk and the Neoliberal State: Why Post-Mitch Lessons Didn't Reduce El Salvador's Earthquake Losses," *Disasters* 25, no. 3 (2001): 251–68.

15 Coutin, *Nation of Emigrants*.

16 Coutin, *Nation of Emigrants*.

17 Christina A. Pryor, "'Aging Out' of Immigration: Analyzing Family Preference Visa Petitions under the Child Status Protection Act," *Fordham Law Review* 80, no. 5 (2012): 2199–239.

18 Immigration and Customs Enforcement, "Immigration Detention Facilities," update March 11, 2021, www.ice.gov.

19 From 2008 to 2014, ICE operated Secure Communities, an information-sharing program operated in tandem with the FBI and state and local criminal justice law enforcement agencies to target removable immigrants. This occurred via the automatic sharing of FBI fingerprint database information with ICE, which would run fingerprint checks against its own records; in the event that such checks revealed that an individual was "not a U.S. citizen or [was] removable from the United States because of their criminal history," ICE would flag the individual for immigration enforcement, often placing a detainer on the individual and requesting that s/he be transferred into ICE custody for processing. U.S. Immigration and Customs Enforcement, "Secure Communities," www.ice.gov. In July 2015, Secure Communities was replaced with the Priority Enforcement Program (PEP), which enables "DHS to work with state and local law enforcement to take custody of individuals who pose a danger to public safety before those individuals are released into our communities." Immigration and Customs Enforcement, "Priority Enforcement Program," www.ice.gov. PEP prioritizes individuals who have violated civil immigration law, individuals who have intentionally participated in gang activity, or individuals who pose a national security threat (ibid.).

20 Kevin R. Johnson et al., *Understanding Immigration Law* (Newark, NJ: Matthew Bender & Company, Inc., 2009).

21 For example, approximately two-thirds of all those deported in FY2019 and FY2020 were initially arrested by CBP, and approximately one-third were initially arrested by ICE. U.S. Immigration and Customs Enforcement, "Fiscal Year 2019

Enforcement and Removal Operations Report," www.ice.gov; U.S. Immigration and Customs Enforcement, "Fiscal Year 2020 Enforcement and Removal Operations Report," www.ice.gov.

22 Executive Office for Immigration Review, "FY 2014 Statistical Year Book," U.S. Department of Justice, www.justice.gov; Executive Office for Immigration Review, "Statistics Yearbook Fiscal Year 2018," U.S. Department of Justice, www.justice. gov.

23 "ISAP I" was a ten-city pilot program funded by Congress for a period of five years beginning in 2004. Office of the Inspector General, "U.S. Immigration and Customs Enforcement's Alternatives to Detention (Revised)," U.S. Department of Homeland Security, February 4, 2015, www.oig.dhs.gov. In 2009, "ISAP II" expanded the supervision program nationwide (ibid.). ISAP services are provided by government contractors (ibid.).

24 Office of the Inspector General, "U.S. Immigration and Customs Enforcement's Alternatives to Detention (Revised)."

25 TRAC Immigration, "New ICE Data Show Both Immigrants Detained and Monitored on ATD Increase in May," https://trac.syr.edu; U.S. Immigration and Customs Enforcement, "ICE Alternatives to Detention Data, F21," www.ice.gov.

26 Abed Ayoub and Khaled Beydoun, "Executive Disorder: The Muslim Ban, Emergency Advocacy, and the Fires Next Time," *Journal of Race and Law* 22, no. 2 (2017): 215–41.

27 TRAC Immigration, "The Life and Death of Administrative Closure," September 10, 2020, https://trac.syr.edu.

28 Austin Kocher, "Migrant Protection Protocols and the Death of Asylum," *Journal of Latin American Geography* 20, no. 1 (2021): 249–58.

29 Protecting Immigrant Families, "What Advocates Need to Know Now," National Immigration Law Center, May 13, 2021, www.nilc.org.

30 Maria Sacchetti and Nick Miroff, "Trump Administration Preparing to Close International Immigration Offices," *Washington Post*, March 12, 2019, www.washingtonpost.com.

31 Beginning in 2017, the Trump administration took a number of controversial steps to increase immigration court efficiency and address the courts' backlog, including the implementation of case completion quotas for immigration judges. Office of the Attorney General, "Renewing Our Commitment to the Timely and Efficient Adjudication of Immigration Cases to Serve the National Interest," Memorandum for the Executive Office for Immigration Review (Washington, D.C.: U.S. Department of Justice, 2017), www.justice.gov; Executive Office for Immigration Review, "Case Priorities and Immigration Court Performance Measures," Memorandum to Office of the Chief Immigration Judge, All Immigration Judges, All Court Administrators, and All Immigration Staff (Washington, D.C.: U.S. Department of Justice, 2018), www.justice.gov; Executive Office for Immigration Review, "No Dark Courtrooms," Memorandum to All of EOIR (Washington, D.C.: U.S. Department of Justice, 2019), www.justice.gov.

32 The Trump administration moved to restrict the grounds for asylum. In *Matter of A-B-* (2018), then–Attorney General Jeff Sessions overruled the BIA's previous decision in *Matter of A-R-C-G-* (2014), setting new case precedent restricting asylum claims based on domestic violence and gang violence. Office of the Attorney General, "Matter of A-B-, Respondent," U.S. Department of Justice, June 11, 2018, www.immpolicytracking.org.

33 Coutin, *Legalizing Moves*; Coutin, *Nation of Emigrants*; McKenzie and Menjívar, "The Meanings of Migration"; Menjívar, "Liminal Legality"; Cecilia Menjívar, "The Power of the Law: Central Americans' Legality and Everyday Life in Phoenix, Arizona," *Latino Studies* 9, no. 4 (2011): 377–95.

34 8 U.S.C. § 1325.

35 Johnson et al., *Understanding Immigration Law*.

36 Johnson et al., *Understanding Immigration Law*.

37 U.S. Citizenship and Immigration Services, "Temporary Protected Status," update May 24, 2021, www.uscis.gov.

38 In 2020, the Ninth Circuit Court of Appeals reversed a lower court's ruling blocking the Trump administration's plan to phase out TPS for Salvadorans in addition to Haitians, Nicaraguans, and Sudanese. In May 2021, the Biden administration extended TPS for Haitians (Jaclyn Diaz, "More Than 100,000 Haitian Immigrants Can Apply for an Extension to Stay in the U.S.," *NPR*, May 24, 2021, www.npr.org).

39 National Immigration Forum, "Fact Sheet: Temporary Protected Status (TPS)," update March 12, 2021, https://immigrationforum.org.

40 Coutin, *Legalizing Moves*; Coutin, *Nation of Emigrants*; Menjivar, "Liminal Legality."

41 NACARA also created an amnesty program for some Cuban and Nicaraguan nationals continuously present in the United States from 1995 to April 2000 (Johnson et al., *Understanding Immigration Law*).

42 Sílvia Roque, "Between New Terrains and Old Dichotomies: Peacebuilding and the Gangs' Truce in El Salvador," *Contexto Internacional* 39, no. 3 (2017): 499–520.

43 Roque, "Between New Terrains."

44 C. M. Katz, E. C. Hedberg, and L. E. Amaya, "Gang Truce for Violence Prevention, El Salvador," *Bulletin of the World Health Organization* 94, no. 9 (2016): 660–66A; Roque, "Between New Terrains."

45 Joshua Partlow, "Why El Salvador Became the Hemisphere's Murder Capital," *Washington Post*, September 16, 2015, www.washingtonpost.com.

46 InSight Crime, "Gangs in Honduras," report made for review by the United States Agency for International Development, April 21, 2016, https://insightcrime.org.

47 Manu Brabo, "Gang Wars in El Salvador, Bloodiest Year," *Al Jazeera*, September 16, 2015, www.aljazeera.com.

48 For the sake of comparison, this would equate to nearly 551 homicides per hour in the United States; that same year, the United States averaged just 1.8 homicides per hour. Criminal Justice Information Services Division, "Crime in the United States, 2015," Federal Bureau of Investigation, https://ucr.fbi.gov (released Fall 2016).

49 Jocelyn Courtney, "The Civil War That Was Fought by Children: Understanding the Role of Child Combatants in El Salvador's Civil War, 1980–1992," *Journal of Military History* 74, no. 2 (2010): 523–56.

50 Dennis Stinchcomb and Eric Hershberg, "Unaccompanied Migrant Children from Central America: Context, Causes, and Responses," *Center for Latin American and Latino Studies* 7 (December 2014).

51 *Renta*, or "rent," is the slang term commonly used to refer to gang extortion fees. Dean Neu, "Accounting for Extortion," *Accounting, Organizations and Society* 76 (2019): 50–63.

52 InSight Crime, "Gangs in Honduras"; Deborah T. Levenson, *Adiós Niño: The Gangs of Guatemala City and the Politics of Death* (Durham, NC: Duke University Press, 2013); Ruhl, "Honduras Unravels."

53 InSight Crime, "Gangs in Honduras"; Stinchcomb and Hershberg, "Unaccompanied Migrant Children."

54 The deterioration of the political situation in Honduras is also directly related to the 2009 coup d'état ousting former president Manuel Zelaya, which destabilized the government and led to increased migration to the United States. McKenzie and Menjívar, "The Meanings of Migration." For further discussion on corruption and impunity in Guatemala and Honduras, see José Miguel Cruz, "Police Misconduct and Political Legitimacy in Central America," *Journal of Latin American Studies* 47, no. 2 (2015): 251–83; Mike LaSusa, "Judge in Guatemala Corruption Case Charged with Taking Bribes," *InSight Crime*, December, 9, 2015, www.insightcrime.org; Michael Lohmuller, "Assessing El Salvador's Gangs in a Post-Truce Contex," *InSight Crime*, November 30, 2015, www.insightcrime.org; Cameron McKibben, "Corruption Scandal and the International Commission Against Impunity in Guatemala," *Washington Report on the Hemisphere* 35, no. 6 (2015): 7–8.

55 Stinchcomb and Hershberg, "Unaccompanied Migrant Children"; Jie Zong and Jeanne Batalova, "Central American Immigrants in the United States," Migration Policy Institute, September 2, 2015, www.migrationpolicy.org.

56 Stinchcomb and Hershberg, "Unaccompanied Migrant Children."

57 Stinchcomb and Hershberg, "Unaccompanied Migrant Children."

58 TRAC Immigration, "Immigration Court Backlog Tool," data through May 2021, http://trac.syr.edu.

59 J. Rawls, *A Theory of Justice* (Cambridge, MA: Harvard University Press, 1971); E. Allan Lind and Tom R. Tyler, *The Social Psychology of Procedural Justice* (New York: Plenum Press, 1988).

60 John W. Thibaut and Laurens Walker, *Procedural Justice: A Psychological Analysis* (New York: L. Erlbaum Associates, 1975).

61 Krist D. Forrest and Richard L. Miller, "Procedural Justice in the College Classroom," *For Teachers of Introductory Psychology* 18, no. 1 (2008): 1–10.

62 Jonathan D. Casper, Tom Tyler, and Bonnie Fisher, "Procedural Justice in Felony Cases," *Law & Society Review* 22, no. 3 (1988): 483–508.

63 Karin A. Beijersbergen, Anja J. E. Dirkzwager, and Paul Nieuwbeerta, "Does Procedural Justice During Imprisonment Matter?" *Criminal Justice and Behavior* 43,
no. 1 (2016): 63–82; Karin A. Beijersbergen et al., "Procedural Justice, Anger, and
Prisoners' Misconduct," *Criminal Justice and Behavior* 42, no. 2 (2015): 196–218;
Edward R. Maguire, Cassandra A. Atkin-Plunk, and William Wells, "The Effects
of Procedural Justice on Cooperation and Compliance Among Inmates in a Work
Release Program," *Justice Quarterly* 38, no. 6 (2021): 1128–53.

64 Susan L. Miller and M. Kristen Hefner, "Procedural Justice for Victims and Offenders? Exploring Restorative Justice Processes in Australia and the U.S.," *Justice
Quarterly* 32, no. 1 (2015): 142–67.

65 Nusret Sahin et al., "The Impact of Procedurally-Just Policing on Citizen Perceptions of Police During Traffic Stops: The Adana Randomized Controlled Trial,"
Journal of Quantitative Criminology 33 (December 2017): 701–26.

66 For more on procedural justice in the workplace, see Robert J. Bies and Debra L.
Shapiro, "Voice and Justification: Their Influence on Procedural Fairness Judgments," *Academy of Management Journal* 31, no. 3 (1988): 676–85; Steven L. Blader
and Tom R. Tyler, "A Four-Component Model of Procedural Justice: Defining the
Meaning of a 'Fair' Process," *Personality and Social Psychology Bulletin* 29 (June
2003): 747–58; Robert Folger, "Distributive and Procedural Justice: Combined
Impact of 'Voice' and Improvement on Experienced Inequity," *Journal of Personality and Social Psychology* 35, no. 2 (1977): 108–99.

67 Rebecca Hollander-Blumoff and Tom R. Tyler, "Procedural Justice in Negotiation: Procedural Fairness, Outcome Acceptance, and Integrative Potential," *Law &
Social Inquiry* 33, no. 2 (2008): 477.

68 Jeffrey Fagan and Tom R. Tyler, "Legal Socialization of Children and Adolescents,"
Social Justice Research 18, no. 3 (2005): 217–42.

69 Kees Van den Bos and E. Allan Lind, "Uncertainty Management by Means of Fairness Judgments," in M. P. Zanna, ed., *Advances in Experimental Social Psychology*
34 (New York: Academic Press, 2002), 19; Irina Elliot, Stuart Thomas, and James
Ogloff, "Procedural Justice in Victim-Police Interactions and Victims' Recovery
from Victimisation Experiences," *Policing and Society* 25, no. 2 (2014): 588–601.

70 Van den Bos and Lind, "Uncertainty Management," 19.

71 Raymond Paternoster et al., "Do Fair Procedures Matter? The Effect of Procedural
Justice on Spouse Assault," *Law & Society Review* 31, no. 1 (1997): 163–204; Tom R.
Tyler, "Procedural Justice, Legitimacy, and the Effective Rule of Law," *Crime and
Justice* 30 (2003): 283–357.

72 Blader and Tyler, "A Four-Component Model"; Tom R. Tyler, "What Is Procedural
Justice? Criteria Used by Citizens to Assess the Fairness of Legal Procedures," *Law
& Society Review* 22, no. 1 (1998): 103–36.

73 For a discussion of profiling and police legitimacy, see T. R. Tyler and C. J. Wak-
slak, "Profiling and Police Legitimacy: Procedural Justice, Attributions of Motive,
and Acceptance of Police Authority," *Criminology* 42, no. 2 (2004): 253–81.

74 Jacinta M. Gau and Rod K. Brunson, "Procedural Justice and Order Maintenance Policing: A Study of Inner-City Young Men's Perceptions of Police Legitimacy," *Justice Quarterly* 27, no. 2 (2010): 255–79; Lyn Hinds, "Building Police-Youth Relationships: The Importance of Procedural Justice," *Youth Justice* 7, no. 3 (2007): 195–209; Paternoster et al., "Do Fair Procedures Matter?"; Jason Sunshine and Tom R. Tyler, "The Role of Procedural Justice and Legitimacy in Shaping Public Support for Policing," *Law & Society Review* 37, no. 3 (2003): 513–48; Tyler, "Procedural Justice, Legitimacy, and the Effective Rule of Law."

75 Tyler, "What Is Procedural Justice?"

76 Gau and Brunson, "Procedural Justice and Order Maintenance Policing"; Hinds, "Building Police-Youth Relationships"; Joel Brockner et al., "Culture and Procedural Justice: The Influence of Power Distance on Reactions to Voice," *Journal of Experimental Social Psychology* 37 (2001): 300–15; Folger, "Distributive and Procedural Justice"; E. Allan Lind, P. Christopher Earley, and Ruth Kanfer, "Voice, Control, and Procedural Justice: Instrumental and Noninstrumental Concerns in Fairness Judgments," *Journal of Personality and Social Psychology* 59, no. 5 (1990): 952–59; Paternoster et al., "Do Fair Procedures Matter?"; Sunshine and Tyler, "The Role of Procedural Justice and Legitimacy"; Tyler, "Procedural Justice, Legitimacy, and the Effective Rule of Law."

77 Bies and Shapiro, "Voice and Justification."

78 As Bies and Shapiro examine hiring decisions, they caution against applying their findings to other settings, such as in the case of criminal justice decisions relying upon "policy and rules" (Bies and Shapiro, "Voice and Justification").

79 Barrett-Howard and Tyler find that bias suppression, decision quality, consistency, and representation matter more to individuals in formal settings than informal ones when making procedural justice assessments. Edith Barret-Howard and Tom Tyler, "Procedural Justice as a Criterion in Allocation Decisions," *Journal of Personality and Social Psychology* 50, no. 2 (1986): 296–304.

80 Barrett-Howard and Tyler also find that individuals care more about consistency, decision quality, and ethicality in cooperative situations. Barret-Howard and Tyler, "Procedural Justice as a Criterion."

81 Tyler notes that opportunities for input and consistency of treatment matter more in assessments of dispute resolution processes than they do in nondispute contexts. Tyler, "What Is Procedural Justice?"

82 Tyler also finds that individuals give more weight to decision quality, bias, and correctability in courtroom encounters than in police encounters. Tyler, "What Is Procedural Justice?"

83 Casper, Tyler, and Fisher, "Procedural Justice in Felony Cases"; Tyler, "What Is Procedural Justice?"

84 Devon Johnson et al., "Race and Perceptions of Police: Experimental Results on the Impact of Procedural (In)Justice," *Justice Quarterly* 34, no. 7 (2017): 1184–1212; Robin Shapiro Engel, "Citizens' Perceptions of Distributive and Procedural

Injustice during Traffic Stops with Police," *Journal of Research in Crime and Delinquency* 42 (2005): 445–81; Tom R. Tyler, "Policing in Black and White: Ethnic Group Differences in Trust and Confidence in the Police," *Police Quarterly* 8 (2005): 322–42; Patricia Warren, "Perceptions of Police Disrespect during Vehicle Stops: A Race-Based Analysis," *Crime & Delinquency* 57 (2011): 356–76.

85 Blader and Tyler, "A Four-Component Model."

86 Casper, Tyler, and Fisher, "Procedural Justice in Felony Cases."

87 Tyler, "Procedural Justice, Legitimacy, and the Effective Rule of Law," 1.

88 Devon Johnson, Edward R. Maguire, and Joseph B. Kuhns, "Public Perceptions of the Legitimacy of the Law and Legal Authorities: Evidence from the Caribbean" *Law & Society Review* 48, no. 4 (2014): 947–78.

89 See also Robert J. Bies, "The Predicament of Injustice: The Management of Moral Outrage," in L. L. Cummings and Barry M. Staw, eds., *Research in Organizational Behavior* 9 (Greenwich, CT: JAI Press, 1987), 289–319; Karl E. Weick, *The Social Psychology of Organizing*, 2nd ed. (Reading, MA: Addison Wesley, 1979).

90 Kennth Sebastián León, "Latino Criminology: Unfucking Colonial Frameworks in 'Latinos and Crime' Scholarship," *Critical Criminology* 29 (2021): 11–35.

91 Similarly, Baćak and Apel argue that most European studies of procedural justice treat "the continent as a homogenous whole" or focus exclusively on "established democracies." Valerio Baćak and Robert Apel, "Police Fairness and Legitimacy across the Post-Communist Divide in Europe," *Law & Society Review* 55 (2021): 474.

92 The criminologist Daniel K. Pryce argues for the expansion of procedural justice research "beyond the *majority* community into different sociological or sociopolitical contexts to increase scholars' understanding of *all* community members' experiences with, assessments of, and beliefs about the police." Daniel K. Pryce, "Ghanaian Immigrants' Experiences with and Perceptions of U.S. Police: A Qualitative Study," *Criminal Justice Review* 41, no. 4 (2016): 469–87. See also Ivan Y. Sun et al., "Procedural Justice, Legitimacy, and Public Cooperation with Police: Does Western Wisdom Hold in China?" *Journal of Research in Crime and Delinquency* 54, no. 4 (2017): 454–78.

93 Doron Dorfman, "Re-claiming Disability: Identity, Procedural Justice, and the Disability Determination Process," *Law & Social Inquiry* 42, no. 1 (2017): 195–231.

94 Dorian Schaap and Elsa Saarikkomäki, "Rethinking Police Procedural Justice," *Theoretical Criminology* (2022): 1–18.

95 Schaap and Saarikkomäki, "Rethinking Police Procedural Justice."

96 Joseph R. Tatar II, Suzanne O. Kaasa, and Elizabeth Cauffman, "Perceptions of Procedural Justice Among Female Offenders: Time Does Not Heal All Wounds," *Psychology, Public Policy, and Law* 18, no. 2 (2012): 268–96.

97 Toby Miles-Johnson, "Confidence and Trust in Police: How Sexual Identity Difference Shapes Perceptions of Police," *Current Issues in Criminal Justice* 25, no. 2 (2013): 685–702; Kevin L. Nadal et al., "Lesbian, Gay, Bisexual, and Queer People's Perceptions of the Criminal Justice System: Implications for Social Services," *Journal of Gay & Lesbian Social Services* 27, no. 4 (2015): 457–81.

98 However, for a discussion of the interplay of race/ethnicity and gender in defining citizens' experiences and perceptions of police encounters, see Joshua C. Cohran and Patricia Y. Warren, "Racial, Ethnic, and Gender Differences in Perceptions of the Police: The Salience of Officer Race Within the Context of Racial Profiling," *Journal of Contemporary Criminal Justice* 28, no. 2 (2012): 210. For a discussion of the effects of the intersections of gender, race, parenthood, and poverty on legal cynicism, see Monica C. Bell, "Situational Trust: How Disadvantaged Mothers Reconcile Legal Cynicism," *Law & Society Review* 50, no. 2 (2016): 314–47.

99 Kimberlé Crenshaw, "Demarginalizing the Intersection of Race and Sex: A Black Feminist Critique of Antidiscrimination Doctrine, Feminist Theory and Antiracist Politics," *University of Chicago Legal Forum* 1989, no. 1 (1989): 139–67; Kimberlé Crenshaw, "Mapping the Margins: Intersectionality, Identity Politics, and Violence Against Women of Color," *Stanford Law Review* 43, no. 6 (1991): 1241–99.

100 Maya Barak, "Fairness and the Law: Central American Experiences in U.S. Immigration Court," in Samantha Fletcher and Holly White, eds., *Emerging Voices: Critical Social Research by European Group Postgraduate and Early Career Researchers* (Weston-super-Mare, UK: European Group Press, 2017), 3–14.

101 Miles-Johnson, "Confidence and Trust in Police."

102 Toby Miles-Johnson, "'They Don't Identify with Us': Perceptions of Police by Australian Transgender People," *International Journal of Transgenderism* 16, no. 3 (2015): 169–89.

103 Hinds, "Building Police-Youth Relationships"; for a discussion on urban youths' perceptions of the police, see Patrick J. Carr, Laura Napolitano, and Jessica Keating, "We Never Call the Cops and Here Is Why: A Qualitative Examination of Legal Cynicism in Three Philadelphia Neighborhoods," *Criminology* 45, no. 2 (2007): 445–80.

104 Rod K. Brunson and Jody Miller, "Young Black Men and Urban Policing in the United States," *British Journal of Criminology* 46, no. 4 (2006): 613–40; Carr, Napolitano, and Keating, "We Never Call the Cops."

105 Fagan and Tyler, "Legal Socialization of Children and Adolescents."

106 For a discussion of Ghanaian immigrants' perceptions of distributive and procedural justice, see Pryce, "Ghanaian Immigrants' Experiences."

107 Richard Sparks and Anthony Bottoms, "Legitimacy and Imprisonment Revisited: Some Notes on the Problem of Order Ten Years After," in J. Byrne, F. Taxman, and D. Hummer, eds., *The Culture of Prison Violence* (Boston: Pearson, 2007), 91–104.

108 Valerie Jenness and Kitty Calavita, "It Depends on the Outcome: Prisoners, Grievances, and Perceptions of Justice," *Law & Society Review* 52, no. 1 (2018): 41–72.

109 Lyn Hinds and Kristina Murphy, "Public Satisfaction with Police: Using Procedural Justice to Improve Police Legitimacy," *Australian and New Zealand Journal of Criminology* 40 (2007): 27–43; Natasha S. Madon, Kristina Murphy, and Elise Sergeant, "Promoting Police Legitimacy Among Disengaged Minority Groups: Does Procedural Justice Matter More?," *Criminology and Criminal Justice* 17, no. 5 (2017): 624–42; Lorraine Mazerolle et al., "Shaping Citizen Perceptions of

Police Legitimacy: A Randomized Field Trial of Procedural Justice," *Criminology* 51 (February 2013): 33–64; Miller and Hefner, "Procedural Justice for Victims and Offenders?"; Kristina Murphy, "Policing at the Margins: Fostering Trust and Cooperation Among Ethnic Minority Groups," *Journal of Policing, Intelligence and Counter Terrorism* 8, no. 2 (2013): 184–99.

110 Maarten Van Craen, "Explaining Majority and Minority Trust in the Police," *Justice Quarterly* 30, no. 6 (2013): 1042–67.

111 Thiago R Oliveira, André Zanetic, and Ariadne Natal, "Preditores e Impactos da Legimidade Policial: Testando a Teoria da Justeza Procedimental em São Paulo," *DADOS: Revista de Ciências Sociais* 63, no. 1 (2020): 1–40.

112 Sun et al., "Procedural Justice, Legitimacy, and Public Cooperation."

113 T. Jonathan-Zamir and D. Weisburd, "The Effects of Security Threats on Antecedents of Police Legitimacy: Findings from a Quasi-Experiment in Israel," *Journal of Research in Crime and Delinquency* 50 (2013): 3–32.

114 Michael D. Reisig and Camille Lloyd, "Procedural Justice, Police Legitimacy, and Helping the Police Fight Crime," *Police Quarterly* 12 (2009): 42–62.

115 Daniel K. Pryce and George Wilson, "Police Procedural Justice, Lawyer Procedural Justice, Judge Procedural Justice, and Satisfaction with the Criminal Justice System: Findings from a Neglected Region of the World," *Criminal Justice Policy Review* 31, no. 9 (2020): 1286–1311.

116 Michael D. Reisig, Justice Tankebe, and Gorazd Meško, "Compliance with the Law in Slovenia: The Role of Procedural Justice and Police Legitimacy," *European Journal on Criminal Policy and Research* 20, no. 2 (2013): 259–76. However, study findings suggest that the effects of legitimacy on compliance are more limited in some cultural contexts than others. See also Justice Tankebe, Michael D. Reisig, and Gorazd Meško, "Procedural Justice, Police Legitimacy, and Public Cooperation with the Police Among Young Slovene Adults," *Journal of Criminal Justice and Security* 14, no. 2 (2012): 147–64.

117 Anjuli Van Damme, Lieven Pauwels, and Robert Svensson, "Why Do Swedes Cooperate with the Police? A SEM Analysis of Tyler's Procedural Justice Model," *European Journal of Criminal Policy Research* 21, no. 1 (2015): 15–33; Simon Wallengren et al., "Trust Toward the Criminal Justice System Among Swedish Roma: A Mixed-Methodology Approach," *Race and Justice* 10, no. 10 (June 2020): 1–24.

118 See Tammy R. Kochel, Roger B. Parks, and Stephen M. Mastrofski, "Examining Police Effectiveness as a Precursor to Legitimacy and Cooperation with Police," *Justice Quarterly* 2011, no. 5 (November 2011). However, research on police-citizen interactions in Trinidad and Tobago indicates that legitimacy and procedural justice may not be distinct concepts, raising questions about the relationship between procedural justice and legitimacy, as well as the way both concepts are understood and operationalized. Johnson, Maguire, and Kuhns, "Public Perceptions".

119 Mustafa Demir et al., "Body Worn Cameras, Procedural Justice, and Police Legitimacy: A Controlled Experimental Evaluation of Traffic Stops," *Justice Quarterly* 37, no. 1 (2020): 53–84.

120 Ben Bradford, "Policing and Social Identity: Procedural Justice, Inclusion and Cooperation between Police and Public," *Policing & Society* 24, no. 1 (2014): 22–43; Justice Tankebe, "Viewing Things Differently: The Dimensions of Public Perceptions of Police Legitimacy," *Criminology* 51, no. 3 (2013): 103–35.

121 Brockner et al., "Culture and Procedural Justice."

122 Rajnandini Pillai, Eric S. Williams, and J. Justin Tan, "Are the Scales Tipped in Favor of Procedural or Distributive Justice? An Investigation of the U.S., India, Germany, and Hong Kong (China)," *International Journal of Conflict Management* 12, no. 4 (2001): 312–32.

123 Reisig, Tankebe, and Meško, "Compliance with the Law in Slovenia." For a similar discussion on the legacies communist policing practices in Europe, see Baćak and Apel, "Police Fairness and Legitimacy."

124 Kristina Murphy and Adrian Cherney, "Fostering Cooperation with the Police: How Do Ethnic Minorities in Australia Respond to Procedural Justice-Based Policing?" *Australian & New Zealand Journal of Criminology* 44 (2011): 235–57.

125 Sarah MacQueen and Ben Bradford, "Enhancing Public Trust and Police Legitimacy During Road Traffic Encounters: Results from a Randomised Controlled Trial in Scotland," *Journal of Experimental Criminology* 11 (2015): 419–43.

126 Adrian Cherney and Kristina Murphy, "Understanding the Contingency of Procedural Justice Outcomes," *Policing* 5, no. 3 (2011): 228–35.

127 Tankebe, "Viewing Things Differently."

128 Similarly, Hinds finds that, although process fairness is related to Australian youths' perception of police legitimacy, so, too, are perceptions of police effectiveness and fear of the consequences of police action. Hinds, "Building Police-Youth Relationships." Moreover, in a study of Australian police-citizen encounters, Murphy finds that both procedural justice and police performance influence ratings of police satisfaction, with the former being most important in police-initiated contacts and the latter being most important in citizen-initiated contacts. Murphy, "Public Satisfaction with Police." Finally, both procedural justice and police effectiveness have been found to influence willingness to cooperate with the police in China (Sun et al., "Procedural Justice, Legitimacy, and Public Cooperation") and the United Kingdom (Bradford, "Policing and Social Identity").

129 Justice Tankebe, "Public Cooperation with the Police in Ghana: Does Procedural Fairness Matter?," *Criminology* 47, no. 4 (2009): 1265–93.

130 Tankebe, "Public Cooperation with the Police in Ghana," 1279. For a similar discussion on the legacies of communist policing practices in Europe, see Baćak and Apel, "Police Fairness and Legitimacy."

131 Daniel K. Pryce, "The Relative Effects of Normative and Instrumental Models of Policing on Police Empowerment: Evidence from Sample of Sub-Saharan African Immigrants," *Criminal Justice Policy Review* 30, no. 3 (2019): 428–50. This is consistent with the work of Garth Davies and Jeffrey Fagan, "Crime and Enforcement in Immigrant Neighborhoods: Evidence from New York City," *Annals of the American Academy of Political and Social Science* 641, no. 1 (2012): 99–124.

However, Pryce, Johnson, and Maguire find not only that police effectiveness has no bearing on Ghanaian immigrants' obligation to obey the police but also that their views of the police in Ghana do not influence obligation or cooperation with the police. Daniel K. Pryce, Devon Johnson, and Edward R. Maguire, "Procedural Justice, Obligation to Obey, and Cooperation with Police in a Sample of Ghanaian Immigrants," *Criminal Justice and Behavior* 44, no. 5 (2017): 733–55.

132 Pryce, Johnson, and Maguire, "Procedural Justice."

133 Belén Lowrey-Kinberg, Maya Barak, and Hillary Mellinger, "Perceptions of Justice Among Guatemalan-Mayans and Latinos of South Florida: A Call for Further Study of Procedural Justice in Minority Communities," *Social Justice: A Journal of Crime, Conflict & World Order* 47 no. 1/2 (2020): 171–93; Pryce, "Ghanaian Immigrants' Experiences."

134 Ben Bradford and Jonathan Jackson, "Police Legitimacy Among Immigrants in Europe: Institutional Frames and Group Positions," *European Journal of Criminology* 15, no. 5 (2018): 567–88; Ben Bradford et al., "A Leap of Faith? Trust in the Police Among Immigrants in England and Wales," *British Journal of Criminology* 57, no. 2 (2017): 381–401.

135 Emily Ryo, "Legal Attitudes of Immigrant Detainees," *Law & Society Review* 51, no. 1 (2017): 99–131.

136 Kristina Murphy and Lorraine Mazerolle, "Policing Immigrants: Using a Randomized Control Trial of Procedural Justice Policing to Promote Trust and Cooperation," *Australian and New Zealand Journal of Criminology* 51, no. 1 (2016): 3–22.

137 Reisig, Tankebe, and Meško, "Compliance with the Law in Slovenia."

138 In explaining why procedural justice does not appear to affect ethnic minorities' willingness to cooperate with the police in Australia, Murphy and Cherney highlight this group's lack of identification with mainstream Australian culture, also noting that this group "may have two distinct reference points when making judgments about whether or not to assist the police: (a) experience with the police in their country of origin; and (b) experience with the police in Australia." Murphy and Cherney, "Fostering Cooperation with the Police."

139 Jon. B. Gould and Maya Pagni Barak, *Capital Defense: Inside the Lives of America's Death Penalty Lawyers* (New York: New York University Press, 2019).

2. JUSTICE AND IMMIGRATION COURT

1 TRAC Immigration, "Immigration Court Backlog Tool: Pending Cases and Length of Wait by Nationality, State, Court, and Hearing Location," July 15, 2022, https://trac.syr.edu.

2 Executive Office for Immigration Review, "Office of the Chief Immigration Judge," U.S. Department of Justice, update December 7, 2020, www.justice.gov.

3 Executive Office for Immigration Review (EOIR Office of the Director), "Case Priorities and Immigration Court Performance Measures," Memorandum to the Office of the Chief Immigration Judge, All Immigration Judges, All Court Administrators, and All Immigration Court Staff, January 17, 2018, www.justice.gov.

4   TRAC Immigration, "The Life and Death of Administrative Closure," September 10, 2020, https://trac.syr.edu.

5   Shuting Chen, "Hon. Dana Leigh Marks," *Judicial Profile*, May 2017, www.naij-usa.org.

6   Beginning in 1956, inspection officials handling immigration adjudication decisions were required to have law degrees. Kevin R. Johnson et al., *Understanding Immigration Law* (Newark, NJ: Matthew Bender & Company, Inc., 2009).

7   Johnson et al., *Understanding Immigration Law*.

8   Executive Office for Immigration Review, "EOIR Immigration Court Listing," U.S. Department of Justice, update June 28, 2021, www.justice.gov/eoir; Executive Office for Immigration Review, "Office of the Chief Immigration Judge," U.S. Department of Justice, update December 7, 2020, www.justice.gov.

9   The Trump administration created two "adjudication centers" to "address backlogs," but the centers have been criticized for lack of transparency and due process concerns. Katie Shepherd, "The Judicial Black Sites the Government Created to Speed Up Deportations," *Immigration Impact*, January 7, 2019, https://immigrationimpact.com; FOIA Litigation, "Government Faces Lawsuit for Failing to Disclose Information on Expansion of Immigration Courts and Immigration Adjudication Centers," American Immigration Council, October 30, 2020, www.americanimmigrationcouncil.org.

10   Dana Leigh Marks, "An Urgent Priority: Why Congress Should Establish an Article I Immigration Court," *Bender's Immigration Bulletin* 13 (January 2008): 3–21.

11   In 2018, about 75% of immigration court hearings involved Guatemalan, Honduran, Mexican, or Salvadoran nationals. Executive Office for Immigration Review, "FY 2018 Statistical Year Book," U.S. Department of Justice, 2019, www.justice.gov. After cases involving Mexican nationals, cases involving Guatemalans, Hondurans, and Salvadorans have consistently been the most frequent, the number two, three, and four spots—although not always in this order—on the list of "Top 25 Countries by Nationality" in immigration court since 2006. Executive Office for Immigration Review, "FY 2008 Statistical Year Book," U.S. Department of Justice, 2009, www.justice.gov; Executive Office for Immigration Review, "FY 2013 Statistical Year Book," U.S. Department of Justice, 2014, www.justice.gov; EOIR, "FY 2018 Statistical Year Book."

12   EOIR, "FY 2018 Statistical Year Book."

13   Johnson et al., *Understanding Immigration Law*; see also *Padilla v. Kentucky*, 130 S. Ct. 1473, 1481 (U.S. 2010); *Fong Yue Ting v. United States*, 149 U.S. 698, 730 (1893).

14   Johnson et al., *Understanding Immigration Law*.

15   Jennifer Chacón, "A Diversion of Attention? Immigration Courts and the Adjudication of Fourth and Fifth Amendment Rights," *Duke Law Journal* 59, no. 15 (2010): 1563–1633.

16   Johnson et al., *Understanding Immigration Law*.

17   Philip L. Torrey, "Rethinking Immigration's Mandatory Detention Regime: Politics, Profit, and the Meaning of 'Custody,'" *University of Michigan Journal of Law Reform* 48 (2015): 879–913.

18 John R. B. Palmer, Stephen W. Yale-Loehr, and Elizabeth Cronin, "Why Are So Many People Challenging Board of Immigration Appeals Decisions in Federal Court? An Empirical Analysis of the Recent Surge in Petitions for Review," *Georgetown Immigration Law Journal* 20 (Fall 2005): 1–100.

19 Johnson et al., *Understanding Immigration Law.*

20 TRAC Immigration, "New Filings Seeking Removal Orders in Immigration Courts Through February 2022," data through February 2022, https://trac.syr.edu/.

21 Again, although technically referred to as "removal," I use the colloquial term "deportation" throughout this book.

22 Executive Office for Immigration Review, *Immigration Court Practice Manual* (Falls Church, VA, 2020), www.justice.gov.

23 Marks, "An Urgent Priority."

24 Marks, "An Urgent Priority."

25 In December 2020, the former EOIR director effectively eliminated Master Calendar hearings via Policy Memo 21–05, but the Biden administration revoked this Trump-era policy on April 2, 2021. Jean King, Acting Director, "Cancellation of Policy Memorandum 21–05," Memorandum to All of EOIR, April 2, 2021, https://immpolicytracking.org.

26 Marks, "An Urgent Priority."

27 However, this often occurs in a perfunctory manner, as opposed to the work of a prosecutor proving a criminal defendant guilty beyond a reasonable doubt.

28 *Jesus Aguilera-Enriquez v. Immigration and Naturalization Service (INS)*, 516 F.2d 565 (1975).

29 Ingrid V. Eagly and Susan Shafer, "A National Study of Access to Counsel in Immigration Court," *University of Pennsylvania Law Review* 164, no. 1 (2015): 1–9.

30 TRAC Immigration, "State and County Details on Deportation Proceedings in Immigration Court," data through May 2021, https://trac.syr.edu.

31 Richard L. Abel, "Practicing Immigration Law in Filene's Basement," *North Carolina Law Review* 84 (2006): 1449–1500; Sabrineh Ardalan, "Access to Justice for Asylum Seekers: Developing an Effective Model of Holistic Asylum Representation," *University of Michigan Journal of Law Reform* 48, no. 4 (2015): 1001–38; Jennifer Barnes, "Practice Context: The Lawyer-Client Relationship in Immigration Law," *Emory Law Journal* 52 (2003): 1215–20; Peter L. Markowitz, "Barriers to Representation for Detained Immigrants Facing Deportation: Varick Street Detention Facility, A Case Study," *Fordham Law Review* 78 (2009): 541–72; Hillary Mellinger, *Access to Justice at the Asylum Office*, American University, PhD dissertation, 2020; Marjorie Zatz and Nancy Rodriguez, *Dreams and Nightmares: Immigration Policy, Youth, and Families* (Oakland: University of California Press, 2015).

32 *Notarios,* or "notaries"—typically found in the immigration context—are non-attorneys who claim to have the capability to assist with legal matters, sometimes even falsely identifying as attorneys and/or illegally practicing law without a

license. Barnes, "Practice Context"; Markowitz, "Barriers to Representation." *Notario* fraud is relatively common in the United States and is facilitated by the fact that, in many Latin American countries, *notarios* are individuals with law degrees and additional specialized legal training. This sharply contrasts with notaries in the U.S. context, who are public officials with the ability to administer oaths, witness the signing of documents, and notarize said documents.

33 Eagly and Shafer, "A National Study"; Banks Miller, Linda Camp Keith, and Jennifer S. Holmes, "Leveling the Odds: The Effect of Quality Legal Representation in Cases of Asymmetrical Capability," *Law & Society Review* 49, no. 1 (2015): 209–39; Jennifer Stave et al., *Evaluation of the New York Immigrant Family Unity Project: Assessing the Impact of Legal Representation on Family and Community Unity* (New York: Vera Institute of Justice, November 2017).

34 Johnson et al., *Understanding Immigration Law.*

35 The Trump administration moved to restrict the grounds for asylum. In *Matter of A-B-* (2018), then–Attorney General Jeff Sessions overruled the BIA's previous decision in *Matter of A-R-C-G-* (2014), setting new case precedent restricting asylum claims based on domestic violence and gang violence. Office of the Attorney General, "Matter of A-B-, Respondent," U.S. Department of Justice, June 11, 2018, https://immpolicytracking.org.

36 Johnson et al., *Understanding Immigration Law.*

37 Johnson et al., *Understanding Immigration Law.*

38 Johnson et al., *Understanding Immigration Law.*

39 Jaya Ramji-Nogales, Andrew Schoenholtz, and Philip G. Schrag, "Refugee Roulette: Disparities in Asylum Adjudication," *Stanford Law Review* 60 (2008): 295–412.

40 Johnson et al., *Understanding Immigration Law.*

41 EOIR, "FY 2013 Statistical Year Book"; EOIR, "FY 2018 Statistical Year Book."

42 Gerald L. Neuman, "Discretionary Deportation," *Georgetown Immigration Law Journal* 20, no. 4 (2005–2006): 611–56.

43 Although the Supreme Court held judicial review provisions of the Administrative Procedure Act (APA) to be applicable to deportation proceedings in *Shaughnessy v. Pedreiro*, 349 U.S. 48 (1955), Congress, in passing IIRIRA (1996), AEDPA (1996), and the REAL ID ACT (2005), subsequently exempted deportation proceedings from full adherence to the APA. Neuman, "Discretionary Deportation"; see also Johnson et al., *Understanding Immigration Law.*

44 Emily Ryo, "Detained: A Study of Immigration Bond Hearings," *Law & Society Review* 50, no. 1 (2016): 117–54; *Jennings v. Rodriguez*, 138 S. Ct. 830 (2018).

45 Torrey, "Rethinking."

46 Torrey, "Rethinking."

47 *Saavedra–Figueroa v. Holder*, 625 F.3d 621, 626 (9th Cir. 2010); *Robles-Urrea v. Holder*, 678 F.3d 702, 708 (9th Cir. 2012).

48 Torrey, "Rethinking."

49 Torrey, "Rethinking."

50 Ryo, "Detained."

51 Jeremey Pepper, "Pay Up or Else: Immigration Bond and How a Small Procedural Change Could Liberate Immigrant Detainees," *Boston College Law Review* 60, no. 3 (2019): 951–88.

52 Pepper, "Pay Up or Else."

53 See also Zatz and Rodriguez, *Dreams and Nightmares*.

54 Laura Abel, *Language Access in Immigration Courts* (Brennan Center for Justice at New York University School of Law, 2011), www.brennancenter.org.

55 Jayesh Rathod, "The Transformative Potential of Attorney Bilingualism," *University of Michigan Journal of Law Reform* 46 (2013): 863–920.

56 EOIR, *Immigration Court Practice Manual*.

57 Eugenio Mollo Jr., "The Expansion of Video Conferencing Technology in Immigration Proceedings and Its Impact on Venue Provisions, Interpretation Rights, and the Mexican Immigrant Community," *Journal of Gender, Race & Justice* 9 (2005): 702.

58 U.S. Department of Justice, "Contract Award Number: 15JPSS20D00000366" (2020), https://sam.gov; David Noriega and Adolfo Flores, "Immigration Courts Could Lose a Third of Their Interpreters," *BuzzFeed.News*, 2015, www.buzzfeednews.com.

59 When I began this study, contract interpretation was provided to the court by Lionbridge, a private company offering artificial intelligence, content creation and marketing, and interpretation and translation services worldwide. In 2015, EOIR signed a six-year contract with SOS International (SOSi), "the largest private, family-owned and operated technology and services integrator in the aerospace, defense, and government services industry," for all interpretation needs. SOSi (SOS International), "Home," n.d., www.sosi.com. SOSi cut interpreter pay by nearly half, reducing rates from $65/hour to $35/hour. This and other exploitative practices led to several labor disputes over interpreter wages, employee classification, and union-busting. Nina Agrawal, "Judge Orders Compensation, Reclassification for Immigration Court Interpreters," *Los Angeles Times*, March 14, 2018, www.latimes.com. For a detailed account and analysis of labor conditions for immigration court interpreters, see Sonya Rao, "Privatizing Language Work: Interpreters and Access in Los Angeles Immigration Court" (PhD diss., University of California, Los Angeles, 2021).

60 Blake Gentry, "O'odham Niok? In Indigenous Languages, U.S. 'Jurisprudence' Means Nothing," *Chicanx-Latinx Law Review* 37, no. 1 (2020): 30–63.

61 Melissa Wallace and Carlos I. Hernández, "Language Access for Asylum Seekers in Borderland Detention Centers in Texas," *Journal of Language and Law* 68 (2017): 143–56.

62 Katherine L. Beck, "Interpreting Injustice: The Department of Homeland Security's Failure to Comply with Federal Language Access Requirements in Immigration Detention," *Havard Latinx Law Review* 20 (2017): 15–50; Sahar Fathi, "The

Right to Understand and to Be Understood: Urban Activism and US Migrants' Access to Interpreters," in Rebecca Ruth Gould and Kayvan Tahmasebian, eds., *The Routledge Handbook of Translation and Activism* (New York: Routledge, 2020), 297–316.

63 Gentry, "O'odham Niok?"

64 National Lawyers Guild (NLG), "Fundamental Fairness: A Report on the Due Process Crisis in New York City Immigration Courts" (New York: NLG, 2011).

65 EOIR, *Immigration Court Practice Manual*.

66 Abel, *Language Access in Immigration Courts*.

67 Muneer I. Ahmad, "Interpreting Communities: Lawyering Across Language Difference," *UCLA Law Review* 54 (2007): 999–1086.

68 Ahmad, "Interpreting Communities"; John R. Bowels, "Court Interpreters in Alabama State Court: Present Perils, Practices, and Possibilities," *American Journal of Trial Advocacy* 31 (2007): 619–49.

69 Ahmad, "Interpreting Communities," 108.

70 Abel, *Language Access in Immigration Courts*.

71 Susan Berk-Seligson, *The Bilingual Courtroom: Court Interpreters in the Judicial Process*, 2nd ed. (Chicago: University of Chicago Press, 2017).

72 NLG, "Fundamental Fairness."

73 Abel, *Language Access in Immigration Courts*; Gentry, "O'odham Niok?"

74 Ahmad, "Interpreting Communities," 103.

75 M. Rosario Martín Ruano, "From Suspicion to Collaboration: Defining New Epistemologies of Reflexive Practice for Legal Translation and Interpreting," *Journal of Specialized Translation* 22 (January 2014), www.jostrans.org.

76 Martín Ruano, "From Suspicion to Collaboration."

77 Ahmad, "Interpreting Communities," 103.

78 Ahmad, "Interpreting Communities"; Philipp Sebastian Angermeyer, "Translation Style and Participant Roles in Court Interpreting," *Journal of Sociolinguistics* 13, no. 1 (2009): 3–28; Bowels, "Court Interpreters in Alabama State Court."

79 During my court observations, I witnessed several instances when the court failed to provide interpretation in the language needed or simply failed to provide interpretation altogether. Such mistakes were stated, on the record, to be logistical errors, and attempts were made to correct them at subsequent hearings. Still, these were outliers, not the norm.

80 *El Rescate Legal Services v. EOIR*, 959 F.2d 742 (9th Cir. 1991).

81 National Association of Judiciary Interpreters and Translators (NAJIT), *Modes of Interpreting: Simultaneous, Consecutive, and Sight Translation* (Atlanta: National Association of Judiciary Interpreters and Translators, 2006).

82 NAJIT, *Modes of Interpreting*.

83 NAJIT, *Modes of Interpreting*.

84 Abel, *Language Access in Immigration Courts*.

85 Abel, *Language Access in Immigration Courts*, 5.

86 Abel, *Language Access in Immigration Courts*, 5.

87 Deborah D. Kuchler and Leslie C. O'Toole, "How Technological Advances in the Courtroom Are Changing the Way We Litigate," *FDCC Quarterly* 58, no. 2 (2008): 210.

88 Diane M. Hartmus, "Videotrials," *Ohio Northern University Law Review* 23 (1996): 1–15.

89 Anne B. Poulin, "Criminal Justice and Video Conferencing Technology: The Remote Defendant," *Tulsa Law Review* 78 (2003–2004): 1089–1167.

90 Poulin, "Criminal Justice and Video Conferencing Technology."

91 Poulin, "Criminal Justice and Video Conferencing Technology."

92 Shari Seidman Diamond et al., "Efficiency and Cost: The Impact of Videoconference Hearings on Bail Decisions," *Journal of Criminal Law & Criminology* 100, no. 3 (2010): 869–902; Fredric I. Lederer, "Technology Comes to the Courtroom, and . . ." *Emory Law Journal* 43 (1994): 1095–1122.

93 *Thornton v. Snyder*, 428 F.3d 690 (7th Cir. 2005); *Rusu v. INS*, 296 F.3d 316 (4th Cir. 2002).

94 *Rusu v. INS*, 296 F.3d 316 (4th Cir. 2002).

95 Ryo, "Detained."

96 Sara DeStefano, "Unshackling the Due Process Rights of Asylum-Seekers," *Virginia Law Review* 105 (2019): 1667–1716.

97 Ingrid V. Eagly, "Remote Adjudication in Immigration," *Northwestern University Law Review* 109, no. 4 (2015): 934–1020.

98 Nathaniel Flanders and Amber Williams, "Memorandum on the History of Agency Video Teleconferencing Adjudications," Administration Conference of the United States, 2014, www.acus.gov.

99 Aaron Haas, "Video Conferencing in Immigration Proceedings," *University of New Hampshire Law Review* 5, no. 1 (2006): 59–90.

100 Frank M. Walsh and Edward M. Walsh, "Effective Processing or Assembly-Line Justice? The Use of Teleconferencing in Asylum Removal Hearings," *Georgetown Immigration Law Journal* 22 (2008): 259–83.

101 Walsh and Walsh, "Effective Processing or Assembly-Line Justice?"

102 Eagly, "Remote Adjudication in Immigration."

103 Legal Assistance Foundation of Metropolitan Chicago and Chicago Appleseed Fund for Justice, *Videoconferencing in Removal Hearings: A Case Study of the Chicago Immigration Court*, August 2, 2005, http://chicagoappleseed.org.

104 Ahmad, "Interpreting Communities."

105 Abel, *Language Access in Immigration Courts.*

106 Abel, *Language Access in Immigration Courts,* 8.

107 Abel, *Language Access in Immigration Courts,* 8.

108 Mollo, "The Expansion of Video Conferencing Technology."

109 Mark Federman, "On the Media Effects of Immigration and Refugee Board Hearings via Videoconference," *Journal of Refugee Studies* 19, no. 4 (2006): 433–52.

110 Walsh and Walsh, "Effective Processing or Assembly-Line Justice?," 265; See also Emily B. Leung, "Technology's Encroachment on Justice: Video Conferencing in Immigration Court Proceedings," *Immigration Briefings* 1 (2014).

111 Abel, *Language Access in Immigration Courts.*

112 Eagly, "Remote Adjudication in Immigration," 941.

113 Eagly, "Remote Adjudication in Immigration."

114 Eagly, "Remote Adjudication in Immigration."

115 In cases of inadmissibility, the burden is on the respondent.

116 For an extended discussion on court communities, see James Eisenstein, Roy B. Flemming, and Peter F. Nardulli, *Contours of Justice: Communities and Their Courts* (Boston: Little, Brown and Co., 1988); James Eisenstein and H. Jacob, *Felony Justice: An Organizational Analysis of Criminal Courts* (Boston: Little, Brown and Co., 1977).

117 Although the Supreme Court held judicial review provisions of the Administrative Procedure Act to be applicable to deportation proceedings in *Shaughnessy v. Pedreiro*, 349 U.S. 48 (1955), Congress, in passing IIRIRA (1996), AEDPA (1996), and the REAL ID ACT (2005), subsequently exempted deportation proceedings from full adherence to the APA. Neuman, "Discretionary Deportation"; Hon. Denise Noonan Slavin and Hon. Dana Leigh Marks, "Conflicting Roles of Immigration Judges: Do You Want Your Case Heard by a 'Government Attorney' or by a 'Judge'?," *Bender's Immigration Bulletin* 16 (2011): 1786.

118 Marks, "An Urgent Priority."

119 Although Congress granted immigration judges the authority to sanction attorneys under IIRIRA, these powers have yet to be implemented by the Department of Justice, rendering them useless (Slavin and Marks, "Conflicting Roles," 1791). However, there is an attorney discipline process within EOIR; see Executive Office for Immigration Review, "EOIR's Attorney Discipline Program and Professional Conduct Rules for Immigration Attorneys and Representatives," 2014, www.justice.gov.

120 Fatma E. Marouf, "Implicit Bias and Immigration Courts," *New England Law Review* 45 (2010–2011): 417–48.

121 Neuman, "Discretionary Deportation."

122 For an exploration of widespread discretion-based disparities in asylum grant rates across the country—including asylum applications linked to deportation proceedings and heard by EOIR and BIA judges—see Ramji-Nogales, Schoenholtz, and Schrag, "Refugee Roulette." Of note, the authors found that judges' gender and prior work experience with INS/DHS, the military, and NGOs greatly impacts asylum grant rates. Specifically, female judges are more likely to grant asylum than male judges and judges with NGO work experience are more likely to grant asylum than judges with military or INS/DHS work experience (ibid.).

123 The Trump administration added dozens of immigration judges to the court, filling about two-thirds of all seats. The majority of Trump appointees either had ICE enforcement and prosecutorial backgrounds or little to no experience with immigration law. Rebecca Beitsch, "Biden Fills Immigration Court with Trump Hires," *The Hill*, May, 8, 2021, thehill.com. In May 2021, in a move that shocked many immigration advocates, the Biden administration continued

this practice, hiring 17 new immigration judges initially picked by the Trump administration (ibid.).

124 Depending on the facts of the case, claims pertaining to sexual orientation or gender identity are recognized as membership in a particular social group (or "PSG") and, in nexus with persecution, may provide the basis for an asylum claim. The nexus analysis rests upon the consideration of whether the persecutor perceives the asylum applicant as possessing a protected characteristic (whether the applicant does possess it or the persecutor imputes it to the applicant) and whether the persecutor acted or would act against the applicant because of the persecutor's perception of that protected characteristic. See *Matter of Toboso-Alfonso*, 20 I. and N. Dec. 819, 822–23 (1990).

125 On average, for every six immigration judges there is one clerk, whom judges must share. Peter L. Markowitz, "Straddling the Civil-Criminal Divide: A Bifurcated Approach to Understanding the Nature of Immigration Removal Proceedings," *Harvard Civil Rights–Civil Liberties Law Review* 43 (2008): 289–352.

126 Dana Leigh Marks, "Immigration Judge: Death Penalty Cases in a Traffic Court Setting," *CNN*, June 26, 2014, www.cnn.com.

127 Jacinta M. Gau and Rod K. Brunson, "Procedural Justice and Order Maintenance Policing: A Study of Inner-City Young Men's Perceptions of Police Legitimacy," *Justice Quarterly* 27, no. 2 (2010): 255–79; Lyn Hinds, "Building Police-Youth Relationships: The Importance of Procedural Justice," *Youth Justice* 7, no. 3 (2007): 195–209; Rebecca Hollander-Blumoff and Tom R. Tyler, "Procedural Justice in Negotiation: Procedural Fairness, Outcome Acceptance, and Integrative Potential," *Law & Social Inquiry* 33, no. 2 (2008): 473–500; Raymond Paternoster et al., "Do Fair Procedures Matter? The Effect of Procedural Justice on Spouse Assault," *Law & Society Review* 31, no. 1 (1997): 163–204; Jason Sunshine and Tom R. Tyler, "The Role of Procedural Justice and Legitimacy in Shaping Public Support for Policing," *Law & Society Review* 37, no. 3 (2003): 513–48; Tom R. Tyler, "Procedural Justice, Legitimacy, and the Effective Rule of Law," *Crime and Justice* 30 (2003): 283–357.

128 Edith Barret-Howard and Tom Tyler, "Procedural Justice as a Criterion in Allocation Decisions," *Journal of Personality and Social Psychology* 50, no. 2 (1986): 296–304; Steven L. Blader and Tom R. Tyler, "A Four-Component Model of Procedural Justice: Defining the Meaning of a 'Fair' Process," *Personality and Social Psychology Bulletin* 29 (2003): 747–58; Gau and Brunson, "Procedural Justice and Order Maintenance Policing"; Hollander-Blumoff and Tyler, "Procedural Justice in Negotiation"; Tom R. Tyler, "What Is Procedural Justice? Criteria Used by Citizens to Assess the Fairness of Legal Procedures," *Law & Society Review* 22, no. 1 (1988): 103–36.

129 Beginning in 2017, the Trump administration took a number of controversial steps to increase immigration court efficiency and address the court's backlog, including the implementation of case-completion quotas for immigration judges. Office of the Attorney General, "Renewing Our Commitment to the Timely and Efficient Adjudication of Immigration Cases to Serve the National Interest," Memorandum

for the Executive Office for Immigration Review, December 5, 2017, www.justice.gov; EOIR, "Case Priorities and Immigration Court Performance Measures"; Executive Office for Immigration Review, Office of the Director, "No Dark Courtrooms," Memorandum to All of EOIR, March 29, 2019, www.justice.gov.

130 Jonathan D. Casper, Tom Tyler, and Bonnie Fisher, "Procedural Justice in Felony Cases," *Law & Society Review* 22, no. 3 (1988): 483–508; Robert Folger, "Distributive and Procedural Justice: Combined Impact of 'Voice' and Improvement on Experienced Inequity," *Journal of Personality and Social Psychology* 35, no. 2 (1977): 108–99; Gerald S. Leventhal, "What Should Be Done with Equity Theory?" in K. J. Gergen, M. S. Greenberg, and R. H. Willis, eds., *Social Exchange: Advances in Theory and Research* (New York: Plenum Press, 1980), 27–55; John W. Thibaut and Laurens Walker, *Procedural Justice: A Psychological Analysis* (New York: L. Erlbaum Associates, 1975).

131 See also Lederer, "Technology Comes to the Courtroom"; Mollo, "The Expansion of Video Conferencing Technology"; Poulin, "Criminal Justice and Video Conferencing Technology."

3. TRACING IMMIGRANT LEGAL CONSCIOUSNESS

1 The 1994 Violence Against Women Act (VAWA) and the 2000 Victims of Trafficking and Violence Protection Act (VTVPA) contain provisions that allow victims of domestic violence, trafficking, and other crimes to apply for a T visa, U visa, or I-360 Petition; all three visas can lead to Lawful Permanent Residency for eligible recipients. Kevin R. Johnson et al., *Understanding Immigration Law* (Newark, NJ: Matthew Bender & Company, Inc., 2009).

2 "Legal consciousness" has been used by some scholars to refer specifically to the consciousness of those in the legal profession. However, this body of work is more akin to the study of legal culture than that of legal consciousness explored here; see Marc Galanter, "Changing Legal Consciousness in America: The View from the Joke Corpus," *Cardozo Law Review* 23, no. 6 (2001): 2223–40; Curtis Nyquist, "Llewellyn's Code as a Reflection of Legal Consciousness," *New England Law Review* 40 (2005): 419–36.

3 Sally Engel Merry, *Getting Justice and Getting Even: Legal Consciousness Among Working-Class Americans* (Chicago: University of Chicago Press, 1990) 5.

4 Sally Engle Merry, "Culture, Power, and the Discourse of Law," *New York Law School Law Review* 37 (1992): 209–25. Similarly, Avi Brisman defines "legal consciousness" as "the ways people understand, imagine, and use the law, as well as their attitudes and feelings towards the law." Avi Brisman, "Fictionalized Criminal Law and Youth Legal Consciousness," *New York Law School Law Review* 55 (2010): 1047.

5 Laura Beth Nielsen, *License to Harass: Law, Hierarchy, and Offensive Public Speech* (Princeton, NJ: Princeton University Press, 2004), 6.

6 Austin Sarat, "'. . . The Law Is All Over': Power, Resistance and the Legal Consciousness of the Welfare Poor," *Yale Journal of Law & the Humanities* 2 (1990): 343–79.

7 Patricia Ewick and Susan S. Silbey, *The Common Place of Law: Stories from Everyday Life* (Chicago: University of Chicago Press, 1998).

8 Patricia Ewick and Susan S. Silbey, "Conformity, Contestation, and Resistance: An Account of Legal Consciousness," *New England Law Review* 26 (1991–1992): 742.

9 For instance, in their study of the disabled, Engel and Munger find that age at which disability presents itself, the passage of the Americans with Disabilities Act of 1990, and personal relationships all play a role in shaping individual legal consciousness. David M. Engel and Frank W. Munger, *Rights of Inclusion: Law and Identity in the Life Stories of Americans with Disabilities* (Chicago: University of Chicago Press, 2003).

10 Brisman, "Fictionalized Criminal Law."

11 *Notarios*, or "notaries," typically found in the immigration context, are nonattorneys who claim to have the capability to assist with legal matters, sometimes even falsely identifying as attorneys and/or illegally practicing law without a license. Jennifer Barnes, "The Lawyer-Client Relationship in Immigration Law," *Emory Law Journal* 52 (2003): 1215–20; Peter L. Markowitz, "Barriers to Representation for Detained Immigrants Facing Deportation: Varick Street Detention Facility, a Case Study," *Fordham Law Review* 78 (2009): 541–71. *Notario* fraud is relatively common in the United States. It is facilitated by the fact that, in many Latin American countries, *notarios* are individuals with law degrees and additional, specialized legal training. This sharply contrasts with notaries in the U.S. context, who are public officials with the ability to administer oaths, witness the signing of documents, and notarize said documents.

12 For a discussion of procedural justice assessments of immigrant detainees in the United States, see Emily Ryo, "Legal Attitudes of Immigrant Detainees," *Law & Society Review* 51, no. 1 (2017): 99–131.

13 For a discussion of changing norms regarding legal advertising among the legal profession, see Joel Henning, "Bar Associations, Law Firms, and Other Medieval Guilds," *Litigation* 32, no. 1 (2005): 17–21.

14 Sally Engle Merry, "Legal Pluralism," *Law & Society Review* 22, no. 5 (1988): 869–96.

15 Merry, "Legal Pluralism."

16 Merry, "Culture, Power, and the Discourse of Law," 13.

17 For a discussion of the important role vicarious experience plays in shaping people's perceptions of the law, legal systems, and legal actors, see Rod K. Brunson and Ronald Weitzer, "Negotiating Unwelcome Police Encounters: The Intergenerational Transmission of Conduct Norms," *Journal of Contemporary Ethnography* 40, no. 4 (2011): 425–56; see also Blanca A. Ramirez, "Excluding Criminals or Mothers? How Vicarious Experiences Shape Legal Attitudes on Immigration Enforcement," *Social Problems* (2021), https://doi.org/10.1093/socpro/spab071.

18 Daniel K. Pryce et al., "Understanding the Effects of Personal and Vicarious Trauma on African Americans' Attitudes Toward the Police," *Criminal Justice and Behavior* 10, no. 10 (2021): 1–24. See also Dennis P. Rosenbaum et al., "Attitudes

Toward the Police: The Effects of Direct and Vicarious Experience," *Police Quarterly* 8, no. 3 (2005): 343–65; Patricia Y. Warren, "Perceptions of Police Disrespect During Vehicle Stops: A Race-Based Analysis," *Crime & Delinquency* 57 (2011): 356–76.

19 Pryce et al., "Understanding the Effects"; see also Monica C. Bell, "Police Reform and the Dismantling of Legal Estrangement," *Yale Law Journal* 126, no. 7 (2017): 2054–2150.

20 Simon Wallengren et al., "Trust Toward the Criminal Justice System Among Swedish Roma: A Mixed-Methodology Approach," *Race and Justice* 10, no. 10 (2020): 13.

21 See Susan B. Coutin, *Legalizing Moves: Salvadoran Immigrants' Struggle for U.S. Residency* (Ann Arbor: University of Michigan Press, 2000); Susan B. Coutin, *Nation of Emigrants: Shifting Boundaries of Citizenship in El Salvador and the United States* (Ithaca, NY: Cornell University Press, 2007); Cecilia Menjívar, "Liminal Legality: Salvadoran and Guatemalan Immigrants' Lives in the United States," *American Journal of Sociology* 111, no. 4 (2006): 999–1037; Cecilia Menjívar, "The Power of the Law: Central Americans' Legality and Everyday Life in Phoenix, Arizona," *Latino Studies* 9, no. 4 (2011): 377–95; Cecilia Menjívar, "Transnational Parenting and Immigration Law: Central Americans in the United States," *Journal of Ethnic and Migration Studies* 38, no. 2 (2012): 301–22.

22 Regarding the history of exclusionary immigration policies in the United States, see, e.g., Bill Ong Hing, *Defining America: Through Immigration Policy* (Philadelphia: Temple University Press, 2003); Peter Schrag, *Not Fit for Our Society: Immigration and Nativism in America* (Berkeley: University of California Press, 2010). Regarding limitations on immigrants' participation in everyday American society, see, e.g., Alissa R. Ackerman and Rich Furman, eds., *The Criminalization of Immigration: Contexts and Consequences* (Durham, NC: Carolina Academic Press, 2014); Jamie Longazel, *Undocumented Fears: Immigration and the Politics of Divide and Conquer in Hazleton, Pennsylvania* (Philadelphia: Temple University Press, 2016).

23 For more on immigrant legal consciousness, see Leisy Abrego, "Legal Consciousness of Undocumented Latinos: Fear and Stigma as Barriers to Claims-Making for First- and 1.5-Generation Immigrant," *Law & Society Review* 45 no. 2 (2011): 337–70; Leisy Abrego, "Illegality as a Source of Solidarity and Tension in Latino Families," *Journal of Latino/Latin American Studies* 8, no. 1 (2016): 5–21.

4. WHO SAYS THE COURT CAN'T BE FAIR?

1 Robert J. Bies and Debra L. Shapiro, "Voice and Justification: Their Influence on Procedural Fairness Judgments," *Academy of Management Journal* 31, no. 3 (1988): 676–85; Steven L. Blader and Tom R. Tyler, "A Four-Component Model of Procedural Justice: Defining the Meaning of a 'Fair' Process," *Personality and Social Psychology Bulletin* 29 (2003): 747–58; Joel Brockner et al., "Culture and Procedural Justice: The Influence of Power Distance on Reactions to Voice," *Jour-

nal of Experimental Social Psychology 37 (2001): 300–15; Robert Folger, "Distributive and Procedural Justice: Combined Impact of 'Voice' and Improvement on Experienced Inequity," *Journal of Personality and Social Psychology* 35, no. 2 (1977): 108–99; E. Allan Lind, P. Christopher Earley, and Ruth Kanfer, "Voice, Control, and Procedural Justice: Instrumental and Noninstrumental Concerns in Fairness Judgments," *Journal of Personality and Social Psychology* 59, no. 5 (1990): 952–59; Tom R. Tyler, "What Is Procedural Justice? Criteria Used by Citizens to Assess the Fairness of Legal Procedures," *Law & Society Review* 22, no. 1 (1988): 103–36.

2 For a detailed account of the migrant paths across Mexico by train, see *The Beast: Riding the Rails and Dodging Narcos on the Migrant Trail* by Óscar Martinez (New York: Verso, 2013).

3 For immigrants like Alex, appearing for court via videoconferencing is described as less intimidating than having to face courtroom actors in person. It also provides a means of sidestepping uncomfortable—and perhaps demoralizing—transportation from the detention center to the courthouse, handcuffed the whole way.

4 TRAC Immigration, "Immigration Court Backlog Tool," data through May 2022, https://trac.syr.edu.

5 As its name indicates, TPS is a temporary legal status designated by the secretary of homeland security and granted to noncitizens from a country to which it is temporarily deemed unsafe and/or unsuitable to return. Countries or regions within countries may be designated for TPS due to temporary conditions such as ongoing armed conflict, environmental disaster, or epidemic.

6 The term *permiso* is often used in Spanish as a catch-all for a number of types of legal status in the United States, some granting individuals permission to work or live temporarily and others affording a path to citizenship.

7 Bies and Shapiro, "Voice and Justification"; Blader and Tyler, "A Four-Component Model"; Brockner et al., "Culture and Procedural Justice"; Folger, "Distributive and Procedural Justice"; Lind, Earley, and Kanfer, "Voice, Control, and Procedural Justice"; John W. Thibaut and Laurens Walker, *Procedural Justice: A Psychological Analysis* (New York: L. Erlbaum Associates, 1975); Tyler, "What Is Procedural Justice?"

8 Blader and Tyler, "A Four-Component Model"; Jonathan D. Casper, Tom Tyler, and Bonnie Fisher, "Procedural Justice in Felony Cases," *Law & Society Review* 22, no. 3 (1988): 483–508; Tyler, "What Is Procedural Justice?"; Tom R. Tyler, "Policing in Black and White: Ethnic Group Differences in Trust and Confidence in the Police," *Police Quarterly* 8 (2005): 322–42; Tom R. Tyler, Jonathan D. Casper, and Bonnie Fisher, "Maintaining Allegiance Toward Political Authorities: The Role of Prior Attitudes and the Use of Fair Procedures," *American Journal of Political Science* 33, no. 3 (1989): 629–52.

9 For instance, Casper, Tyler, and Fisher in "Procedural Justice in Felony Cases" find that feeling listened to and believed by legal actors is crucial to a criminal defendant's positive evaluations of the procedural fairness of hearings. See also

Bies and Shapiro, "Voice and Justification"; Folger, "Distributive and Procedural Justice"; Lind, Earley, and Kanfer, "Voice, Control, and Procedural Justice.

10 Philipp Sebastian Angermeyer, "Translation Style and Participant Roles in Court Interpreting," *Journal of Sociolinguistics* 13, no. 1 (2009): 3–28.

11 TRAC Immigration, "Immigration Court Backlog Tool: Pending Cases and Length of Wait by Nationality, State, Court, and Hearing Location," May 2022, https://trac.syr.edu.

12 Julia Preston and Andrew R. Calderon, "Trump Tried to Deport People Faster. Immigration Courts Slowed Down Instead," The Marshall Project, July 16, 2019, www.themarshallproject.org.

13 "ISAP I" was a ten-city pilot program funded by Congress for a period of five years beginning in 2004. Beginning in 2009, "ISAP II" expanded the supervision program nationwide. ISAP services are provided by government contractors.

14 Steve Fisher, "Getting Immigrants Out of Detention Is Very Profitable," *Mother Jones*, 2016, www.motherjones.com.

15 Jack Holmes, "An Expert on Concentration Camps Says That's Exactly What the U.S. Is Running at the Border," *Esquire*, June 13, 2019, www.esquire.com.

16 Thibaut and Walker, *Procedural Justice*.

17 Gerald S. Leventhal, "What Should Be Done with Equity Theory?," in K. J. Gergen, M. S. Greenberg, and R. H. Willis, eds., *Social Exchange: Advances in Theory and Research* (New York: Plenum Press, 1980), 27–55; Tyler, "What Is Procedural Justice?"

18 Brockner et al., "Culture and Procedural Justice."

19 See Jacinta M. Gau and Rod K. Brunson, "Procedural Justice and Order Maintenance Policing: A Study of Inner-City Young Men's Perceptions of Police Legitimacy," *Justice Quarterly* 27, no. 2 (2010): 255–79; Lyn Hinds, "Building Police-Youth Relationships: The Importance of Procedural Justice," *Youth Justice* 7, no. 3 (2007): 195–209; Rebecca Hollander-Blumoff and Tom R. Tyler, "Procedural Justice in Negotiation: Procedural Fairness, Outcome Acceptance, and Integrative Potential," *Law & Social Inquiry* 33, no. 2 (2008): 473–500; Raymond Paternoster et al., "Do Fair Procedures Matter? The Effect of Procedural Justice on Spouse Assault," *Law & Society Review* 31, no. 1 (1997): 163–204; Jason Sunshine and Tom R. Tyler, "The Role of Procedural Justice and Legitimacy in Shaping Public Support for Policing," *Law & Society Review* 37, no. 3 (2003): 513–48; Tom R. Tyler, "Procedural Justice, Legitimacy, and the Effective Rule of Law," *Crime and Justice* 30 (2003): 283–357.

20 Casper, Tyler, and Fisher, "Procedural Justice in Felony Cases."

21 Rajnandini Pillai, Eric S. Williams, and J. Justin Tan, "Are the Scales Tipped in Favor of Procedural or Distributive Justice? An Investigation of the U.S., India, Germany, and Hong Kong (China)," *International Journal of Conflict Management* 12, no. 4 (2001): 312–32.

22 Justice Tankebe, "Public Cooperation with the Police in Ghana: Does Procedural Fairness Matter?" *Criminology* 47, no. 4 (2009): 1265–93.

23 This is not to say that U.S.-born citizens do not rely upon informal legal knowledge when forming expectations and evaluations of procedural justice, only that immigrants are an example of such groups. To my knowledge, no other procedural justice studies have examined this relationship.

24 Tyler, "What Is Procedural Justice?"

25 Tyler, "What Is Procedural Justice?" 131–132.

5. DEPORTATION HEARINGS, LEGITIMACY, AND THE RULE OF LAW

1 For a discussion of widespread gang-related systemic and opportunistic ("copycat") extortion in El Salvador, see Carlos Ponce, "Street Corner Decisions: An Empirical Investigation of Extortionist Choices in El Salvador," *Global Crime* 22, no. 2 (2021): 143–65. For a discussion of the accounting practices associated with gang-related extortion from the perspectives of business owners, gang members, and law enforcement in El Salvador and Honduras, see Dean Neu, "Accounting for Extortion," *Accounting, Organizations & Society* 76 (2019): 50–63.

2 For a detailed discussion of the criminal operations of gang members while incarcerated in El Salvador, see Neu, "Accounting for Extortion"; Steven Dudley and Juan José Martínez D'Aubuisson, "El Salvador Prisons and the Battle for the MS13's Soul," *InSight Crime*, February 16, 2017, www.insightcrime.org.

3 "Tough on crime" policies approach crime control through deterrence and incapacitation. Such policies often target violent and/or repeat offenders through determinate and mandatory sentencing practices, such as "three strikes" and "truth-in-sentencing" laws. For further discussion, see Marc Mauer, "Why Are Tough on Crime Policies So Popular?" *Stanford Law and Policy Review* 11, no. 1 (1999): 9–17.

4 Raymond Paternoster et al., "Do Fair Procedures Matter? The Effect of Procedural Justice on Spouse Assault," *Law & Society Review* 31, no. 1 (1997): 163–204; Tom R. Tyler, "Procedural Justice, Legitimacy, and the Effective Rule of Law," *Crime and Justice* 30 (2003): 283–357.

5 Valerie Jenness and Kitty Calavita, "It Depends on the Outcome: Prisoners, Grievances, and Perceptions of Justice," *Law & Society Review* 52, no. 1 (2018): 41–72.

6 Rajnandini Pillai, Eric S. Williams, and J. Justin Tan, "Are the Scales Tipped in Favor of Procedural or Distributive Justice? An Investigation of the U.S., India, Germany, and Hong Kong (China)," *International Journal of Conflict Management* 12, no. 4 (2001): 312–32; Justice Tankebe, "Public Cooperation with the Police in Ghana: Does Procedural Fairness Matter?" *Criminology* 47, no. 4 (2009): 1265–93.

7 See Justice Tankebe, "Viewing Things Differently: The Dimensions of Public Perceptions of Police Legitimacy," *Criminology* 51, no. 3 (2013): 103–35.

8 In Slovenia, for example, procedural justice remains a predictor of police legitimacy, but the effects of legitimacy on compliance are limited. Michael D. Reisig, Justice Tankebe, and Gorazd Meško, "Compliance with the Law in Slovenia: The Role of Procedural Justice and Police Legitimacy," *European Journal on Criminal Policy and Research* 20, no. 2 (2013): 259–76.

6. THE CASE FOR SUBSTANTIVE JUSTICE

1 Kees Van den Bos and E. Allan Lind, "Uncertainty Management by Means of Fairness Judgments," in M. P. Zanna, ed., *Advances in Experimental Social Psychology* 34 (New York: Academic Press, 2002), 19; Irina Elliot, Stuart Thomas, and James Ogloff, "Procedural Justice in Victim-Police Interactions and Victims' Recovery from Victimisation Experiences," *Policing and Society* 25, no. 2 (2014): 588–601.

2 Van den Bos and Lind, "Uncertainty Management," 19.

3 Jeffrey Fagan and Tom R. Tyler, "Legal Socialization of Children and Adolescents," *Social Justice Research* 18, no. 3 (2005): 217–42.

4 Jerald Greenberg, "Looking Fair vs. Being Fair: Managing Impressions of Organizational Justice," *Research in Organizational Behavior* 12 (1990): 111–57.

5 Greenberg, "Looking Fair vs. Being Fair," 137.

6 Maya Barak, "A Hollow Hope? The Empty Promise of Rights in the U.S. Immigration System," in Jorge González del Pozo and Javier Campelo Bermejo, eds., *Las Cadenas Que Amamos: Una Panorámica sobre el Retroceso de Occidente a Todos los Niveles* (Valladolid, Spain: Editorial Paramo, 2021) 71–94.

7 Stuart Scheingold, *The Politics of Rights: Lawyers, Public Policy, and Political Change* (Ann Arbor: University of Michigan Press, 1974).

8 Scheingold, *The Politics of Rights.*

9 Scheingold, *The Politics of Right,* 9.

10 Guttmacher Institute, "State Policy Trends 2021: The Worst Year for Abortion Rights in Almost Half a Century," January 5, 2022, www.guttmacher.org.

11 Guttmacher Institute, "State Policy Trends 2021."

12 "Dobbs v. Jackson Women's Health Organization," *Oyez*, February 28, 2022, www.oyez.org.

13 Gerald N. Rosenberg, *The Hollow Hope: Can Courts Bring about Social Change?* (Chicago: University of Chicago Press, 1991).

14 David M. Engel and Frank W. Munger, *Rights of Inclusion: Law and Identity in the Life Stories of Americans with Disabilities* (Chicago: University of Chicago Press, 2003).

15 Alissa R. Ackerman and Rich Furman, "The Criminalization of Immigration and the Privatization of the Immigration Detention: Implications for Justice," *Contemporary Justice Review* 16, no. 2 (2013): 251–63; Charles E. Kubrin, Marjorie S. Zatz, and Roberto Martinez Jr., eds., *Punishing Immigrants: Policy, Politics, and Injustice* (New York: New York University Press, 2012).

16 Kimberlé Crenshaw, "Demarginalizing the Intersection of Race and Sex: A Black Feminist Critique of Antidiscrimination Doctrine, Feminist Theory and Antiracist Politics," *University of Chicago Legal Forum* 1989, no. 1 (1989): 139–67.

17 Charles R. Epp, *The Rights Revolution: Lawyers, Activists, and Supreme Courts in Comparative Perspective* (Chicago: University of Chicago Press, 1998); Michael W. McCann, *Rights at Work: Pay Equity Reform and the Politics of Legal Mobilization* (Chicago: University of Chicago Press, 1994).

18 William F. Felstiner, Richard L. Able, and Austin Sarat, "The Emergence and Transformation of Disputes: Naming, Blaming, Claiming . . . ," *Law & Society Review* 15, no. 3/4 (1980): 631–54.

19 Scheingold, *The Politics of Rights*, 9.

20 Philip L. Torrey, "Rethinking Immigration's Mandatory Detention Regime: Politics, Profit, and the Meaning of 'Custody,'" *University of Michigan Journal of Law Reform* 48 (2015): 879–913.

21 Torrey, "Rethinking."

22 Kevin R. Johnson et al., *Understanding Immigration Law*, 3rd ed. (Durham, NC: Carolina Academic Press, 2019).

23 Jennifer Chacón, "A Diversion of Attention? Immigration Courts and the Adjudication of Fourth and Fifth Amendment Rights," *Duke Law Journal* 59, no. 15 (2010): 1563–1633.

24 Johnson et al., *Understanding Immigration Law*.

25 Matt Adams, "Advancing the 'Right' to Counsel in Removal Proceedings," *Seattle Journal for Social Justice* 9, no. 1 (2010): 169–83; Ingrid V. Eagly, "*Gideon's* Migration," *Yale Law Journal* 122 (2013): 2282–2314; Mark T. Fennell, "Preserving Process in the Wake of Policy: The Need for Appointed Counsel in Immigration Removal Proceedings," *Notre Dame Journal of Law, Ethics, and Public Policy* 23 (2009): 261–89; Michale Kagan, "Toward Universal Deportation Defense: An Optimistic View," *Wisconsin Law Review* (2018): 305–16; J. C. Salyer, *Court of Injustice: Law Without Recognition in U.S. Immigration* (Palo Alto, CA: Stanford University Press, 2020).

26 The Bronx Defenders, "New York Immigrant Family Unity Project," May 27, 2020, www.bronxdefenders.org.

27 Alameda County Public Defender, "Immigration," May 27, 2020, www.co.alameda.ca.us.

28 Annie Chan, "Safety and Fairness for Everyone (SAFE) Network," May 27, 2020, Vera Institute of Justice, www.vera.org.

29 *Jennings v. Rodriguez* 583 U.S. __ (2018).

30 *Nielsen v. Preap* 586 U.S. __ (2019).

31 *Hernandez v. Sessions* No. 15-72181 (9th Cir., May 21, 2018).

32 Jennifer Huynh, "La Charla: Documenting the Experience of Unaccompanied Minors in Immigration Court," *Journal of Ethnic and Migration Studies* (2019): 1–15; Christina Jewett and Shefali Luthra, "From Crib to Court: At Least 70 Children Under 1 Summoned for Deportation Proceedings," *USA Today*, 18 July 2018, www.usatoday.com.

33 Ackerman and Furman, "The Criminalization of Immigration"; Dora Schriro, *Immigration Detention Overview and Recommendations* (Washington, DC: U.S. Dept. of Homeland Security, Immigration and Customs Enforcement, 2009).

34 Cheryl Little, "INS Detention in Florida," *University of Miami Inter-American Law Review* 30, no. 3 (1999): 551–75; Fatma E. Marouf, "Alternatives to Immigration Detention," *Cardozo Law Review* 38, no. 6 (2017): 2141–92.

35 Office of Inspector General, "U.S. Immigration and Customs Enforcement's Alternatives to Detention (Revised)," (Washington, DC: U.S. Department of Homeland Security, 2015).

36 Maya Barak, "Can You Hear Me Now? Attorney Perceptions of Interpretation, Technology, and Power in Immigration Court," *Journal on Migration and Human Security* 9, no. 4 (2021): 207–23.

37 Again, the Supreme Court has rejected challenges to the use of indefinite detention (*Jennings v. Rodriguez*) and the use of mandatory detention to hold certain categories of immigrants facing deportation who have been convicted of crimes, including those who are clearly eligible for relief from deportation (*Nielsen v. Preap*). In 2017, the Ninth Circuit Court of Appeals upheld a preliminary injunction by a lower court in a class-action lawsuit filed by the American Civil Liberties Union requiring that immigration judges consider immigrants' financial circumstances when setting bond amounts (*Hernandez v. Sessions*). This decision, however, applies only to immigration judges working within the jurisdiction of the Ninth Circuit. Indeed, prior to the COVID-19 pandemic, the use of detention was trending upward. Although detention numbers fell during the COVID-19 pandemic (see Sarah R. Tosh, Ulla D. Berg, and Kenneth Sebastian León, "Migrant Detention and COVID-19: Pandemic Responses in Four New Jersey Detention Centers," *Journal on Migration and Human Security* 9, vol. 2 (2021): 44–62), it seems that previous detention trends have begun to resume. For example, in June 2021 the Supreme Court effectively eliminated detained immigrants' right to request bond if they have previously been deported (*Johnson v. Guzman Chavez*).

38 Community supervision effectively ensures immigrants appear in immigration court. See Office of Inspector General, "U.S. Immigration and Customs Enforcement's Alternatives to Detention (Revised)." It also helps immigrants avoid physical, psychological, and sexual harms often associated with detention. See Ackerman and Furman, "The Criminalization of Immigration." However, such alternatives to detention have been criticized as perpetuating harmful anti-immigrant practices of the state by "shroud[ing them] in a feminized, infantilized, and benevolent discourse of care for families and children." Andrea Gómez Cervantes, Cecilia Menjívar, and William G. Staples, "'Humane' Immigration Enforcement and Latina Immigrants in the Detention Complex," *Feminist Criminology* 12, no. 3 (2017): 285.

39 Donald Kerwin, "Unlocking Human Dignity: A Plan to Transform the US Immigrant Detention System," *Journal on Migration and Human Security* 3, vol. 2 (2015): 159–204.

40 Racial biases in the technology used to capture and reproduce images in facial recognition software, film, and video affect how we view "the other." Joy Buolamwini and Timnit Gebru, "Gender Shades: Intersectional Accuracy Disparities in Commercial Gender Classification," *Proceedings of Machine Learning Research* 81, vol. 1 (2018): 1–15; Sarah Lewis, "The Racial Bias Built into Photography," *New York Times*, April 25, 2019, www.nytimes.com.

41 For example, immigration court should consider the adoption of team interpreting, in which two or more interpreters share interpretation responsibilities. The National Association of Judiciary Interpreters and Translators (NAJIT) contends that team interpreting is perhaps "the most effective tool for protecting the integrity of interpretation, the liberty and rights of defendants/litigants, and . . . is critical to the administration of justice and the safeguarding of due process." National Association of Judiciary Interpreters and Translators, *Team Interpreting in Court-Related Proceedings* (Atlanta: NAJIT, 2020), 1.

42 Ingrid V. Eagly and Steven Shafer, "A National Study of Access to Counsel in Immigration Court," *University of Pennsylvania Law Review* 164, no. 1 (2015): 1–91; Richard L. Abel, "Practicing Immigration Law in Filene's Basement," *North Carolina Law Review* 84 (2006): 1449–1500; Sabrineh Ardalan, "Access to Justice for Asylum Seekers: Developing an Effective Model of Holistic Asylum Representation," *University of Michigan Journal of Law Reform* 48, no. 4 (2015): 1001–38; Jennifer Barnes, "Practice Context: The Lawyer-Client Relationship in Immigration Law," *Emory Law Journal* 52 (2003): 1215–20; Peter L. Markowitz, "Barriers to Representation for Detained Immigrants Facing Deportation: Varick Street Detention Facility, A Case Study," *Fordham Law Review* 78 (2009): 541–72; Hillary Mellinger, "Quality over Quantity: Legal Representation at the Asylum Office," *Law & Policy* 43, no. 4 (2021): 368–89; Marjorie Zatz, *Dreams and Nightmares: Immigration Policy, Youth, and Families* (Berkeley: University of California Press, 2015).

43 Eagly and Shafer, "A National Study."

44 Eagly and Shafer, "A National Study"; Banks Miller, Linda Camp Keith, and Jennifer S. Holmes, "Leveling the Odds: The Effect of Quality Legal Representation in Cases of Asymmetrical Capability," *Law & Society Review* 49, no. 1 (2015): 209–39; Jennifer Stave et al., *Evaluation of the New York Immigrant Family Unity Project: Assessing the Impact of Legal Representation on Family and Community Unity* (New York: Vera Institute of Justice, November 2017).

45 On the legacies of slavery, Jim Crow, and legalized racism in the U.S. criminal justice system, see Michelle Alexander, *The New Jim Crow: Mass Incarceration in the Age of Colorblindness* (New York: New Press, 2012); Douglas A. Blackmon, *Slavery by Another Name: The Re-Enslavement of Black Americans from the Civil War to World War II* (New York: Anchor Books, 2008); Glenn McNair, *Criminal Injustice: Slaves and Free Blacks in Georgia's Criminal Justice System* (Charlottesville: University of Virginia Press, 2009); Austin Sarat, *From Lynch Mobs to the Killing State: Race and the Death Penalty in America* (New York: New York University Press, 2006).

46 Jeffrey Reiman and Paul Leighton, *The Rich Get Richer and the Poor Get Prison: Ideology, Class, and Criminal Justice*, 10th ed. (New York: Routledge, 2016); Loïc Wacquant, *Punishing the Poor: The Neoliberal Government of Social Insecurity* (Durham, NC: Duke University Press, 2009).

47 Marc Mauer and Meda Chesney-Lind, *Invisible Punishment: The Collateral Consequences of Mass Imprisonment* (New York: New Press, 2003).

48 Alexander, *The New Jim Crow.*

49 James Forman Jr., *Locking Up Our Own: Crime and Punishment in Black America* (New York: Farrar, Straus, and Giroux, 2017); Tanya Golash-Boza, *Deported: Immigrant Policing, Disposable Labor and Global Capitalism* (New York: New York University Press, 2015).

50 Samuel Gross, Maurice Possley, and Klara Stephens, "Race and Wrongful Convictions in the United States," National Registry of Exonerations (Irvine: University of California, Irvine, 2017).

51 *Gideon v. Wainwright,* 374 U.S. 335 (1963).

52 Cara H. Drinan, "The National Right to Counsel Act: A Congressional Solution to the Nation's Indigent Defense Crisis," *Harvard Journal on Legislation* 47 (2010): 487–522.

53 Saul M. Kassin and Rebecca J. Norwick, "Why People Waive Their Miranda Rights: The Power of Innocence," *Law and Human Behavior* 28, no. 2 (2004): 211–21.

54 Kassin and Norwick, "Why People Waive Their Miranda Rights."

55 Donald B. Verrilli Jr., "The Eighth Amendment and the Right to Bail: Historical Perspectives," *Columbia Law Review* 82, no. 2 (1982): 328–62.

56 "H.R.5865—98th Congress (1983–1984): Bail Reform Act of 1984," Congress.gov, Library of Congress, October 12, 1984, www.congress.gov.

57 *United States v. Salerno,* 481 U.S. 739 (1987).

58 Andrea Woods and Portia Allen-Kyle, "America's Pretrial System Is Broken. Here's Our Vision to Fix It," American Civil Liberties Union, May 27, 2020, www.aclu.org.

59 Samuel R. Wiseman, "Pretrial Detention and the Right to Be Monitored," *Yale Law Journal* 12 (2014): 1345–1404.

60 Wiseman, "Pretrial Detention and the Right to Be Monitored," 1398.

61 Wiseman, "Pretrial Detention and the Right to Be Monitored."

62 Jayashri Srikantiah, "Reconsidering Money Bail in Immigration Detention," *UC Davis Law Review* 52, no. 1 (2019): 521–49.

63 Wiseman, "Pretrial Detention and the Right to Be Monitored."

64 Ava Kofman, "Digital Jail: How Electronic Monitoring Devices Drives Defendants into Debt," ProPublica, July 3, 2019, www.propublica.org.

65 Kofman, "Digital Jail."

66 Steve Fisher, "Getting Immigrants Out of Detention Is Very Profitable," *Mother Jones*, September–October 2016, www.motherjones.com; Pew Charitable Trusts, "Use of Electronic Offender-Tracking Devices Expands Sharply: Number of Monitored Individuals More Than Doubled in 10 Years," *A Brief from the Pew Charitable Trusts*, September 2016, www.pewtrusts.org.

67 Michael E. Miller, "This Company Is Making Millions from America's Broken Immigration System," *Washington Post*, March 9, 2017, www.washingtonpost.com.

68 Miller, "This Company Is Making Millions."

69 Mellinger, "Quality over Quantity."

70 Regarding the history of exclusionary immigration policies in the United States, see, e.g., Bill Ong Hing, *Defining America: Through Immigration Policy* (Philadelphia: Temple University Press, 2003); Peter Schrag, *Not Fit for Our Society: Immigration and Nativism in America* (Berkeley: University of California Press, 2010).

71 Regarding limitations on immigrants' participation in everyday American society, see, e.g., Jamie Longazel, *Undocumented Fears: Immigration and the Politics of Divide and Conquer in Hazleton, Pennsylvania* (Philadelphia: Temple University Press, 2016).

72 Regarding the criminalization of immigrants, see, e.g., Juliet Stumpf, "The Crimmigration Crisis: Immigrants, Crime, and Sovereign Power," *American University Law Review* 56 (2006–2007): 367–419.

73 See Devon Johnson, Edward R. Maguire, and Joseph B. Kuhns, "Public Perceptions of the Legitimacy of the Law and Legal Authorities: Evidence from the Caribbean," *Law & Society Review* 48, no. 4 (2014): 947–78. The authors advocate for rigorous testing of construct validity to determine the underlying meaning of "procedural justice" and how best to capture and operationalize it. The authors stress that, as "concepts are the building blocks of theory, knowledge about their nature and structure and the relationships between them is vital for building, testing and refining theory. Conversely, conceptual ambiguity inhibits the development of a robust and meaningful body of social theory" (954). Steven L. Blader and Tom R. Tyler, "A Four-Component Model of Procedural Justice: Defining the Meaning of a 'Fair' Process," *Personality and Social Psychology Bulletin* 29 (2003): 747–58.

74 Mariana Valverde, *Chronotopes of Law: Jurisdiction, Scale and Governance* (New York: Routledge, 2015), 22.

75 Valverde, *Chronotopes of Law*, 27.

76 Rita Shah, editor's introduction to "Centering the Margins: Addressing the Implementation Gap of Critical Criminology," special issue, *Critical Criminology* 29 (2021): 4.

CONCLUSION

1 Regarding health care access challenges and corruption in Honduras, see, e.g., Jessica Blatt, "Political Corruption and Healthcare in Honduras," *Borgen Magazine*, August 6, 2020, www.borgenmagazine.com; Nina Lakhani, "How Hitmen and High Living Lifted Lid on Looting of Honduran Healthcare System," *The Guardian*, June 10, 2015, www.theguardian.com; Catherine A. Pearson et al., "Access and Barriers to Healthcare Vary among Three Neighboring Communities in Northern Honduras," *International Journal of Family Medicine* (2012): 1–6; Felipe Puerta, "US Arrests Honduras Elite for Allegedly Laundering Corruption Proceeds," *InSight Crime*, May 3, 2018, https://insightcrime.org.

2 Regarding alternatives to immigration detention and electronic monitoring, see, e.g., Andrea Gómez Cervantes, Cecilia Menjívar, and William G. Staples,

"'Humane' Immigration Enforcement and Latina Immigrants in the Detention Complex," *Feminist Criminology* 12, no. 3 (2017): 269–92; Mary Holper, "Immigration E-Carceration: A Faustian Bargain," *Boston College Law School Legal Studies Research Paper Series*, Research Paper 539 (2020): 1–41; Michael E. Miller, "This Company Is Making Millions from America's Broken Immigration System," *Washington Post*, March 9. 2017, www.washingtonpost.com.

3 A "green card," officially a Permanent Resident Card, permits immigrants to live and work permanently in the United States.

4 Regarding medical hardship and deportation relief, see, e.g., Anita Gupta, "Proving Medical and Psychological Hardship for Non-LPR Cancellation of Removal," *Practice Advisory* (San Francisco: Immigrant Legal Resource Center, June 2020); Kevin R. Johnson et al., *Understanding Immigration Law*, 3rd ed. (Durham, NC: Carolina Academic Press, 2019); Adela de la Torre, Rosa Gomez-Camacho, and Alexis Alvarez, "Making the Case for Health Hardship: Examining the Mexican Health Care System in Cancellation of Removal Proceedings," *Georgetown Immigration Law Journal* 93 (2010–2011): 94–115.

5 In *Slavery and Social Death*, Orlando Patterson used the term "social death" to describe the physical and psychological processes by which the enslaved were systematically and symbolically severed from their former lives, heritages, and communities. Orlando Patterson, *Slavery and Social Death* (Cambridge, MA: Harvard University Press, 1982). Social death has also been applied to other forms of state harm, or crimes of the powerful, such as genocide (see, e.g., Claudia Card, "Genocide and Social Death," *Hypatia: A Journal of Feminist Philosophy* 18, no. 1 (2003): 63–69), incarceration (see, e.g., Joshua M. Price, *Prison and Social Death* (New Brunswick, NJ: Rutgers University Press, 2015)), and (im)migration controls (see, e.g., Lisa Marie Cacho, *Social Death: Racialized Rightlessness and the Criminalization of the Unprotected* (New York: New York University Press, 2012); Heide Castañeda, *Borders of Belonging: Struggle and Solidarity in Mixed-Status Immigrant Families* (Stanford, CA: Stanford University Press, 2019)).

6 Robert J. Bies and Debra L. Shapiro, "Voice and Justification: Their Influence on Procedural Fairness Judgments," *Academy of Management Journal* 31, no. 3 (1988): 676–85; Steven L. Blader and Tom R. Tyler, "A Four-Component Model of Procedural Justice: Defining the Meaning of a 'Fair' Process," *Personality and Social Psychology Bulletin* 29 (2003): 747–58; Joel Brockner et al., "Culture and Procedural Justice: The Influence of Power Distance on Reactions to Voice," *Journal of Experimental Social Psychology* 37 (2001): 300–15; Robert Folger, "Distributive and Procedural Justice: Combined Impact of 'Voice' and Improvement on Experienced Inequity," *Journal of Personality and Social Psychology* 35, no. 2 (1977): 108–99; E. Allan Lind, P. Christopher Earley and Ruth Kanfer, "Voice, Control, and Procedural Justice: Instrumental and Noninstrumental Concerns in Fairness Judgments," *Journal of Personality and Social Psychology* 59, no. 5 (1990): 952–59; John W. Thibaut and Laurens Walker, *Procedural Justice: A Psychological Analysis* (New York: L. Erlbaum

Associates, 1975); Tom R. Tyler, "What Is Procedural Justice? Criteria Used by Citizens to Assess the Fairness of Legal Procedures," *Law & Society Review* 22, no. 1 (1988): 103–36.

7 Maya Barak, "A Hollow Hope? The Empty Promise of Rights in the U.S. Immigration System," in Jorge González del Pozo and Javier Campelo Bermejo, eds., *Las Cadenas Que Amamos: Una Panorámica sobre el Retroceso de Occidente a Todos los Niveles* (Valladolid, Spain: Editorial Paramo, 2021), 71–94.

8 Regarding the criminalization of immigrants, see, e.g., Juliet Stumpf, "The Crimmigration Crisis: Immigrants, Crime, and Sovereign Power," *American University Law Review* 56 (2006–2007): 367–419.

9 See also Cervantes, Menjívar, and Staples, "'Humane' Immigration Enforcement."

EPILOGUE

1 Southern Poverty Law Center, "Family Separation Under the Trump Administration—A Timeline," June 17, 2020, www.splcenter.org.

2 Maya Barak, "Family Separation as State-Corporate Crime," *Journal of White Collar and Corporate Crime* 2, no. 2 (2021): 109–21; Stephen Lee, "Family Separation as Slow Death," *Columbia La Review* 119, no. 8 (2019): 2319–84.

3 Fernando Ramirez, "Texas Border Agents Tell Migrant Moms They'll Bathe Their Kids. Instead, They Separate Them," *Houston Chronicle*, June 12, 2018, www.chron.com.

4 Physicians for Human Rights, *"You Will Never See Your Child Again": The Persistent Psychological Effects of Family Separation* (Boston: Physicians for Human Rights, 2020), 3.

5 Physicians for Human Rights, *"You Will Never See Your Child Again,"* 3.

6 Caitlin Dickerson, "The Youngest Child Separated from His Family at the Border Was 4 Months Old," *New York Times*, June 16, 2019, www.nytimes.com.

7 Sergio Garcia, "The Unconstitutional Prosecution of Asylum-Seeking Parents Under Trump's Family Separation," *Hastings Constitutional Law Quarterly* 47, no. 1 (2019): 49–82; Lee, "Family Separation as Slow Death."

8 Barak, "Family Separation as State-Corporate Crime."

9 Barak, "Family Separation as State-Corporate Crime," 111.

10 Jacob Soboroff, *Separated: Inside an American Tragedy* (New York: Custom House, 2020).

11 Soboroff, *Separated.*

12 Soami Calles-Rios Sosa, "Sosa: Am I the Person Who Puts Children in Cages?" *Iowa State Daily*, July 7, 2020, www.iowastatedaily.com.

13 Hannah Critchfield, "Migrant Fathers Seek Damages from USA for Family Separations," *Phoenix New Times*, September 9, 2019, www.phoenixnewtimes.com.

14 Aura Bogado et al., "Migrant Children Sent to Shelters with Histories of Abuse Allegations," *Reveal News*, June 20, 2018, www.revealnews.org.

15 U.S. Department of Health and Human Services, *Frequently Asked Questions Regarding Unaccompanied Alien Children*, August 7, 2018, www.hhs.gov.

16 See, for example, the Immigration and Nationality Act (INA) and the *Flores* settlement agreement. See Rebecca M. López, "Codifying the *Flores* Settlement Agreement: Seeking to Protect Immigrant Children in U.S. Custody," *Marquette Law Review* 95, no. 4 (2012): 1635–77; and U.S. Department of Health and Human Services, Administration for Children & Families, Office of Refugee Resettlement, *ORR Guide: Children Entering the United States Unaccompanied* (Washington, DC: HHS, January 30, 2015), www.ohchr.org.

17 Barak, "Family Separation as State-Corporate Crime."

18 Matt Stieb, "The Inhumane Conditions at Migrant Detention Camps," *New York Magazine*, July 2, 2019, www.nymag.com.

19 Marisa Schultz and Nikki Schwab, "DHS Report Details 'Dangerous Overcrowding' in Border Facilities," *New York Post*, July 2, 2019, www.nypost.com.

20 Richard Gonzales, "Sexual Assault of Detained Migrant Children Reported in the Thousands since 2015," *NPR*, February 26, 2019, www.npr.org.

21 Jacob Soboroff and Julia Ainsley, "Migrant Kids in Overcrowded Arizona Border Station Allege Sex Assault, Retaliation from U.S. Agents," *NBC News*, July 9, 2019, www.nbcnews.com.

22 Nicole Acevedo, "Why Are Migrant Children Dying in U.S. Custody?" *NBC News*, May 29, 2019, www.nbcnews.com; Adolfo Flores, "A 2-Year-Old Boy Detained at the Border Has Died After Weeks in the Hospital," *BuzzFeed.News*, May 15, 2019, www.buzzfeednews.com; Maria Sacchetti, "Mother Blames Toddler's Death on Poor Medical Care in U.S. Immigration Jail," *Washington Post*, August 28, 2018, www.washingtonpost.com.

23 Lizzie O'Leary, "'Children Were Dirty, They Were Scared, and They Were Hungry,'" *The Atlantic*, June 25, 2019, www.theatlantic.com.

24 Jasmine Aguilera, "Homeland Security Chief Calls for a Pathway to Citizenship for Families Separated by Trump," *Time*, February 2, 2022, https://time.com; Aline Barros, "Five Years Later, Work of Reuniting Families Separated at US-Mexico Border Remains Unfinished," *Voice of America News*, June 11, 2022, www.voanews.com.

25 U.S. Department of Health and Human Services, Office of Inspector General, *Unaccompanied Alien Children Care Provider Facilities Generally Required Background Checks but Faced Challenges in Hiring, Screening, and Retaining Employees*, 2019, https://oig.hhs.gov.

26 Lee, "Family Separation as Slow Death," 2322.

27 Lee, "Family Separation as Slow Death," 2322.

28 Lee, "Family Separation as Slow Death," 2322.

29 See Lauren Berlant, "Slow Death (Sovereignty, Obesity, Lateral Agency)," *Critical Inquiry* 33, no. 4 (2007): 754–80.

30 Jacquelyn Doyon-Martin, "The Flint Water Crisis: A Case Study of State-Sponsored Environmental (In)Justice," in Avi Brisman and Nigel South, eds., *Routledge International Handbook of Green Criminology*, 2nd ed. (London: Routledge, 2020), 317–332.

31 Laura Gottesdiener, "The Children of Fallujah: The Medical Mystery at the Heart of the Iraq War," *The Nation*, November 9, 2020, www.thenation.com.

32 Josh Akers and Eric Seymore, "Instrumental Exploitation: Predatory Property Relations at City's End," *Geoforum* 91 (2018): 127–40; Mark Betancourt, "Detroit's Housing Crisis Is the Work of Its Own Government," *Vice News*, December 29, 2017, www.vice.com; Aaron Mondry, "New Report Shows Detroit's Tax Foreclosure Crisis Was Even Worse than We Thought," *Curbed Detroit*, January 16, 2020, https://detroit.curbed.com.

33 For a discussion of nativism, discrimination, and U.S. immigration policy, see Peter Schrag, *Not Fit for Our Society: Immigration and Nativism in America* (Berkeley: University of California Press, 2010); see also Bill Ong Hing, *Defining America: Through Immigration Policy* (Philadelphia: Temple University Press, 2003).

34 Jessica Bolter, Emma Israel, and Sarah Pierce, *Four Years of Profound Change: Immigration Policy during the Trump Presidency* (Washington, DC: Migration Policy Institute, 2022).

35 Despite legal challenges, a third version of the ban was allowed to take effect by the U.S. Supreme Court (*Trump v. Hawaii*, 138 S. Ct. 2392, 585 U.S. __ (2018)).

36 Jennifer Rogers, "Dreaming of the Future: Reflections of a Latina College Student Receiving DACA Protection in the Trump Era," *Journal of Hispanic Higher Education* (2020): 1–14.

37 Sarah E. Baranik de Alarcón, David H. Secor, and Norma Funetes-Mayorga, "'We Are Asking Why You Treat Us This Way. Is It Because We Are Negroes?': A Reparations-Based Approach to Remedying the Trump Administration's Cancellation of TPS Protections for Haitians," *Michigan Journal of Race & Law* 26 (2020): 1–47; Stephanie M. Huezo, "Nada sobre Nosotros sin Nosotros: Reflections on the TPS Movement and its Fight for Permanent Residency," *Latino Studies* 18, no. 1 (2020): 114–21.

38 Lindsay M. Harris, "Asylum Under Attack: Restoring Asylum Protections in the United States," *Loyal Law Review* 67, no. 1 (2021): 1–69.

39 Harris, "Asylum Under Attack."

40 Bolter, Israel, and Pierce, *Four Years of Profound Change*.

41 For example, the length of immigration forms and the amount and type of accompanying supporting evidence increased. For a discussion of immigration, see Catherine Rampell, "Trump Didn't Build His Border Wall with Steel. He Built It Out of Paper," *Washington Post*, October 29, 2020, www.washingtonpost.com.

42 David J. Bier, "Visualizing a 4-Year Assault on Legal Immigration: Trends Biden Must Reverse," Cato Institute, December 11, 2020, www.cato.org.

43 The Trump administration obtained $16.3 billion for border wall construction and built 458 miles of barriers, of which 52 miles were in areas that previously lacked a barrier. Bolter, Israel, and Pierce, *Four Years of Profound Change*.

44 The Obama administration's policy of prioritizing "criminal aliens" for deportation was not without criticism, particularly as the vast majority of immigrants

deported under this practice did not have serious criminal convictions but rather nonviolent misdemeanor and traffic violations. For further discussion, see Angélica Cházaro, "Challenging the 'Criminal Alien' Paradigm," *UCLA Law Review* 53, no. 3 (2016): 594–664.

45 Immigration and Customs Enforcement, "Prosecutorial Discretion and the ICE Office of the Principal Legal Advisor (OPLA)," December 9, 2021, www.ice.gov.

46 Bolter, Israel, and Pierce, *Four Years of Profound Change.*

47 Office of the Attorney General, *Renewing Our Commitment to the Timely and Efficient Adjudication of Immigration Cases to Serve the National Interest* (Washington, DC: U.S. Department of Justice, 2017); Executive Office for Immigration Review, "Case Priorities and Immigration Court Performance Measures," Memorandum to Office of the Chief Immigration Judge, All Immigration Judges, All Court Administrators, and All Immigration Staff (Washington, DC: U.S. Department of Justice, 2018); Executive Office for Immigration Review, "No Dark Courtrooms," Memorandum to All of EOIR (Washington, DC: U.S. Department of Justice, 2019).

48 Ashley Binetti Armstrong, "Co-opting Coronavirus, Assailing Asylum," *Georgetown Immigration Law Journal* 35, no. 2 (2021): 361–98; Michele Goodwin and Erwin Chemerinsky, "The Trump Administration: Immigration, Racism, and COVID-19," *University of Pennsylvania Law Review* 169, no. 2 (2021): 313–82.

49 Bolter, Israel, and Pierce, *Four Years of Profound Change.*

50 David J. Bier, "76 Percent of Consulates Are Fully or Partly Closed Even After Tests and Vaccinations," Cato Institute, April 9, 2021, www.cato.org.

51 Bolter, Israel, and Pierce, *Four Years of Profound Change.*

52 American Immigration Council, "Fact Sheet: A Guide to Title 42 Expulsions at the Border," October 15, 2021, www.americanimmigrationcouncil.org.

53 Jasmine Aguilera, "Biden Is Expelling Migrants on COVID-19 Grounds, but Health Experts Say That's All Wrong," *Time*, October 12, 2021, https://time.com.

54 Amnesty International, "Biden Administration Continues to Fail Asylum-Seekers as Title 42 Is Extended," December 3, 2021, www.amnestyusa.org.

55 Jasmine Aguilera and Madeleine Carlisle, "Federal Judge Blocks Biden from Ending Controversial Border Policy, Title 42," *Time*, May 20, 2022, www.time.com.

56 John Gramlich, "Key Facts about Title 42, the Pandemic Policy That Has Reshaped Immigrantion Enforcement at the U.S.-Mexico Border," Pew Research, April 27, 2022, www.pewresearch.org.

57 Ginger Thompson, "Listen to Children Who've Just Been Separated from Their Parents at the Border," ProPublica, June 18, 2018, www.propublica.org.

INDEX

Abel, Laura, 47–48; on interpretation, 52
abortion, right to, 126
addiction, of immigrant, 111
administrative closure, of immigration judges, 36
Administrative Law Judges (ALJ), immigration judges as, 54
Administrative Office, U.S. Courts, 43
Administrative Procedure Act (APA), 189n43, 193n117
advertisements, for immigration services, misinformation in, 76
AEDPA. *See* Anti-Terrorism and Effective Death Penalty Act
Ahmad, Muneer I., 43
AILA. *See* American Immigration Lawyers Association
Alameda County Public Defender, 128–29
Alex (pseudonym): asylum sought by, 81–82; court experience of, 82–83, 198n3; on jailhouse lawyers, 74
ALJ. *See* Administrative Law Judges
American Civil Liberties Union, 129, 132, 203n37
American Immigration Lawyers Association (AILA), 9
Americans with Disabilities Act (1990), 196n9
Angelica (pseudonym), 116, 150; on corruption, 115; court experience of, 92, 94–95; on immigrant knowledge, 71, 72; on immigration attorneys, 100; TPS of, 91

Anti-Terrorism and Effective Death Penalty Act (AEDPA), 189n43, 193n117; mandatory detention relation to, 41
APA. *See* Administrative Procedure Act
Aracely (pseudonym), 68–69; on immigration system, 119
Árbenz, Jacobo, military overthrow of, 16
Ashcroft, John, 40
assistance of counsel, ineffective, prevalence of, 77
asylum: for Alex, 81–82; bias against seekers of, 56, 57–58; for Eduardo, 87, 89; gang violence relation to, 22, 26–27; grant rates of, 6, 193n122; policy effect on, 89, 178n32; for PSG, 194n124
attorney, ICE, 39, 53–54; case backlog effect on, 59, 142; perceptions of, 89, 91
Attorney General U.S., 40; immigration judges appointed by, 54; Sessions as, 22, 178n32, 189n35
attorneys, immigration, 188n32, 196n11; detained client relation to, 41–42; difficulty in obtaining, 131; EOIR discipline process for, 193n119; fraudulent experiences with, 69, 73, 76–77; gender of, 9; ICE, 39, 53–54, 59, 89, 91, 142; on immigrant knowledge, 73–75; on immigration judges, 55–57, 59; on interpretation, 44–45, 47–48; legal knowledge from, 66, 68, 78; for nonprofit organizations, 8, 9, 137; perceptions of, 102, 142, 143–44; pressures on, 2; pro bono, 82, 137; procedural justice view of, 11–12, 35; quality of, 100, 134; workload of, 5

ties, 71–72, 73–74, 144; from immigration attorneys, 66, 68, 78; misinformation in, 74–76, 77; of procedural justice, 101; of TPS, 67, 71
"know your rights" trainings, of nonprofit organizations, 72

languages, immigrant: in court, 42–43, 44, 191n79; dialects in, 45–46; English as, 44, 59–60, 87, 93–94; Spanish as, 46, 90–91; videoconferencing effect on, 51–52
Language Services Unit, EOIR, 43
Lara (pseudonym), 57; on *notario* fraud, 76
law, immigration, 118; compliance with, 122; fairness of, 119; inescapability of, 80; legalization in, 4, 120; perceptions of, 1, 2–3, 12, 61–62, 65, 73–77, 78, 121, 195n4. *See also* knowledge, legal
law, rule of: human rights pitted against, 156; immigrants seeking, 105–6, 112, 144–45; perceptions of, 115–16; in U.S., 118
Lee, Stephen, 152
legal consciousness, 195n2, 195n4; developed in detention, 63, 64; of the disabled, 196n9; law inescapability in, 80; perceptions relation to, 60; politics of rights in, 125–26; procedural justice relation to, 12, 141–42; socialization in, 69–70, 78, 144; storytelling in, 11, 79, 100
legal culture, in U.S., 6, 11, 124
legalization: absence of path to, 4; in immigration law, 120
legal socialization: as dynamic, 69, 78, 144; effect on perceptions, 31; "jailhouse lawyers" in, 74; in legal consciousness, 69–70, 78, 144; storytelling in, 78–79
legitimacy, state: belief in, 3–4, 12, 31, 99, 105–6, 107, 115–16, 121, 144–45, 147; compliance relation to, 29, 102,

184n116, 200n8; fairness relation to, 123–24, 185n128; procedural justice relation to, 117–18, 184n118; rights relation to, 127; security as, 114
LEP. *See* limited English proficiency
lesbian, gay, bisexual, and transgender community (LGBT+): bias against, 56; fairness perceptions of, 31; persecution based on, 89, 95
limited English proficiency (LEP), 42
Lionbridge, translation services of, 190n59
litigant disengagement, videoconferencing associated with, 52
litigation, for rights, 126–27
Los Angeles, Salvadoran gangs in, 25
Luis (pseudonym), 111–12, 116, 150; on corruption, 115

Maguire, Edward R., 33
Mara Salvatrucha-13 (MS-13), 24; Alex relation to, 81–82; Eddie relation to, 25–26
marginalized groups: in criminal justice system, 132; oppression of, 136; rights of, 127
María (pseudonym), 137–38, 140; hearing postponement of, 139
Marks, Dana, 58
Marouf, Fatma, 54–55
Martín Ruano, María Rosario, 44
Master Calendar day, 38–39
Mauricio (pseudonym), 77; on ICE attorneys, 53; on judge caseload, 58
media, legal knowledge from, 75
medical treatment, immigrant seeking, 138–40
Menjívar, Cecilia, on legal limbo, 9–10
Merry, Sally Engel, 70; on storytelling, 78–79
la migra (immigration enforcement officers), 20
migration, as human right, 120, 122
Migration Protection Protocols, 155

ABOUT THE AUTHOR

MAYA PAGNI BARAK is Associate Professor of Criminal Justice Studies and affiliate of Women's and Gender Studies at the University of Michigan–Dearborn. She holds a PhD in Justice, Law, and Criminology from American University. Her research brings together the areas of law, deviance, immigration, and power.

www.ingramcontent.com/pod-product-compliance
Lightning Source LLC
Chambersburg PA
CBHW020251030426
42336CB00010B/717